S0-CAE-182

To

Henry Huntington Rosstacher
from
his grand-mother
Christmas. 1959

Esquire's THE ART OF KEEPING FIT

Esquire's

OR HOW THE SUCCESSFUL MALE CAN

BY THE EDITORS OF ESQUIRE MAGAZINE

HARPER & BROTHERS

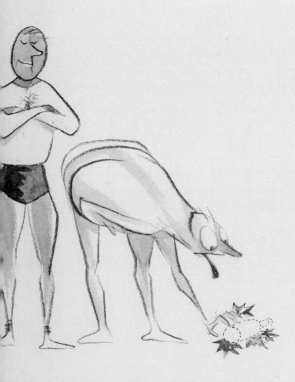

THE ART OF KEEPING FIT

AVOID GOING TO SEED

ILLUSTRATED BY ROBERT OSBORN

NEW YORK

ESQUIRE'S THE ART OF KEEPING FIT

Copyright © 1940, 1941, 1942, 1944, 1945, 1946, 1947, 1948, 1949, 1950, 1951, 1952, 1953, 1954, 1956, 1957, 1958, 1959 by Esquire, Inc.

Printed in the United States of America

All rights in this book are reserved. No part of the book may be used or reproduced in any manner whatsoever without written permission except in the case of brief quotations embodied in critical articles and reviews. For information address Harper & Brothers 49 East 33rd Street, New York 16, N. Y.

Library of Congress catalog card number: 59-6331

CONTENTS

v

How It Can Be Prevented; Is There a Heart Attack Type?
Why Does Heart Disease Hit Men More Than Women?
Does Diet Affect Your Heart? Heredity?

Gunning—Wing Shooting, Bird Dogs, the Safari, Skeet,
Hand-Trap Shooting, Shooting the Pistol

PREFACE

In the preparation of this book, there was the special necessity of getting a qualified medical review of the content. This essential service and protection to the reader has been performed by the distinguished head of the American Medical Association's Department of Health Education, Dr. W. W. Bauer.

In his note giving this book a clean bill of health, medically speaking,

Dr. Bauer has correctly diagnosed its chief element of value as being a sort of helpful specific against "the tensions of the age."

In this Age of Anxiety, when best-sellerdom is virtually assured for books that promise peace of mind, we might appear to be bucking the trend in offering a book that might seem to be adding to the reader's anxieties instead of giving him some get-happy-quick formula for minimizing them.

But we believe there are many men who would rather know their own health score, before it's too late, and do something about improving it, rather than go on looking for ways to tranquilize themselves into an ignorant euphoria, as concerns the main question of their lives.

It is to such wise men that this book is addressed, and for them it is written. May their tribe increase, because today's world needs them.

Before we move on to examine the body, we feel impelled to explain and to credit the role of Mary Scott Welch in the making of this book from the pages of *Esquire*.

While it is a fact that the original editing source of this book is "the editors of *Esquire*," still it is one of those facts that, left to themselves, fall far short of the whole truth. As Rose Franken pointed out long ago, in a play called *Another Language*, there are times when you can say, "Those are only the facts—that's still not the truth."

The truth is that the job of shaping past writings from past issues of a magazine into a cohesive and coherent whole, as was done in this book, is a task which goes about as far beyond mere editing as midwifery goes beyond pedicuring.

This job was done, as it has been so often and so well before, by Mary Scott Welch, whose present perfect presentation of our past imperfect editings so far transforms the original new material as to make us wish that there were some more laudatory word than "editing" for the truly creative contribution that she brings to the making of books out of *Esquire*.

ARNOLD GINGRICH
Publisher, *Esquire*

INTRODUCTION–FOR MEN ONLY

Figures tell us—the pear-shaped figures on our friends as insistently as the scary figures on mortality tables*—that men go to pot.

* This year, 200,000 more men than women will die, swelling our already formidable population of widows (nearly eight million). Heart disease will claim 78 per cent more men than women, and of the five leading causes of death not a one will be nearly so unfair to the fair sex as to men. (Only diabetes mellitus, among major diseases, "favors" women, and only 2 per cent of all deaths are ascribed to it.) As George Bugbee, president

They go to pot gradually (so they can tell themselves, for a lifetime of *mañanas,* that they'll "go to work on it" as soon as they "have time"). . . .

Sometimes they do it comfortably ("I wouldn't be young again if you paid me").

Occasionally they manage to fool themselves about it ("Doesn't *everybody* take pep pills?").

But they do it *definitely.* They go to pot.

That, sad to say, is man's nature.

BUT . . .

Nature is a woman, and like any woman worth cultivating she will gladly bow to the strong, intelligent management of a man.

As an adversary, she is no push-over. (Read Part I of this book if you have any doubt about what Nature holds in store for a man who lets her have her way.) Managing her begins with a cautious respect for the punch she packs.

But she's a sucker for a guy who has enough sense, and enough will power, to "wear the pants." She bestows her favors—vitality, effectiveness, zest for living—on the man who knows how to take care of her by taking care of himself.

This book will tell you how. How to manage Nature. How *not* to go to pot.

Keeping fit is an art, in the sense that art rises above and improves on Nature, but it is also a science. Hence the scientific authority for every word in this book. Doctors have written or checked every medical fact and theory you'll read here. Writers have reviewed their articles in the light of steadily advancing medical science. And the entire book has been

**read and reviewed by Dr. W. W. Bauer,
head of the Department of Health Education,
American Medical Association.**

Dr. Bauer says . . .

"As modern life makes more and greater demands upon men—and particularly upon ambitious and successful men, who come up against the tensions of the age every day in their lives—keeping fit becomes at once more difficult and more important. Keeping fit becomes, in fact, a matter of

---

of the Health Information Foundation, says, "American males, especially those at age forty-five and beyond, are becoming, in effect, an underprivileged segment of our population." Taking care of yourself, as you infer, is not "vain" nor "womanly"—or if it *is,* look at the results! (Women, by the way, consult doctors more regularly than men do—not counting visits related to childbirth—and most hospital patients—not counting Veterans hospitals—are men.)

life and death. This book is worth a million times its weight in 'happy pills' to any man who will take it to heart."

Hopefully supposing that you're going to take it to heart (and to stomach, liver, muscles and all the rest of your vulnerable body), we'll convey your thanks, along with ours to Dr. Bauer and to the many experts who helped to make this book, among whom are:

Tommy Armour
Edwin Becker
Carolyn Bird
Raymond Browne
Coleman Clark
Dr. Logan Clendening
Robert Coates
Rod Cooper
Nicholas David
Bernard Davis
John Drieman
F. Scott Fitzgerald
Eric Frances
Paul Gallico
Herb Graffis
Thomas Haney
Tom Harmon
Robert Hart
James Hilton
Al Hirschfeld
Ben Hogan
Travis Hoke
Morton Hunt
E. C. Janes
Manya Kahn
Paul Kearney
O. B. Keeler
H. B. Knoll
David Lavender

Richard Lewis
Dr. Miriam Lincoln
George Mann
Robert Marks
Henry McLemore
Dr. Bess M. Mensendieck
David Newell
Glen Perry
Karl G. Pfeiffer
James Poling
Fletcher Pratt
William Reichenbach
Dr. J. B. Rice
Critchell Rimington
Walter Ross
Charles Roth
Robert Ruark
Stephanie Sargent
William Schaldach
Arthur Schlesinger, Jr.
Sanderson Smith
M. H. Soglow
Dr. Peter J. Steincrohn
Hart Stillwell
Clarence Streit
Donald Vaughan, Jr.
Edmund Ware
Dr. Charles Williams
George Wiswell

To Your Good Health!
—The Editors of *Esquire*

PART I THE HANDWRITING ON THE WALL

We don't mean to scare you—no more, at least, than is necessary to loosen your grip on that second martini at lunch—but here, to help you make up your mind to do something about your health, is what you're up against. Here is the medical information you need about the maladies most common to men today.

In the old days, men apparently believed that illness did not exist until it was confirmed by medical diagnosis: the way to treat a spot of breathlessness or indigestion or a little twinge here or there was, simply, not to notice it. More recently, the "miracles" performed by new and newer drugs have led some of us to believe that the cure for whatever ails us is available in some pill or other; and we'll try them all. Somewhere in between the dangerous extremes of ignorance and overconfidence there lies an attitude that can add years to a man's life, and zest to each of the years. It consists in knowing when you should go to a doctor, and what to tell him when you get there. Neither fatalistic nor hypochondriacal, the new attitude is matter-of-fact.

1. YOUR HEART

You cannot, by taking thought, add a single cubit to your stature, but heart specialists think they have proved that you can add perhaps years to your life span by intelligent living. To do this you must understand about coronary heart disease—what it is, what causes it, how it can be prevented.

Here are the facts you need:

Coronary heart disease used to be called "acute indigestion" because attacks are sometimes precipitated by overeating, and because the severe pain that is typical of an attack is not always felt in the chest but occasionally in the abdomen instead.

The fundamental process involved is the early hardening of the arteries—just plain aging.

The blood vessels of a child are like smooth elastic, resilient as rubber tubing. Each illness and each year of life injures the flexibility and the smoothness of these vessels. They begin, by the time we are thirty-five years old, to show signs of wear and tear in even the sturdiest of us. They become thicker, less elastic; and along the smooth walls are deposited tiny, pinhead-sized patches of lime and fat.

Year by year these deposits continue, perhaps becoming so closely placed that they coalesce—that is, they grow together. The vessels, especially the arteries where pressure is high, grow thick and narrow. Less blood can be transported. In time, the arteries may become so thick and brittle that the vessel walls will crunch between the fingers, crumbling like a crushed eggshell. Doctors see such vessels at operations and speak of them as "pipestem" because they resemble a narrow, clay pipestem.

How narrowing of arteries affects a heart is illustrated by what happens when a tight elastic band is wound about a finger. This produces numbness, throbbing and pain. The finger grows pale, then swollen and purple. In time it will become gangrenous and "die" if the band is not removed so that blood, bearing oxygen, can be carried to the cells in the tissue of the finger.

Similar changes occur in the area of the heart muscle deprived of blood. The tissue dies. The victim experiences perhaps numbness, almost always pain of a severe viselike quality, usually in the chest but sometimes in the arms, neck or abdomen. Because it was first described when Latin was the language of science, such pain is called *angina pectoris*, "distress in the breast." Because there is injury, even death of tissue, the victim may have a drop in blood pressure, followed by fever, a higher white-blood-cell count, an elevated sedimentation rate, and almost always changes in his electrocardiogram (a photo of the electrical impulses of the heart muscle, as recorded by the swing of a string galvanometer. The electrocardiogram is the most helpful laboratory test for diagnosing coronary artery diseases.)

If the arteries are but little constricted, distress may come only when the demands on the heart are increased—on exertion, or under emotional stress. But if they are greatly narrowed, so that only a trickle of blood can circulate, then pain may come without apparent provocation.

Occasionally—and this is a common cause of sudden death—a brittle artery lining may deteriorate, crumbling and completely plugging the channel suddenly, so that all blood supply is cut off in the area nourished by that twig of coronary artery. The area of heart muscle so left without blood supply is called *infarct*. The injured tissue shows on the heart wall as a patch of different color, as large as a nickel or quarter or even bigger. Coronary disease leaves a truly scarred heart.

When this occurs, the victim's chances of survival depend on three factors:

First, on how large an area is damaged or infarcted. The larger, the more dangerous, in general.

Second, on how good the circulation is to the rest of the heart muscle. If the victim can live long enough to allow other intact vessels to form new communications with the injured area, re-establishing an adequate blood supply, then continued life is possible.

Third, on what strain the heart as a whole must bear. If the man is obese or has high blood pressure, forcing the heart constantly to bear a great burden, the chance for survival is less.

Prompt medical care is imperative. A doctor cannot supply the victim of coronary occlusion with new arteries, but he can institute measures like rest, oxygen, medication, which may tide the victim over a period long enough to permit healing and the establishment of a new substitute blood supply from some neighboring blood vessel. Healing takes a minimum of about six weeks, usually many months and sometimes even years.

Many men do recover and live long happy lives. One man was climbing a mountain, seventeen years after his first attack, when he died of his second infarction. Men are reported to have lived as long as thirty years between a first and a fatal coronary occlusion. Such men learned how to live new and much less strenuous lives.

The time when the doctor can be of most use is early, before the arteries are irreparably damaged. How many men reading this have already been cautioned against hurry and fatigue, too much overwork, too much weight?

Heart specialists know that we need more facts about this disease. In medical schools and under grants from the American Heart Association, research projects are afoot, seeking the answers to many questions:

IS THERE A "HEART ATTACK TYPE"?

Some studies have suggested that the men most likely to succeed are those most likely to drop dead.

A Massachusetts General Hospital study of a hundred coronary victims under forty found that the average victim is always in a hurry. He seldom takes a vacation, works rather than plays at his hobbies, saves time by talking business at lunch, drinks and smokes more than most men.

Advertising Age recently surveyed its obituary columns and announced that newsworthy admen were dying at an average age of fifty-eight, eight years sooner than the population as a whole. Another trade magazine calls the advertising executive the "Man in the Black Wooden Suit." His coronary arteries succumb to "the intensity of competition, the relative insecurity of tenure of agency appointments, the absence of scientific standards which would make decisions less of a gamble."

As early as 1937, doctors at the Mayo Clinic found that hardening of the coronary arteries was four times as frequent among physicians and twice

as frequent among bankers and lawyers as among humble farmers and laborers.

Psychiatrists have suggested that repression is a factor: the heart victim is mad at someone he doesn't dare fight. Psychiatrist Daniel E. Schneider suggests that the coronary candidate is a man who drives himself to success to overcome a subconscious fear that his heart will run away from him. Dominating mothers have appeared as a factor, and so has a man's self-doubt about his masculinity.

But these and comparable theories have yet to be proved.

WHY DOES HEART DISEASE HIT MEN MORE THAN WOMEN?

In some series, 93 per cent of the victims are men. Women are affected only if they have high blood pressure, diabetes or great age. Recent biochemical discoveries indicate that men are weaker because they don't bear children. Female hormones active during childbearing years protect women against coronary attacks and can protect animals who have endured some modification of male characteristics. But if hormones were the only cause, why is it that American Negro women are about as vulnerable as American Negro men? Why is the gap between the sexes wider in the United States than in countries with a lower coronary rate, and why has the gap widened in the United States in the last generation? We may learn more about this when we find out exactly how female hormones influence the arteries and the heart.

DOES DIET HAVE ANY EFFECT ON HARDENING OF THE ARTERIES?

Dr. Ancel Keys, the biochemist, thinks that if successful people are more vulnerable to coronary disease, it's because they take more of their calories in butter, meat and animal fats. These animal fats line the arteries with a fatty substance called cholesterol, which encourages the fatal plugging of coronary arteries just as rusty pipes encourage plumbing stoppages. A "better" diet, rather than cultural or racial differences, might account for the fact that Spaniards, Italians, Bantus and Orientals have less coronary disease than Americans, that rich, fat-fed Spaniards have more coronary disease than Spanish peasants, and that African Bantus in the wild have less coronary disease than racially related American Negroes or Bantus treated to a civilized diet. And if stress were the cause, Keys argues, why didn't Northern Europeans have more heart disease during the fat-short war years? They had less.

However, radioactive tracer studies show that the animal fat a person eats isn't the only source of the raw materials out of which the body manufactures cholesterol. And one man's internal chemistry may favor the production of cholesterol where another's does not. Physiologists are not even sure that the rise in cholesterol deposit which accompanies coronary disease actually causes it. And animal fat can't be the whole answer, for women eat as much fat as their menfolk without getting anywhere near as much coronary disease.

DOES HEART DISEASE RUN IN FAMILIES?

Practicing physicians traditionally say so, but statisticians find the observation haphazard. Good diagnosis of coronary occlusion is less than thirty years old, so it's hard to go very far back in anyone's family tree. For the same reason, many figures you see published are suspect. Heart disease is bound to loom larger as a killer as we save people from other deaths, and larger in the United States because we have done a better job on the infectious killers than the low-heart-rate Mediterranean, African and Oriental nations. Comparisons are misleading because other nations don't keep their figures the way we do.

IN SUM . . .

So we have a long way to go in finding the answers to our questions about the heart. But heart specialists say that many men could be saved from the fate of the coronary victims if they could only be taught early enough in life to avoid what invites artery damage. Worry, tension, overwork, over-fatigue—these all seem to predispose to coronary artery damage. Hard physical work in itself does not appear to cheat a man of long life, but work involving nervous and mental strain may. Hurry, constant deadlines, too little relaxation, too few vacations—there is a long list of such predisposing factors.

If you're a man . . . if you're ambitious and energetic . . . if you're thirty or over . . . start your lifesaving program now. Here's what the doctor orders:

Avoid overeating and its twin, overweight.

Shun overwork and overfatigue. Easier said than done?

Then learn to recognize the times when you *are* overtense, over-tired, so you can pay your heart back with rest and relaxation when you need it most.

Take annual or semiannual holidays that break the strain.

Court outdoor relaxation in golf (only if played for fun), gardening or fishing. Enforce *daily* recreation through hobbies, music, play or study.

These are palatable medicines for any man. They should help postpone the aging process.

2. YOUR DIGESTIVE SYSTEM

ULCERS: THE PRICE OF ABILITY?

Hollywood and New York are supposed to be in a neck-and-neck race for the dubious honor of being the ulcer capital of these United States. Frankly, it is not so much a question of where a man lives; what is important is what is going on beneath his hat. In other words, you can get an ulcer in Podunk if you are that kind of man.

Unquestionably, ulcer feeds on those who feed on themselves. It finds its habitat in the man who is tearing at his vitals by indulging in indecision, worry, chronic anxiety, simmering jealousy, fear of losing his job, hatred of his job, or a vague insecurity experienced since childhood. Such are characteristics which prevent him from meeting the changing vicissitudes of his environment head on—and without tension.

That's what will do it—whether it be in Podunk, Hollywood or New York. Of course, we realize that there may be other precipitating causes. For example, overwork, hasty snacks instead of regular, leisurely meals, too much smoking or drinking, focal infections such as bad teeth or a chronically infected gall bladder. All these things add up to a predisposition to ulcer.

Yet if you were to ask the most prominent physicians in the field of gastroenterology just what causes ulcer they could only answer, "I wish we knew the *actual* cause." If you were to press further and ask about the role of fears and tensions and unconscious insecurity, then their faces would light up. "Now there you have something," they would say. There seems to be complete agreement that gastric and duodenal ulcer are definitely tied up with emotions that are out of hand more than they are in hand.

Recent tests at the University of Illinois proved that dogs can develop ulcers of the stomach. They get that way by being frustrated: by not receiving expected food. If it can happen to a dog, is it unusual to find it in man, who is frustrated in more ways than you can keep a bone from a dog?

What are your chances of having a three-quarter-inch gastric ulcer or a one-quarter-inch duodenal ulcer? According to some statistics, at least a half-million of us have ulcers. This is a conservative estimate. Others say 10 per cent of us have ulcer of the stomach or duodenum.

Ulcer of the stomach and duodenum was listed as the sixteenth commonest cause of death in the latest U.S. tally. Doctors, lawyers, executives, advertising men and diplomats have more than their share of ulcers. Chinese coolies, Latin-American Indians, primitives, farmers and mental defectives have less than their share. The Army is worried because officers—and the most valuable ones at that—have ulcers almost twice as frequently as enlisted men. Men in the productive years between twenty and forty have four times the ulcer rate of women their age.

HOW YOUR INNER MAN WORKS

No understanding of the problem of ulcers is possible without some concept of the basic physiology of digestion. Scientific facts are gleaned in curious ways. It took an alert young Army surgeon, a fur trapper, and a stray bullet to give us the start of our knowledge of human digestion. It happened this way.

In June, 1822, when the hunters were converging on Fort Mackinac with the winter's fur-trapping harvest, a carelessly packed gun in one of the canoes was accidentally discharged and a nineteen-year-old Canadian trapper named Alexis St. Martin was hit in the abdomen. The shot made a ghastly wound that penetrated deep into his left side, leaving a hole the size of a man's palm in the region of the stomach.

Dr. William Beaumont, a young Army surgeon, was called to attend him. The man survived and eventually his wounds healed and left remaining only a "fistula" or kind of a peephole into the stomach. Alert to the medical research possibilities of this situation, Beaumont hired the trapper as his servant with the understanding that he was to have the privilege of observing and experimenting with the windowed stomach so that facts about human digestion could be collected. It was an arrangement that furthered science considerably and made William Beaumont one of medicine's immortals.

Over a period of years, Dr. Beaumont experimented. He collected stomach juices and learned that they contained hydrochloric acid. He inserted various foods into the open stomach, observed their slow disintegration, and recorded the time required for digestion. He noted the angry redness of the stomach's lining after a bout of drunkenness. He saw the color of the walls of the stomach lining and the speed of digestion change in accord with St. Martin's emotions.

All these facts, set down in scientific exactitude, were published in 1833 in a small book called *Experiments and Observations on the Gastric Juice and the Physiology of Digestion.*

Since Beaumont's pioneer work, the famous Pavlov of old Russia, Cannon of Boston, Ivy and Carlson of Chicago and many other scientists have contributed facts about the physiology of the stomach and digestion acquired through years of research. Those essential for an understanding of the ulcer problem may be summarized:

The stomach is the ballooned-out upper portion of the muscular tubing that forms the entire digestive tract. It is a remarkably flexible organ. Empty, its walls are thick and crinkled. Distended with food, they are thin and smooth. A baby's stomach is no bigger than a man's thumb, yet it dilates to hold a bottle of milk several times a day. When an adult's stomach is empty and contracted, it can be covered by a man's hand.

The walls are four layers thick. The lining and sublining contain the cells and glands that secrete the gastric juices—weak hydrochloric acid and digestive enzymes called pepsin and rennin. Beneath is a sturdy layer of muscle strands that set the walls into kneading motions so that food is well mixed with digestive juices. These movements are waves of contractions descending from the upper or cardiac end to the lower or pyloric end of the stomach. The muscle at the pylorus acts a bit like a purse string and by relaxing allows the mass of semiliquid food to spill into the next portion of digestive tract called the duodenum.

Normally, the stomach empties in about four hours. The stomach varies in shape because the waves of contraction pinch it in here and there as they descend, but it is roughly like a bulgy fishhook in outline. The fourth or outside layer of the walls is a smooth, cellophane-like skin.

When the stomach empties, the partially digested food spills through the pyloric sphincter into the duodenum, a loop of tubing about twelve inches in length. Set at an angle, in an X-ray picture it looks a bit like a fat thumb pointing upward.

The entire digestive tract is about thirty feet in length and each portion has its own specific task in the process of digestion. The enzymes of the saliva digest starches into sugars. The stomach is chiefly concerned with the digestion of proteins. The duodenum continues protein digestion and adds enzymes that break down carbohydrates and fats. The lower intestine is charged with the absorption of water and nutriment.

The stomach takes in crude foods like steak and pie with their mixtures of proteins, carbohydrates and fats. By action of the digestive enzymes working in the acid medium provided by the 0.5 per cent hydrochloric acid of gastric juice, the large, complicated protein molecules are broken into smaller, simpler molecules like peptones and albuminoses. These travel through the rest of the intestines until digested into usable amino acids. By a complicated process, involving diffusion and osmosis, they pass through the intestine walls to enter blood and lymph channels. They are then transported elsewhere for use by the body as fuel for energy and as building blocks for repair and growth.

ENTER THE ULCER

But what about the man with ulcers? What is happening to him? Along the lower third of his stomach or in the walls of the adjacent duodenum (which is much more common), a raw, bleeding, punched-out area develops. Is may be saucer or funnel shaped. This we call an ulcer—gastric if located in the stomach, duodenal if in the duodenum. If we do not wish to be specific, but merely to indicate that it develops in the area where digestion takes place, we call it peptic ulcer.

Peptic ulcers may be either single or multiple; superficial or penetrating deep into the muscle layer. A group of tiny ulcers may coalesce to form a larger single ulcer. Ulcers vary in size from pinhead to the diameter of a dime or even a silver dollar.

There are four complications that make peptic ulcer frightening. The commonest is hemorrhage, usually the slow oozing of tiny amounts of blood. Blood when digested becomes black so this complication is manifested by the appearance of black or tarry stools. Almost every patient with an active, raw ulcer, bleeds a little. If the stools do not show it, the laboratory test for blood will usually reveal its presence. Hemorrhage is a hazard to life only when it is massive. Then there may be fainting, weakness, dizziness, sudden vomiting of frank blood or partly digested blood that looks like coffee grounds. This is one of the few real medical emergencies and calls for immediate hospitalization and transfusions.

The second complication is obstruction, and it is fairly common. Scarring on either side of the pyloric opening of the stomach may cause such distortion that food is prevented from leaving the stomach. This complication sometimes demands surgery to establish a new and adequate opening so that food can pass on for complete digestion.

The third complication also creates a genuine emergency. It is perforation. Sometimes an ulcer becomes so deep that it penetrates through the stomach or duodenal wall, digestive products leak into the abdominal cavity causing inflammation, even death, if not surgically repaired in a matter of hours.

The fourth complication is the development of cancer in an unhealed ulcer crater. Ulcers develop from teen age to old age, but most commonly from thirty to fifty-five. In middle age any injured spot may, in some persons, show changes that we call cancer.

In cancer of the stomach (for it is in gastric ulcer that cancer develops), cure depends on early detection and surgical removal. Human beings can live long and eat lustily after surprisingly large portions of the stomach have been removed. This last complication is mentioned in the hope that more men will take the trouble to be *sure* a gastric ulcer is wholesomely healed before they dismiss persisting symptoms with a casual—"just my old ulcer working."

BUT FIRST!

Before any such complications threaten—long before—any intelligent man will hie himself to a doctor. Ulcer symptoms are perfectly clear.

Usually there is a history of "indigestion" for years in the ulcer patient. There are periodic attacks which alternate with periods of freedom. During the attacks the patient complains of heartburn, belching and eructations, and discomfort under the angle of the ribs. Patients become irritable, edgy, sleepless, and lose weight. Many a man who is "hard to get along with" is the victim of ulcer distress.

When the ulcer is "old," the patient usually has vomiting, pain, and some hemorrhage. But pain is the outstanding symptom. If you have pain which, though relieved by food, disappears and reappears again, most likely you have gastric ulcer. If the pain is almost continuous, if frequent feedings are the only way to relieve it, chances are the ulcer is in the duodenum (the first part of the intestine as it joins the stomach).

Such symptoms are quite suggestive, but the way to be sure is by X-ray examination. Other tests are laboratory examinations of the stomach contents and direct visualization by gastroscopy.

TREATMENT WORKS (IF YOU'LL LET IT)

Modern treatment of peptic ulcer is medical—rest, diet and medicine. In the bulk of all co-operative patients, ulcers will heal with such care in about six weeks—a little less in acute ulcers and a bit longer in chronic ulcers. Surgery saves lives when complications arise. Good ulcer care includes rest, relaxation, peace of mind, a balanced diet free of all rough foods, and all substances like condiments, alcohol and tobacco that increase gastric secretion. Medicines, like belladonna (which relaxes smooth muscle), and alkaline substances (which coat the ulcer and neutralize acid gastric juices) are also standard.

Numerous other treatments have come and gone. Chemicals that inhibit gastric secretion or block off nerve stimulation have been used. Treatments come and go, for none are specific cures as penicillin is a cure for pneumonia, for example. All bodies, human and animal, possess an innate *tendency toward recovery*, an ability to self-heal; it is well for the man with peptic ulcers to remember this and not stack the cards too heavily against his body by poor hygiene and unwise living. It is not so much medicine, but a new adjustment to environment that is important in treatment.

When treatment fails, usually due to the patient's incomplete co-operation, there is always operation to fall back on. But vagotomy—a cutting of the vagus nerve carrying impulses from the brain to the walls of the stomach —is not the answer. Neither is hitching the stomach to the intestine to by-pass the ulcer. Nor is partial or complete removal of the stomach a sure cure. Ulcers can recur after apparently successful surgery.

With operation or without operation the *sine qua non* is the full co-operation of the patient.

So if a doctor ever says anything like this to you, pay attention!

"Physical and mental rest is basic," the physician's injunction to an ulcer patient usually runs. "A trip to Bermuda is often as good as three weeks in a hospital. No physical strain; plenty of rest. No emotional stress to stimulate the gastric flow. Cut out tobacco and alcohol; be wary of coffee. No coarse foods, which are abrasive. No spicy foods, which irritate. No acid foods such as pickles, rhubarb, sauerkraut. Eat slowly; do *everything* at a leisurely pace. Don't catch cold or get run down; your resistance is lowered. And stop

fretting about things, even if I have to give you sedatives to keep you numb up in the top story.

"Now, on the positive side—it's best to eat lightly but often and regularly; catch a snack in the middle of each morning and afternoon. Stick to bland foods. Fill yourself full of milk and cream, in as many varied forms as you can concoct. Take the medicine I prescribe, regularly."

And here he'll probably come to the heart of the problem. "If you have any real emotional problem—jealousy, or frustration, or a guilty conscience, or loneliness—you've got to face it squarely, not try to forget it. Maybe I can help, maybe you'll need to talk to a psychiatrist or your minister. Emotional indigestion can give you an awful bellyache."

Peptic ulcer can be cured. It's only the tendency, or predisposition to it, which is really hard to cure. Some people will always have to walk on eggs, emotionally and gastronomically. But, then, this restriction is no worse to live with than a bad back, weak eyes, or a knee that forecasts weather.

So cheer up, if you're worried. Ulcer is no harder to head off than a forty-two-inch waistline or a case of taut nerves. And if you *should* come up with one, you can still get well enough to lead as vigorous and productive a life, in your own field, as have some other ulcer-owners in theirs—Darwin, Napoleon and Bernard Baruch, for example.

HOW'S YOUR LIVER?

In these hectic days of biliousness and burps, the liver assumes considerable importance. It's wonderfully efficient, seldom appreciated, often abused and—indispensable. Maybe you ought to get a little better acquainted with yours:

The liver is the largest gland in the body and in the adult usually weighs between three and three and three-quarters pounds, or roughly one-fortieth of your total weight. In the newborn infant it is much larger in proportion, nearly filling the abdominal cavity and representing about one-eighteenth of the body weight. The reason for this disproportion is that during the early months of life it serves as a reservoir for iron, preventing anemias from developing during the period when the baby's diet is largely milk.

The liver is located high up under the dome of the diaphragm on the right side of the body and extends to about the margin of the lower ribs. If you feel yours projecting down below that level, better check in with a doctor.

Your digestive system converts the carbohydrates you eat (the starches and sugars) into dextrose. The dextrose is absorbed into your circulation, finding its way to your liver. There the portion that you don't need immediately (for energy and heat) is converted into a compound called glycogen and stored for future use. As your body demands it, then, the liver reconverts the glycogen into sugar, gives it into the blood stream, and keeps you going. This process is called the glycogenic function of the liver.

The liver's best-known function, however, is the secretion of bile. Bile is indispensable in the emulsification and digestion of fats. The liver cells secrete bile continuously. Some of the bile output goes immediately to work in your digestive system. Excess goes into reserve in your gall bladder, a small muscular pear-shaped organ snugly tucked away on the underside of your liver. In the gall bladder, the thin and straw-colored liver bile is concentrated into a thick and viscid fluid, ready to be called into service at a moment's notice when the gourmand decides to stuff himself with fatty foods.

Although the liver is susceptible to various poisons, infections, abscesses, tumors and what not, most of the disorders attributed to it by laymen are in reality derangements of the gall bladder and bile passages, so perhaps it might be well to get the geography of this neighborhood properly lined up. Imagine now you're facing a capital Y. The arm of the letter on your right would then correspond to the main collecting duct from the liver formed by the confluence of the many small collecting tubules and properly called the hepatic (liver) duct. The arm of the letter on your left would correspond to the main duct leading from the gall bladder and is known as the cystic duct. The stem of the letter, comparable to the union of both the liver and gall bladder ducts, conducts the bile into the intestinal tract and is named the common duct. With this arrangement well fixed in mind you can easily see how obstruction of the hepatic or common ducts would cause the bile to dam back into the blood stream and produce that yellowish discoloration of the skin known as jaundice, and that's just what happens when infections or foreign bodies such as gallstones occlude these passages.

Disorders of the biliary apparatus are responsible for more burps, tummy-aches, bouts with indigestion than most people suppose. Infections of these passages may come up from the intestinal tract or down, via the blood and lymph channels, from a source so far removed as bad teeth or infected tonsils. If the infection is confined to the gall bladder it is called a cholecysti-tis; if it's in the ducts it is known as a cholangitis. Both types may, and often do, exist concurrently. Symptoms are somewhat the same in either case, except that jaundice is nearly always present when disturbances of the ducts are severe.

As the gall bladder is the most frequent offender, let's give it a closer look. Its thick lining of mucous membrane, and the more or less stagnant bile it contains, make it peculiarly susceptible. Difficulty here is essentially a disease of middle and later life, and it is more common among females than males, but any age or sex is susceptible. A Henry VIII approach to food and drink lays the foundation.

An acute attack usually comes on suddenly; you feel sick all the way through. There is likely to be considerable upper abdominal pain accompanied by nausea, vomiting, retching. The pain may be dull and fairly mild, or severe and radiating to the back, around the right shoulder blade.

The abdomen feels full and distended and is generally tender in the right upper segment. Many other conditions might present a similar picture—don't diagnose yourself! Get thee to a doctor, and without delay.

More common than the acute attack is the low-grade, chronic infection of the biliary apparatus. Those who are overweight, overeating, overdrinking and over forty should be particularly suspicious of "stomach-ache." Symptoms include that overstuffed feeling, vague upper abdominal distress, considerable burping and belching. The capacity of the stomach seems smaller, and tolerance to fatty or greasy foods nil. Such symptoms may continue for a long time without any complications other than acute distress after an eat-and-drink binge. Sometimes, however, gallstones complicate the picture.

Gallstones derive their name from the site of origin, the gall bladder. They are composed chiefly of calcium bilirubinate, a compound derived from bile pigment, and cholesterol, a substance found in such foods as brain, kidney, cream, egg yolk, bacon, liver. One might go along for years totally unaware that he had these little stowaways in his gall bladder. If, however, a stone of any size should pass into the ducts, it would announce itself with a bang.

The migration of the stone causes the smooth muscle lining of the duct affected to contract and go into spasm. The pain is devastating—sharp, lancinating, often referred to the back and right shoulder blade. It may at times be so overwhelming as to resist the strongest opiates. The name for this particular type of bad news is biliary colic. It is, as you see, nothing you can cheerfully ignore.

Fortunately, it can be diagnosed accurately, with the help of a dye (with an unpronounceable name!) and X-ray. And it can be treated, medically or surgically. In practically all cases, dietary restrictions are imposed: fatty and greasy foods are taboo; fried foods and pork products are out, as are eggs, cream, condiments, alcoholic beverages, fatty cheeses, rich dressings, gravies and squishy desserts. Meats rich in cholesterol are also best left alone.

To the luckless afflicted epicure, the prohibited list appears formidable, but he can still make out fairly well on such things as fish, poultry, lean meats, fruits, vegetables and cereals. Regular exercise and moderate living will doubtless be included in his doctor's orders. He will have to keep reminding himself that knives, forks and goblets cause more casualties than bullets and bayonets, in our civilization.

The rest of us might better remember that ahead of time!

3. YOUR NERVES

Tension can kill you! Whatever is bothering you is not just a pain in the neck; it can turn into a pain in the liver and lights. So take it easy.

To put it in medical terms, life stress—arising out of a job, business worries, marriage difficulties or any of a dozen other problems—can create permanent emotional tensions which actually cause dangerous bodily changes; can make a man more susceptible to infectious diseases and even to accidents. If the tensions are not relieved, they will make him chronically ill and may wind up killing him.

It starts with the fact that an emotion is not just a feeling; it's a bodily process. Fear and anger make your heart beat faster, raise your blood pressure and change your metabolism. When you're happy, your facial and diaphragm muscles contract and you laugh; when you're sad, your lachrymal glands make tears; and when you get mad, your adrenal glands and circulatory system get into the act.

All these are normal daily reactions. But in some people certain emotions become persistent. These people are what the doctors call "overmobilized" —always ready for trouble. Pretty soon they find it, inside themselves.

TENSION'S EFFECT ON YOUR BODY

Dr. H. G. McGregor describes the process: "Normally we feel a sense of well-being . . . but let something upset the even tenor of emotional life; let it be protracted from day to day and from week to week; let there be no end in view but only a featureless waste of anxiety, then . . . the victim becomes conscious of the beat of the heart . . . he feels and hears movements in his stomach . . . anxiety exaggerates the sensations so that they become converted into pains. Often the pains serve to divert his mind from the original anxiety to the worse one of ill health, by which he is enabled in some measure to escape from his difficulty."

Tension affects different people in different ways. In some men the colon is the sensitive organ, in others the nose, in still others the heart, the blood vessels, the stomach, the skin. Each group will get a different disease under the same set of stresses; some, who are never called on strongly for a protective reaction, will never get sick at all.

Much of this knowledge traces back to an odd accident that happened to a nine-year-old Irish-American boy named Tom. He had just come in all hot and sweaty from a street game, and he spied the family growler on the kitchen table. He was alone in the room and he decided to steal a swig of the ice-cold, forbidden beer. But it wasn't beer; the pail was full of piping-hot clam chowder, a gift to his father from the local bartender.

Tom gulped a huge mouthful of the scalding chowder and then was afraid to spit it out onto the kitchen floor. He swallowed the steaming liquid and burned his gullet so badly he was never able to use it again.

They took him to the hospital and tried unsuccessfully to open his esophagus with surgery. Finally the surgeon was forced to suture part of Tom's stomach to the outer wall of his body, just below his chest. Tom has lived with this open stomach for the last forty-nine years. He has had a full life—

wife, kids, a good home. He even takes a glass of beer occasionally, tasting it first and then letting it into his stomach through a funnel and rubber tube.

His stomach became more than a curiosity in 1940, when two Cornell University doctors, Stewart Wolf and Harold Wolff, began to study it. After numerous tests with drugs, poisons, alcohol and strong language, they proved that Tom's stomach was an accurate barometer of his emotions, his mental state and his entire life situation.

They found that Tom's stomach swelled up with blood when he was angry. They watched it as it tried to eject and neutralize a poisonous substance; then they watched an identical reaction as Tom tried to reject an unacceptable life situation. From this work and other experiments doctors have deduced that vomiting and diarrhea are the physical evidence that a person has taken on more than he can handle—his body goes through a "riddance pattern." If this pattern is repeated often enough it can lead to such diseases as peptic ulcer or ulcerative colitis.

Other specific diseases have been linked with attitudes. Psychiatrists say that migraine, which is one of the commonest types of headache, is definitely associated with hostility. They believe that in the majority of painful illnesses arising out of tension situations the victim has a deep-seated desire to hurt someone and that the pain is subconscious self-punishment.

IS THE PAIN REAL?

Sometimes the pain has no real physical cause. A lady once complained of "a frightful pain, Doctor. It begins down in my ankles and moves up my legs into the knees; then up to my thighs and catches me in the groins. It keeps on through my stomach and chest, rolls up into my neck and throat and ends up as wind." The doctor to whom she confided these engaging symptoms comments: "There can, of course, be no doubt that in such a case what terminates in a belch can only originate in wind, from one quarter or another." And Dr. Walter Alvarez of the Mayo Clinic says that the objectivity of a pain is inversely proportionate to its description.

Nevertheless, pains rooted in tension are often very real. Life situations can cause hypertension (high blood pressure): the blood vessels constrict, and the heart must work harder to pump blood through them. This condition comes to men and women who are "constantly in a state of conflict in which they feel a strong need to repress their aggressive drives and to gain approval by maintaining peace." People with this kind of high blood pressure are known as hypertensives. Their "emotional conflicts," says Dr. Franz Alexander, "may cause continued fluctuations of blood pressures which, in time, overtax the vascular (circulatory) system, finally cause organic vascular changes and end in irreversible, malignant cases of hypertension."

Nobody knows exactly how many cases of malignant hypertensions are linked with emotional tension. Some doctors think that most of them are. Several have even attempted to classify a number of diseases as "caused" by emotions. Dr. Flanders Dunbar says that cardiovascular disease, accidents, and nephritis (kidney disease)—which, together, cause more than half the total deaths in this country—are diseases in which emotion is either the cause or a complicating factor. Others place hypertension, peptic ulcer, mucous colitis, diabetes and migraine on the list.

CHERCHEZ LA . . . CAUSE

More and more doctors believe that, for successful treatment of any disease—even infectious diseases like tuberculosis—they must investigate the patient's life situation. They use psychotherapy, which is not a long psychoanalysis but a hurry-up method of getting the patient to talk out his difficulties.

A forty-one-year-old man who had suffered long, painful attacks of hives was cured when he learned why he got them. Many of his attacks had occurred at work when he felt some unjust demand had been made on him; on the two occasions when he had talked back to his boss, he had not developed hives. Eventually he learned not to bottle up his resentments, and he stopped itching after arguments.

Dr. Jed H. Irvine, of New York City, noticed seven years ago that many of his arthritis patients developed tender muscles and arthritis when under

emotional strain. He followed three hundred such cases and discovered that he could diagnose emotional tension in his patients by testing their necks, shoulders, arms and thighs for muscle soreness. He found also that some of his patients lost not only their muscular difficulties but the pains of arthritis under psychotherapy.

ON THE MENTAL SIDE

Tension has a shotgun effect—there's no doubt about it—and if a man escapes its toll in bodily ailments he is still a candidate for a crippling neurosis. Some of the most fascinating evidence against tension, in this field, comes from the Behavior Farm at Cornell. There Dr. Howard S. Liddell and his associates have, for almost thirty years, been turning happy, healthy sheep, goats and pigs into analogues of suffering humanity, tremendously increasing medical understanding of how neurosis is caused and cured. Though an animal's nervous breakdown isn't point for point identical with a man's, the similarities are astonishing.

Consider this typical experiment, for example. Liddell goes out to the pasture and leads in a young ewe who has never been inside before. In a testing cell he fastens a stimulus wire to her right foreleg; otherwise she is free to move about the room. (In some experiments, other wires are used to record pulse, breathing, and so on.)

Suddenly, the lights go dim for ten seconds; then, as they go up again, a slight but startling shock prickles her leg. She jumps, bleats and runs around a bit. All is quiet again for a few minutes; then the cycle repeats.

After ten or twenty stimuli, she begins to get the idea. Now she grows anxious when the lights go dim: she starts running about at once, breathing more heavily, and holding her head tensely erect.

But in later sessions, as the wearing process takes effect, she may give up running about. When the lights go dim, she backs tightly into a corner and crouches there, lifting her leg again and again as if to draw it away from the coming stimulus. Her breathing and pulse are getting faster; she trembles and twitches at outside sounds; you can hear her gritting her teeth. Like a soldier under mortar fire, who hears the slow, awful sound of impending blows, she can only wait and hold tight.

Months later, after five hundred or a thousand shocks, she has probably passed over into a full-fledged nervous breakdown. She may jump and twitch and jerk continuously, no matter whether there are signals and shocks or not. Or she may become rigid as soon as she enters the test cell, with her test leg so stiff that it resists bending by the experimenter.

Back in the pasture she avoids the flock—a truly astonishing thing in so gregarious an animal as the sheep. She sleeps poorly, and paces up and down at night. At the oat trough, in the morning, she is afraid to fight her way in with the rest and hangs back until they are finished. She is a very sick sheep.

Like her human counterparts, she has acquired a full-fledged phobia. If dimming lights have been the preshock signal, any dimming now frightens her.

Professor Jules Masserman, formerly at Chicago University, once taught some cats to open a food box, after a light was flashed, and get a morsel of salmon. Later on, though, when they opened the box they might instead get a startling jet of air across their noses. The conflict between the two desires —to get the food and to avoid the air blast—made nervous wrecks of them. Even a semistarved cat, seeing the food box brought near, would run to the far corner and huddle there, face to the wall, in cataleptic rigidity, not even daring to turn around and look at the box.

Sheep and cats have taught psychiatrists that some of the ills we think are due to our great human intelligences aren't so at all. An overwrought sheep, for instance, can behave as if he had a bona fide hallucination. Not long ago, a big ram was being tested in Liddell's laboratory. In the long quiet pauses between buzzer signals, he'd frequently jerk his leg upward and jump, just as he did when he got a real stimulus. His straining nervous system must have "thought" it received stimuli, again and again. If he'd been a man, he might have been seeing snakes or ghosts, or talking to invisible companions.

Animals can be made into "perfectionists"; they can develop "compulsive behavior" that is very like a human's. An accumulation of annoyances can turn even the meek and mild sheep into an aggressive beast.

The first work on animal neuroses grew out of tests of what scientists called "difficult differentiations." Over thirty years ago, the great Russian physiologist, Ivan Pavlov, was teaching a dog to expect food wherever he saw a circle, but not when he saw an oval. Day by day Pavlov showed him ovals that were nearer and nearer to being perfect circles.

One day the dog suddenly went wild—howling and showing what could only be called "neurotic" behavior. He had had a near nervous breakdown from trying to make too difficult a decision, just as human beings sometimes do.

Anxiety and tension occurring at reasonably frequent and regular intervals will wear away the nervous system. In the animal experiments it would appear that the tension is more destructive than the actual shock. An animal can be shocked without warning signals hundreds of times; he'll be startled, but he won't become neurotic. But the warning signal touches off an alarm reaction in the body. Adrenalin spurts into the blood, the heart speeds up, muscles get tense, blood pressure increases, the brain races madly—and the real damage is under way.

Even though a goat or sheep learns to avoid a shock by lifting his leg, he can become neurotic just from the repeated strain of the warning, tension and waiting. He may look a lot quieter than a new animal just experiencing stimuli for the first time, who thrashes about excitedly, for he has learned that mere thrashing does no good and he imposes restraint on himself, tensely waiting for the shock or the end of the signal. But this quiet, restrained

phase is the real sign, to Howard Liddell, that his animal is on the way to trouble.

IN YOUR OWN CASE . . .

And what has all this to do with you? Know anyone who has migraine, or ulcers, or that "tired feeling"? Ever have lunch with an executive who takes a pill or two along with his meal? Perhaps you yourself are up against any of these four contributing factors to businessmen's ailments:

> Friction generated by competitive internal politicking top management ignores, and sometimes encourages;
>
> Expense-account living that often warps the individual's sense of values;

Anxiety produced by the relentless pressure to acquire status and "status symbols";

Recreational activities that are too competitive or aggravating, too apt to repeat the friction and expense and status problems they are intended to relieve.

Take the first letter of each of those points and you have a staple of modern life—F E A R. Probably you have to live with fear and doubt and worry in some form or another—that's life—but you don't have to die of it. Not if you recognize what you're up against. Not if you learn to be alert to the signals your body will send you when the screw begins to turn too tight.

THE POUND OF PREVENTION

The best a man can do for himself is to prevent disease by recognizing in advance the physical effects of stresses and strains in his daily life. Disease resulting from tension does not come suddenly. All through a man's life there are signs and portents to tell him which organs of his body are most endangered by tension. Then, either alone or with the help of a doctor, a man can avoid the dangerous tensions that may make him sick. In most cases he can learn to relax.

Mild, noncompetitive exercises such as golf are often recommended as relaxation. "But don't imagine that golf or painting or any one hobby is a cure for everyone," a doctor said recently. "Some men get more tense playing golf than working in the office. They go at the game with the same competitive drive that causes their tension. One man can relax by walking up and down his office, another may take a trip around the world—and still not lose his tension."

Most doctors don't believe much in self-help, certainly not after a man is sick, but one has proved that relaxation can be learned by most people if they try hard enough. Dr. Edmund Jacobson, who wrote *Progressive Relaxation* for the medical profession and *You Must Relax!* for everybody else, holds that a man who can control a muscle can also relax it, and that the way to control it is to tense it until it hurts. Then every time it tenses unconsciously you can relax it consciously.

Jacobson suggests that you lie comfortably on your back on a cot or bed with your arms at your sides and your legs not crossed. Then, one by one, you can tense your muscles and relax them—the biceps, triceps, hand flexors, hand extensors, elevators of shoulders, even the face muscles of smiling and frowning, of mouth opening and of swallowing.

As a doctor, Jacobson is careful not to make any large claims for his theories. But his relaxation methods have shown positive results on patients with a wide variety of disorders such as convulsive tic, mucous colitis, asthma, chronic insomnia and Graves' disease.

The ability to relax is always a useful quality, and in some people it's vital. "If you go through life under tension," one doctor said recently, "you're like an automobile steadily racing its motor at full throttle, in high gear, with the clutch out and the brake on. Sooner or later something lets go—and there are damned few spare parts to repair a human body."

DANGER AHEAD?

If it is your spirit that "lets go"—nothing so precise as a stomach-ache or a skin disorder—this too can be restored to effective working order. Neurosis is curable if it is recognized early and fought early. Just remember that it *could* happen to you.

Every one of us is a potential neurotic. It is only a question of time when an event or events will try our stability. Dr. William C. Menninger has said, "No one, no matter how calm and complacent, is immune to psychoneurosis if the emotional strain gets tough enough."

The neurotic man is only half living. Half living is half dying. Although there are spirited neurotics who make great contributions to mankind (at, as Marcel Proust once wrote, great cost "in sleepless nights, tears, spasmodic laughter, rashes, asthmas, epilepsies, and the fear of death, which is worse than all the rest"), the more common variety of neurotic is listless, passive, emotionally empty and devoid of feeling. He is anesthetized against the enjoyments of life, and prevented by his neurosis from the effectiveness, the accomplishments and the happiness that might otherwise be his.

How can you tell when you have a neurosis? The answer is not always simple. Usually, the doctor has to make that decision for you. Nevertheless, even without a doctor's help, a person can sense that everything is just not right. Most people are not neurotic all their lives. They pass through childhood, adolescence, the twenties and the thirties apparently well adjusted and happy. Then, suddenly or slowly, they notice, and perhaps their friends notice, that they are different.

For example, if you have always had an ebullient nature, but if for a number of months you have been depressed and unhappy, you may be suffering from some sort of neurosis. It may be mild, and perhaps will pass over within a few weeks or months; but, nevertheless, it is sufficiently severe to take the so-called joy out of life. Your former interests become stale. If you were a heavy reader, you now read little if at all. If you enjoyed fishing trips with the boys, you now decline to go. You are rarely seen at affairs where people congregate; rather, you tend to keep to yourself. Something obviously is bothering you.

Illness or death in the family may have brought on your neurosis. Financial difficulties are a common cause. Loss of a job and the subsequent development of inferiority feeling is another reason.

But whatever the cause or causes, it is essential that you meet yourself squarely and answer the questions, "Have I really gone off on a tangent? Am I unlike the fellow I used to be?"

If you are not willing and able to answer such questions honestly, you are giving your neurosis opportunity to imbed its tentacles in your personality. Remember that you can partially die in a neurosis by living only part of your life. You must neutralize the destructive urge which is squeezing the fun out of living. The only way to give self-preservation a chance is to ask your doctor how you can strengthen this instinct and lessen the destructive urge.

The cure may be simpler than you think. It is possible that you are in less imbalance than you realize. Your family doctor may easily set you straight. If it is not so simple, a psychiatrist can straighten you out.

And the sooner the better.

4. YOUR SEX

This article by Arthur Schlesinger, Jr., is not, strictly speaking, about health. But it belongs here in this book, we think, prologue to the medical articles concerned with problems of maleness, because it lights the stage on which modern men move. In what direction? With what sense of self? Mr. Schlesinger:

ARE YOU MAN ENOUGH?—<small>A SPECIAL INTRODUCTION</small>

What has happened to the American male? For a long time, he seemed utterly confident in his manhood, sure of his masculine role in society, easy and definite in his sense of sexual identity. The frontiersmen of James Fenimore Cooper, for example, never had any concern about masculinity; they were men, and it did not occur to them to think twice about it. Even well into the twentieth century, the heroes of Dreiser, of Fitzgerald, of Hemingway remain men. But one begins to detect a new theme emerging in some of these authors, especially in Hemingway: the theme of the male hero increasingly preoccupied with proving his virility to himself. And by mid-century, the male role had plainly lost its rugged clarity of outline. Today men are more and more conscious of maleness not as a fact but as a problem. The ways by which American men affirm their masculinity are uncertain and obscure. There are multiplying signs, indeed, that something has gone badly wrong with the American male's conception of himself.

On the most superficial level, the roles of male and female are increasingly merged in the American household. The American man is found as never before as a substitute for wife and mother—changing diapers, washing dishes, cooking meals and performing a whole series of what once were considered female duties. The American woman meanwhile takes over more and more of the big decisions, controlling them indirectly when she cannot do so directly. Outside the home, one sees a similar blurring of function. While men design dresses and brew up cosmetics, women become doctors, lawyers, bank cashiers and executives. "Women now fill many 'masculine' roles," writes the psychologist, Dr. Bruno Bettelheim, "and expect their husbands to assume many of the tasks once reserved for their own sex." They seem an expanding, aggressive force, seizing new domains like a conquering army, while men, more and more on the defensive, are hardly able to hold their own and gratefully accept assignments from their new rulers. A recent book bears the stark and melancholy title *The Decline of the American Male*.

Some of this evidence, it should be quickly said, has been pushed too far. The willingness of a man to help his wife around the house may as well be evidence of confidence in masculinity as the opposite; such a man obviously does not have to cling to masculine symbols in order to keep demonstrating his maleness to himself. But there is more impressive evidence than the helpful husband that this is an age of sexual ambiguity. It appears no accident, for example, that the changing of sex—the Christine Jorgensen phenomenon

—so fascinates our newspaper editors and readers; or that homosexuality, that incarnation of sexual ambiguity, should be enjoying a cultural boom new in our history. Such developments surely express a deeper tension about the problems of sexual identity.

Consider the theater, that faithful mirror of a society's preoccupations. There have been, of course, popular overt inquiries into sexual ambiguities, like *Compulsion* or *Tea and Sympathy*. But in a sense these plays prove the case too easily. Let us take rather two uncommonly successful plays by the most discussed young playwrights of the United States and Great Britain— Tennessee Williams's *Cat on a Hot Tin Roof* and John Osborne's *Look Back in Anger*. Both deal with the young male in a singular state of confusion and desperation. In *Cat on a Hot Tin Roof*, Brick Pollitt, the professional football player, refuses to sleep with his wife because of guilty memories of his relations with a dead team mate. In *Look Back in Anger*, Jimmy Porter, the embittered young intellectual who can sustain a relationship with his wife only by pretending they are furry animals together, explodes with hatred of women and finds his moments of happiness roughhousing around the stage with a male pal.

Brick Pollitt and Jimmy Porter are all too characteristic modern heroes. They are, in a sense, castrated; one is stymied by fear of homosexuality, the other is an unconscious homosexual. Neither is capable of dealing with the woman in his life: Brick surrenders to a strong woman, Jimmy destroys a weak one. Both reject the normal female desire for full and reciprocal love as an unconscionable demand and an intolerable burden. Now not many American males have been reduced to quite the Pollitt-Porter condition. Still the intentness with which audiences have watched these plays suggests that exposed nerves are being plucked—that the Pollitt-Porter dilemma expresses in vivid and heightened form something that many spectators themselves feel or fear.

Or consider the movies. In some ways, the most brilliant and influential American film since the war is *High Noon*. That remarkable movie, which invested the Western with the classic economy of myth, can be viewed in several ways: as an existentialist drama, for example, or as a parable of McCarthyism. It can also be viewed as a mordant comment on the effort of the American woman to emasculate the American man. The sheriff plainly did not suffer from Brick Pollitt's disease. But a large part of the story dealt with the attempt of his girl to persuade him not to use force—to deny him the use of his pistol. The pistol is an obvious masculine symbol, and, in the end, it was the girl herself, in the modern American manner, who used the pistol and killed a villain. (In this connection, one can pause and note why the Gary Coopers, Cary Grants, Clark Gables and Spencer Tracys continue to play romantic leads opposite girls young enough to be their daughters; it is obviously because so few of the younger male stars can project a convincing sense of masculinity.)

Psychoanalysis backs up the theater and the movies in emphasizing the obsession of the American male with his manhood. "Every psychoanalyst knows," writes one of them, "how many emotional difficulties are due to those fears and insecurities of neurotic men who are unconsciously doubting their masculinity." "In our civilization," Dr. Theodor Reik says, "men are afraid that they will not be men enough." Reik adds significantly: "And women are afraid that they might be considered only women." Why is it that women worry, not over whether they can fill the feminine role, but whether filling that role is enough, while men worry whether they can fill the masculine role at all? How to account for this rising tide of male anxiety? What has unmanned the American man?

There is currently a fashionable answer to this question. Male anxiety, many observers have declared, is simply the result of female aggression: what has unmanned the American man is the American woman. The present male confusion and desperation, it is contended, are the inevitable consequence of the threatened feminization of American society. The victory of women is the culmination of a long process of masculine retreat, beginning when Puritanism made men feel guilty about sex and the frontier gave women the added value of scarcity. Fleeing from the reality of femininity, the American man, while denying the American woman juridical equality, transformed her into an ideal of remote and transcendent purity with overriding authority over the family, the home, the school and culture. This habit of obeisance left the male psychologically disarmed and vulnerable when the goddess stepped off the pedestal and demanded in addition equal economic, political and legal rights. In the last part of the nineteenth century, women won their battle for equality. They gained the right of entry into one occupation after another previously reserved for males. Today they hold the key positions of personal power in our society and use this power relentlessly to consolidate their mastery. As mothers, they undermine masculinity through the use of love as a technique of reward and punishment. As teachers, they prepare male children for their role of submission in an increasingly feminine world. As wives, they complete the work of subjugation. Their strategy of conquest is deliberately to emasculate men—to turn them into Brick Pollitts and Jimmy Porters.

Or so a standard indictment runs; and no doubt there is something in it. American women have unquestionably gained through the years a place in our society which American men have not been psychologically prepared to accept. Whether because of Puritanism or the frontier, there has been something immature in the traditional American male attitude toward women —a sense of alarm at times amounting to panic. Almost none of the classic American novels, for example, presents the theme of mature and passionate love. Our nineteenth-century novelists saw women either as unassailable virgins or abandoned temptresses—never simply as women. One looks in vain through *Moby Dick* and *The Adventures of Huckleberry Finn,* through Cooper and Poe and Whitman, for an adult portrayal of relations between men and women. "Where," Leslie Fiedler has asked, "is the American *Madame Bovary, Anna Karenina, Wuthering Heights,* or *Vanity Fair?*"

Yet the implication of the argument that the American man has been unmanned by the emancipation of the American woman is that the American man was incapable of growing up. For the nineteenth-century sense of masculinity was based on the psychological idealization and the legal subjection of women; masculinity so spuriously derived could never—and should never —have endured. The male had to learn to live at some point with the free and equal female. Current attempts to blame "the decline of the American male" on the aggressiveness of the American female amount to a confession that, under conditions of free competition, the female was bound to win. Simple observation refutes this supposition. In a world of equal rights, some women rise; so too do some men; and no pat generalization is possible about the sexual future of society. Women have gained power in certain ways; in others, they have made little progress. It is safe to predict, for example, that we will have a Roman Catholic, perhaps even a Jew, for President before we have a woman. Those amiable prophets of an impending American matriarchy (all men, by the way) are too pessimistic.

Something more fundamental is involved in the unmanning of American men than simply the onward rush of American women. Why is the American man so unsure today about his masculine identity? The basic answer to this is surely because he is so unsure about his identity in general. Nothing is harder in the whole human condition than to achieve a full sense of identity —than to know who you are, where you are going, and what you mean to live and die for. From the most primitive myths to the most contemporary novels—from Oedipus making the horrified discovery that he had married his mother, to Leopold Bloom and Stephen Dedalus searching their souls in Joyce's Dublin and the haunted characters of Kafka trying to make desperate sense out of an incomprehensible universe—the search for identity has been the most compelling human problem. That search has always been ridden with trouble and terror. And it can be plausibly argued that the conditions of modern life make the quest for identity more difficult than it has ever been before.

The predemocratic world was characteristically a world of status in which people were provided with ready-made identities. But modern Western society—free, equalitarian, democratic—has swept away all the old niches in which people for so many centuries found safe refuge. Only a few people at any time in human history have enjoyed the challenge of "making" themselves; most have fled from the unendurable burden of freedom into the womblike security of the group. The new age of social mobility may be fine for those strong enough to discover and develop their own roles. But for the timid and the frightened, who constitute the majority in any age, the great vacant spaces of equalitarian society can become a nightmare filled with nameless horrors. Thus mass democracy, in the very act of offering the individual new freedom and opportunity, offers new moral authority to the group and thereby sets off a new assault on individual identity. Over a century ago Alexis de Tocqueville, the perceptive Frenchman who ruminated on the contradictions of equality as he toured the United States in the eighteen-thirties, pointed to the "tyranny of the majority" as a central problem of democracy. John Stuart Mill, lamenting the decline of individualism in Great Britain, wrote: "That so few now dare to be eccentric marks the chief danger of the time." How much greater that danger seems a century later!

For our own time has aggravated the assault on identity by adding economic and technological pressures to the political and social pressures of the nineteenth century. Modern science has brought about the growing centralization of the economy. We work and think and live and even dream in larger and larger units. William H. Whyte, Jr., has described the rise of "the organization man," working by day in immense business concerns, sleeping by night in immense suburban developments, deriving his fantasy life from mass-produced entertainments, spending his existence, not as an individual, but as a member of a group and coming in the end to feel guilty and lost when he deviates from his fellows. Adjustment rather than achievement becomes the social ideal. Men no longer fulfill an inner sense of what they *must* be; indeed, with the cult of the group, that inner sense itself begins to evaporate. Identity consists, not of self-realization, but of smooth absorption into the group. Nor is this just a matter of passive acquiescence. The group is aggressive, imperialistic, even vengeful, forever developing new weapons with which to overwhelm and crush the recalcitrant individual. Not content with disciplining the conscious mind, the group today is even experimenting with means of violating the subconscious. The subliminal invasion represents the climax of the assault on individual identity.

It may seem a long way from the loss of the sense of self to the question of masculinity. But if people do not know *who* they are, it is hardly surprising that they are no longer sure what sex they are. Nigel Dennis's exuberant novel, *Cards of Identity,* consists of a series of brilliant variations on the quest for identity in contemporary life. It reaches one of its climaxes in the tale of a person who was brought up by enlightened parents to believe that there was no such thing as pure male or female—everyone had elements of both —and who accepted this proposition so rigorously that he (she) could not decide what his (her) own sex was. "In what identity do you intend to face the future?" someone asks. "It seems that nowadays," comes the plaintive reply, "one must choose between being a woman who behaves like a man, and a man who behaves like a woman. In short, I must choose to be one in order to behave like the other." If most of us have not yet quite reached that condition of sexual chaos, yet the loss of a sense of identity is obviously a fundamental step in the decay of masculinity. And the gratification with which some American males contemplate their own decline should not obscure the fact that women, for all their recent legal and economic triumphs, are suffering from a loss of identity too. It is not accidental that the authors of one recent book described modern woman as the "lost sex."

If this is true, then the key to the recovery of masculinity does not lie in any wistful hope of humiliating the aggressive female and restoring the old masculine supremacy. Masculine supremacy, like white supremacy, was the neurosis of an immature society. It is good for men as well as for women that women have been set free. In any case, the process is irreversible; that particular genie can never be put back into the bottle. The key to the recovery of masculinity lies rather in the problem of identity. When a person begins to find out *who* he is, he is likely to find out rather soon what sex he is.

For men to become men again, in short, their first task is to recover a sense of individual spontaneity. And to do this a man must visualize himself as an individual apart from the group, whatever it is, which defines his values and commands his loyalty. There is no reason to suppose that the group is always wrong: to oppose the group automatically is nearly as conformist as to surrender to it automatically. But there is every necessity to recognize that the group is one thing and the individual—oneself—is another. One of the most sinister of present-day doctrines is that of *togetherness.* The recovery of identity means, first of all, a new belief in apartness. It means a determination to resist the overpowering conspiracy of blandness, which seeks to conceal all tension and conflict in American life under a blanket of locker-room affability. And the rebirth of spontaneity depends, at bottom, on changes of attitude *within* people—changes which can perhaps be described, without undue solemnity, as moral changes. These changes will no doubt come about in as many ways as there are individuals involved. But there are some general suggestions that can be made about the techniques of liberation. I should like to mention three such techniques: satire, art, and politics.

Satire means essentially the belief that nothing is sacred—that there is no person or institution or idea which cannot but benefit from the exposure of comedy. Our nation in the past has reveled in satire; it is, after all, the nation of Abraham Lincoln, of Mark Twain, of Finley Peter Dunne, of H. L. Mencken, of Ring Lardner. Indeed, the whole spirit of democracy is that of satire; as Montaigne succinctly summed up the democratic faith: "Sit he on never so high a throne, a man still sits on his own bottom." Yet today American society can only be described as a pompous society, at least in its official manifestations. Early in 1958 Mort Sahl, the night-club comedian, made headlines in New York because he dared make a joke about J. Edgar Hoover! It was not an especially good joke, but the fact that he made it at all was an encouraging sign. One begins to feel that the American people can only stand so much reverence—that in the end our native skepticism will break through, sweep aside the stuffed shirts and the stuffed heads and insist that platitudes are platitudinous and the great are made, among other things, to be laughed at. Irony is good for our rulers; and it is even better for ourselves because it is a means of dissolving the pomposity of society and giving the individual a chance to emerge.

If irony is one source of spontaneity, art is another. Very little can so refresh our vision and develop our vision and develop our values as the liberating experience of art. The mass media have cast a spell on us: the popular addiction to prefabricated emotional clichés threatens to erode our capacity for fresh and direct aesthetic experience. Individual identity vanishes in the welter of machine-made reactions. But thoughtful exposure to music, to painting, to poetry, to the beauties of nature, can do much to restore the inwardness, and thereby the identity, of man. There is thus great hope in the immense cultural underground of our age—the paper-bound books, the long-playing records, the drama societies, the art festivals, the new interest in painting and sculpture. All this represents a disdain for existing values and goals, a reaching out for something more exacting and more personal, an intensified questing for identity.

And politics in a true sense can be a means of liberation—not the banal politics of rhetoric and self-congratulation, which aims at burying all real issues under a mass of piety and platitude; but the politics of responsibility, which tries to define the real issues and present them to the people for decision. Our national politics have become boring in recent years because our leaders have offered neither candid and clear-cut formulations of the problems nor the facts necessary for intelligent choice. A virile political life will be definite and hard-hitting, respecting debate and dissent, seeking clarity and decision.

As the American male develops himself by developing his comic sense, his aesthetic sense and his moral and political sense, the lineaments of personality will at last begin to emerge. The achievement of identity, the conquest of a sense of self—these will do infinitely more to restore American masculinity than all the hormones in the test tubes of our scientists. "Whoso would be a *man*," said Emerson, "must be a nonconformist"; and, if it is the present writer who adds the italics, nonetheless one feels that no injustice is done to Emerson's intention. How can masculinity, femininity, or anything else survive in a homogenized society, which seeks steadily and benignly to eradicate all differences between the individuals who compose it? If we want to have *men* again in our theaters and our films and our novels—not to speak of in our classrooms, our business offices and our homes—we must first have a society which encourages each of its members to have a distinct identity.

HOW YOUR SEX ORGANS WORK—OR FALTER

This is a bull session about sex, but without the bull: the medical facts on sterility, impotence, "change of life" in men, the effect of general health on performance, the answers to a batch of other questions that a man might hesitate to ask out loud. Lock out the locker-room innuendo, now, for these are the straight and basic facts.

The human body is wonderfully engineered, and one of its most fascinating machines is the apparatus set up for the propagation of the species.

The male child is born with all the necessary reproductive parts in miniature. From the time the average boy is seven or eight he has specific evidence of his maleness and his eventual reproductive function. Erection has been known to occur even in infants. Small boys have shown themselves capable of reproductive effectiveness at an extraordinarily early age, and there are cases of proven fatherhood in men of ninety. What are the mechanics of this almost lifetime endowment of sexual power?

At puberty, changes occur in the testis or male sex gland that make it capable of responding to special chemicals spilled into the blood stream by the pituitary gland in the brain. These pituitary chemicals, called hormones, act in combination with the hormones from the thyroid gland in the neck and the adrenal glands above the kidneys and prod the testicles into growth and activity. The action of all these glands together completes sexual maturity. The small boy outgrows all his clothes; his bones and muscles increase in weight and size. He acquires physical strength. His sexual organs become those of an adult male. His voice deepens, and his beard grows. A day comes when father looks at little Johnny and is startled to see that he has produced a man.

This gradual progression from boy to man will not take place unless all the proper hormones are secreted by the endocrine glands in proper sequence and quantity. Of course, there are wide normal variations. Both the male and the female manufacture in their own bodies hormones of the opposite sex. Few of us are one hundred per cent male or one hundred per cent female. The ruggedest of he-men has some traits we consider feminine, the daintiest of women may show a make-up more typical of the male—a mixture that puts spice into everyday living.

Although various endocrine glands secrete hormones that influence the maturing of the male, the characteristics which we associate with maleness result from the action of hormones called androgens, from two Greek words meaning "man" and "produce." Over fifty such substances have been isolated or synthesized. They are secreted by many different tissues and organs in both male and female bodies. The development and maintenance of essential maleness, however, depends on the integrity of the testis. Its most important androgen is called testosterone.

The human testicle is composed of a mass of coils of "seminiferous tubules," somewhat like the copper coils in a radiant-heating system, only arranged throughout a ball rather than over a flat surface. These tubules contain several layers of developing sperm cells. The deeper layers hold the more primitive cells and the outer layer, which lines the tubules, contains the almost mature spermatozoa. At puberty these cells begin to mature, to slough off, and to pass into an adjacent storage structure called the epididymis, where their maturing continues until they become motile and capable of migration.

Because spermatozoa can live only in a limited temperature range, preferring a climate cooler than the normal body temperature, the testicle and epididymis are slung in a sacklike organ, the scrotum, hung between the legs, where the temperature is lower than within the body cavity. When the body is exposed to chilling, the muscles of the scrotum contract, snuggling the testes closer for increased warmth, to protect the fragile spermatozoa from dangerous chilling. When the body is too warm, the muscles relax, letting the scrotum sag lower, into cooler air—a wonderful job of engineering.

The supporting tissue of the testes contains "interstitial cells" which secrete the male sex hormones, testosterone. This complex chemical is responsible for the production and the maintenance of the male characteristics —the deep voice, the beard, the male distribution of body hair, the size and the healthy functioning of the organs of reproduction: testes, epididymes, prostate, penis, etc.

For reproduction, fertile, mature spermatozoa must be deposited at the orifice of the female uterus (womb) so that they can swim through the uterus into the Fallopian tubes and unite with the female germ cells. To effect this union, the penis must be capable of penetration.

The complicated mechanisms of erection and ejaculation are possible because of the anatomy of the penis, which has an intricate network of blood vessels forming a mesh about the shaft of the organ, and a special arrangement of supporting ligaments. Erection is not a matter of muscles; it occurs when nerves stimulate the walls of the multitudinous blood vessels in the penis. The walls promptly dilate, allowing the mesh of vessels to be flooded with blood. This turgidity makes the organ enlarge and become rigid, much as a piece of flexible rubber garden hose becomes rigid when the water is turned on hard. The ligaments attach the penis to the torso in such a way that leverage produces erection when the penis is rigid.

Of course, no erection would take place without nervous stimulation. The mechanism is activated by nerves from the sacral portion of the spinal cord. Stimulation may come from local congestion, as in some nocturnal emissions, from local reaction, as a contact against the penis surface, or even from the higher brain centers. Thought, emotion, memory, sights, smells, all sorts of erotic stimuli may be involved in sex activity, a fact which is important in any discussion of potency.

After a varying period of erection, certain muscles relax while others contract, and about a teaspoonful of mucoid fluid is ejaculated. This contains various proteins, salts, calcium, even sugar, and an average, normally, of 120 million swimming spermatozoa. Following this sequence there is a sense of satiety and lassitude with complete flaccidity of the genital organs. That the tissue in the penis is able to go through such dramatic changes in such a short period is still a matter of wonder to the physiologist.

For reproduction, there must be healthy sex organs, proper nervous response, and mature, motile spermatozoa adequate both as to quality and quantity. Either phase of the function may be lost. When the ability to produce and emit normal spermatozoa is lost, we say the man is infertile or sterile. When the ability to have an erection and coitus is lost, the man is called impotent. It is possible to be impotent but fertile, and potent but sterile. Both of these matters cause a good deal of unnecessary confusion.

INFERTILITY

The first requisite of reproduction is the ability to produce healthy, viable spermatozoa. Many things may interfere with this ability. The pituitary gland may fail to secrete hormone to stimulate the testes into production of male hormone, which means that spermatogenesis does not occur. Some pituitary dwarfs are examples of this failure. Such conditions are uncommon. More usual is damage from malnutrition, exposure to X-rays, or disease.

Malnutrition can be due to food fads and ignorance in balancing the diet, as well as to poverty. A starving man—whether he is a war victim or a prosperous businessman on an inadequate diet—experiences deterioration in body tissue. Diseases which cause high fever may temporarily kill spermatozoa, which require a cool environment. Mumps with testicular complications and syphilis can destroy actual seminiferous tubule tissue and produce permanent sterility. Repeated exposure to radiation may also destroy germ tissue. Gonorrhea usually creates sterility by causing blocking or stricture of the exit channels, thus preventing the emission of spermatozoa. Such blocking may be permanent or relieved by surgery.

These are a few of the common reasons for infertility. It is also possible that couples will fail to produce offspring, although the man shows apparently healthy motile spermatozoa and the woman is normal to all known tests for fertility. Sometimes both of them will have children in new marriages. But more than half the sterile marriages in the United States are due to infertility or subnormal fertility on the part of the male.

IMPOTENCE

Impotence is the inability to have an erection and ejaculation. Its causes may be physical or emotional, permanent or temporary. Actual malformation, injury or disease of the generative organs may make erection impossible. Injury or disease of any part of the complicated nerve structure that initiates the action may impair or abolish erections. Polio or a broken back, paralyzing the victim from the waist down and cutting the nerve circuit, may produce impotence. Fatigue and anxiety may cause temporary impotence, and most men experience a "physiologic impotence" lasting from minutes to hours or days immediately following intercourse.

Much impotence has an emotional cause—*functional*, the doctor calls it. The machinery is all in good order, tests are all normal, but it just doesn't work.

Embarrassment, fears, inhibitions, religious taboos, panic from danger of discovery, sudden concern about disease or pregnancy, conflicts—all these horrid emotions can rise up like ghosts to paralyze a man at just the wrong moment. Then, dismayed, he adds to his troubles by anxiety about his own male capacity. It may take an understanding wife, a wise doctor, even a competent psychiatrist several months to straighten out the situation.

THE EFFECTS OF AGING

In the great over-all plan for the universe, all creatures grow, mature, work, reproduce, then decline and eventually disappear. It takes sixty-three days for the development of a cocker spaniel from fertilization of the egg to birth of a curly-haired puppy, and elephants require from eighteen to twenty-one months to produce another elephant, depending on the breed. Man is between them, manufactured in nine months. He lives six or seven times as long as his companion the dog, and expects to outlive the elephant by fifteen or twenty years. But, like his animal kin, he has periods of development and productivity, and then declines. Physiologists tell us that this decline begins at about thirty-five, but can hardly be noticed until the late forties or fifties. Because man is a thoughtful animal, he is aware of this decline and sometimes foolishly rebellious. Few men have received the gift of acceptance.

This pattern of growth, maturity, reproduction and slow decline is clearly visible in both men and women. It is more obvious in the female because the reproduction mechanism is more intricate. From the age of about twelve, when menstruation begins, until reproductive capacity ends with menopause at about forty-eight, every woman is constantly reminded of her importance as a propagation machine. Anything else she may do with her life—teaching, business, a profession—has to be superimposed on her fundamental body activity as a childbearing creature. Both the onset and the cessation of this complicated function are sudden and dramatic, involving relatively short periods of time. Nature crowds everything into two or three years and forces every woman to hurry through major adjustments in her physical and emotional life.

In men, the transition is usually late and extremely gradual. Few men are ever aware of the changes which are closing out their reproductive lives. Few doctors see men with any of the complaints which characterize the female menopause. It is doubtful that there is anything in man worthy of the important title of the climacteric.

In middle age, many men become physically and mentally slower. They get tired more easily, sometimes suffer a mildly unpleasant dizziness, a moodiness and a loss of zest. Some may note a lessening of interest in sex experience, but they also note a loss in physical stamina, in muscular strength, perhaps some shortness of breath on exertion—a dozen minor inconveniences that can be blamed on Father Time alone.

There is seldom any startling collapse of sex prowess. Gradually, just as he lost the hotheadedness of youth, the man of sixty finds his sex desires less demanding. The intervals between enjoyment become longer, but the satisfaction may be unchanged or even increased. If he is wise enough to accept the adjustments that the years impose, a man may continue both potent and fertile far into old age.

Sterility and impotence may occur at any age. One or both may come, plague the victim for a time, and then disappear. Recovery is sometimes spontaneous, but sometimes long periods of medical or psychiatric treatment are required. These problems have no specific tie-up with the problems of aging and the male climacteric, except that eventually age will supervene, if any man lives long enough.

The effects of aging always depend on the individual: some men and some families are old at fifty-five and others are young at eighty.

Getting older is a problem in a man's sex life only if he lets his mind linger over the past instead of stepping expectantly toward the future. For men, if not for women, there is accuracy in the adage, "You're only as old as you feel."

ARE YOU A FERTILE MALE?

If your answer to that question is a deep sigh, followed by a peroration on the difference between the real costs and the income tax deductions allowed you for raising a big family, you will probably find it hard to believe that lack of fertility could ever be a *problem* to anyone. But the fact is that, according to the findings of Philadelphia's Wistar Institute of Anatomy and Biology, only about 40 per cent of American men are capable of fertilization most of the time during the peak of their reproductive lives. About 20 to 25 per cent probably *never* will become fathers, no matter how much they try. Of the remaining 35 to 40 per cent, many will have fewer children than they want, and some will have none unless they get medical advice and scientific help. And as a final blow to the male ego, the Institute says about two-thirds of the cases of childlessness are the husband's rather than the wife's fault.

Now don't get the idea that subfertile males are all sissies. As far as that goes, the most fertile are not necessarily the most masculine-looking. The heavyweight wrestler isn't always more fertile than the decidedly less rugged artist. We all know a Casper Milquetoast type who has fathered a large, healthy brood, while some heavy-bearded superman of our acquaintance goes childless year after year. We probably say these are exceptions to the rule. The fact is, there isn't any rule. There are about as many strongly masculine types to be found in the fertile group as in the unfertile. This is borne out by the result of a test of eight first-team college football players, all thoroughly masculine types. Two were classified as highly fertile, three as relatively fertile, and three as subfertile. Interestingly, the percentages in each group are about the same for the male population as a whole.

All fertile males can be classified into one of these three groups: *highly fertile, relatively fertile,* and *subfertile.* A few unfortunate males go into a fourth group: *sterile.*

A man's classification depends upon the number of active spermatozoa his system can manufacture at one time. If his body can produce 185 million or more, he is classified as *highly fertile;* if between 80 and 185 million, he is *relatively fertile;* if below 80 million, he is *subfertile.* Sterile men produce no active spermatozoa at all. Except for a temporary drop for a day or two after sexual relations, most men remain in the same category all their reproductive lives.

However, some men may unwittingly reduce their powers of fertility. Venereal disease may affect fertility, as may tuberculosis and mumps.

This doesn't mean that a man is made sterile by one or more of these experiences. In some cases, there may be no effect at all. In others, the sperm count is lowered, but the fertility classification is not necessarily changed. Men whose classification is already subfertile are of course in the greatest danger. A highly fertile male will probably not be affected to the point where he cannot have children, for he has sperm to spare.

CHILDLESSNESS: WHOSE "FAULT"?

Highly fertile men seldom have difficulty in fathering children. When they do have difficulty, the fault is usually the wife's. But childlessness is the wife's fault less often than most men will admit. Childlessness may be due to any one of several hundred causes, in the husband, in the wife, or in both. But a common cause is the relative infertility of the husband.

This is a fact that the childless husband is seldom willing to accept, for he considers it a slur on his manhood. If his sex urge is strong and his sex life active, he is sure that their childlessness is his wife's fault. But unless he submits to a laboratory test he cannot really know.

Completely sterile men are few. Only about 7 per cent of men with fertility problems are actually sterile. Many a man who thinks he is sterile because his wife has not conceived often proves to be merely subfertile or even relatively fertile. If his sperm count is not too low, he should be able to father a child if he goes about it in the right way.

The way most men go about it is not the right way. They think the thing to do is to keep trying, especially if they concentrate their efforts around the middle of the wife's cycle. A woman's cycle is the number of days from the beginning—not the end—of one menstrual period until the beginning of the next. Most women's cycles range between twenty-four and thirty-five days. Since the majority of conceptions take place between the eleventh and fifteenth days—known as the period of ovulation—many couples take this into account and are baffled and disappointed when conception does not result. But the fact is that too frequent sexual relations is often the *cause* rather than the remedy of childlessness.

Fertility rating (the sperm count) drops temporarily after sex relations. After a man in the highly fertile group has relations for three days, his count drops to the relatively fertile level; no problem, since the sperm count of the relatively fertile male is quite enough to fertilize the egg. But suppose the man starts out with a normal rating of relatively fertile. After sexual relations he becomes, temporarily, subfertile. Abstaining from relations for five days will return him to his original reproductive potential, *but*—by that time, his wife's period of ovulation has probably passed.

For it is only during her period of ovulation that a woman can conceive. A normal woman produces a normal egg—and only one—in seven out of eight cycles, approximately two days before the middle of the cycles. This period of ovulation lasts only about twelve hours. If the husband cannot produce sufficient sperm during this short time, conception will not be possible until the next ovulation.

HELP FOR SUBFERTILE MEN

The Wistar Institute developed a rat test which makes it possible to predict the time of ovulation in a particular woman within twelve hours, and often less. Couples who have had previous difficulty in conception have had success when they abstained from sexual relations for five days beforehand, then tried for conception at the predetermined time of the woman's ovulation. The method has worked even for men in the subfertile category, when their sperm count was not too far below the relatively fertile level.

This failing, the subfertile male can sometimes be made fertile by having his sperm count increased, if only temporarily. Some of the measures that have been tried to this end are (1) *thyroid treatment,* (2) *vitamin increase,* and (3) *irradiation of the pituitary gland.* The Wistar Institute found the latter seems to be the most promising. By means of it, some subfertile males have been upped to the relatively fertile classification.

The method usually considered a last resort is artificial insemination, though physicians believe it deserves greater public understanding.

There is one fact about artificial insemination that few husbands know, and when they learn it they often change their attitude. This is the fact that, in most cases, it is the sperm produced by the husband's body that is used—not that of another man. Under these conditions the husband is still the biological father of his wife's child. That brings up the question: How is it that Science can do the job when Nature can't? The Wistar Institute answers that quite simply. Artificial insemination requires fewer spermatozoa than Nature's more profligate method—sometimes as few as twenty million are sufficient compared to the eighty million minimum usually needed. The spermatozoa do not have to travel so far under their own power or depend upon chance to the same extent to find their way to the egg. They are placed where one of the sperm is most likely to fertilize the egg. No method always works, but this one often does where others fail.

If the husband is completely sterile or almost so, insemination by a donor is recommended by the Wistar Institute. But before the Institute will co-operate in this procedure, the husband as well as the wife must fully agree to it.

The selection of a donor is a complicated business. The first requisite is that he have no personal knowledge of the husband or the wife, nor they of him. Neither's identity is ever revealed to the other. The choice of a donor must be made, therefore, by some disinterested group such as the Wistar Institute. One of the most important requisites in the selection of a donor is that there be no taint of hereditary disease in his family background.

Other requirements are that the donor be close to the mental level of the husband and have some of his physical characteristics. Donors' records therefore include information regarding race, religion, hair (straight or curly), eye color, Rh factor (blood), stature, and constitutional type (linear, muscular or lateral). In order to increase the chances of success, only those donors who are in the highly fertile classification are selected.

At present, seniors in medical school and hospital interns are the most frequent donors. In addition to possessing all the other necessary qualifications, most of these men sympathize with the plight of the childless couple and are able to view the problem with scientific detachment.

Much remains to be done to solve problems of sterility, but every year more and more is learned. Thanks to the progress of medical science, the percentage of couples who must remain childless grows steadily smaller. One front where little progress has so far been made is the husband's stubborn lack of willingness to admit that the fault *may* be his. There is only one way to get a dependable answer to the question, "Are you capable of becoming a father?" That is careful examination by a physician.

SEX AND YOUR HEART

Love-making should be a thing of careless rapture and unrestrained concentration, but sometimes an affair of the heart requires a bit of headwork as well. For a man who cherishes both love and life, particularly if he happens to be one of the ten million Americans who has heart disease, this report should help add zest to both. Here is what medical science knows about the effect of the sex act on a man's heart.

Not long ago the heart reactions to intercourse by three married couples were measured by two doctors, Roscoe G. Bartlett of the National Institute of Health and Vernon C. Bohr. The doctors never knew the names of their young (twenty-two- to thirty-year-old) subjects; complete anonymity and privacy were assured to guard against any psychological upset which would impair the results of the experiment. Each couple repeated the sex act three times in a small windowless room. The bed was against one wall through which a tiny opening had been made to permit lead wires to be attached to measuring devices in an adjoining room. And both sides of the openings were completely covered with thin sheets of foam rubber.

The subjects themselves attached the electrocardiogram wires to their upper thighs and upper arms by means of elastic bandages. Each had a button to press which would signal to the outside world that a new stage had begun. Both wore mouthpieces to register their rate of breathing. During the preliminaries, electrocardiogram recordings were taken at regular intervals; during coitus, the recordings were continuous.

PULSE RATES CLIMB HIGH

Doctors Bartlett and Bohr's recordings of the changes in pulse rates give the layman the best idea of what happens to his (or his wife's) heart during intercourse. The simplest statistic is the most staggering: pulse rates for both male and female went as high as 170 heartbeats per minute. This rate, one hundred beats above the heart rate at rest, is far above the rates produced by any but the most strenuous exercise. In several instances, for both sexes, the acceleration to this peak was achieved in a mere sixty seconds!

The male heartbeat tended to go a little higher than the female and followed a definite pattern of slow rise, sudden peak and fast return to near normal. The female in each test had several orgasms, however, and generally equaled or even excelled her partner in the over-all increase of heartbeats.

Findings by other doctors have shown that intercourse has the same radical effect on other bodily functions related to the heart and heart trouble. Arterial blood pressure, stroke volume, output, and even clotting time and the viscosity of the blood are significantly affected.

Some doctors have suggested that sexual excitement may produce chemical changes in the blood which mitigate the strains of intercourse. But so far this has not been confirmed. The certainty remains that during love-making the healthy heart has its work cut out for it—work which may be too much for an aging or diseased heart.

Now if a man has reason to be concerned about his heart, information of this nature will depress him. Yet two real blessings flow from the dissemination of the truth about what sex means to a man's heart.

Blessing Number One: For a man who is approaching middle age in good health and with a minimum of hypochondria, these facts should help him see the wisdom of a yearly checkup visit to his doctor. If he is pronounced O.K., he can forget about his heart.

He should keep in mind, of course, that even though he is healthy, his sex life always has a profound effect on the physical condition of his heart. If love-making were purely a matter of physical exertion, its effect on the heart could be measured exactly and each man could learn his limitations. But love-making in human beings is mostly an emotional phenomenon. Dr. Edward Weiss, the nation's foremost authority on the relation of emotions to heart disease, says: "Emotional stress can be just as damaging to the heart as physical stress. Very often it is more damaging." In his studies at Temple University, where he is professor of clinical medicine, Dr. Weiss has come to the conclusion that "emotional tension, often rising out of sexual maladjustment, not only complicates recovery from heart disease, but helps bring it on in the first place."

Dr. Weiss and his staff compared the life histories of forty-three coronary patients and an equal number of nonheart patients matched for sex, age and race. There was, he found, a great deal more tension and maladjustment, sexual and otherwise, in the background of the heart patients. Again and again, the heart ailment was preceded by a long period of gradually mounting tension culminating in an emotional blow of some kind.

"The sexual problems of middle-aged men often cause great emotional tension," says Dr. Weiss. "Loss of libido, premature ejaculation, a feeling of 'growing old,' preoccupation with 'loss of manhood,' and compensatory efforts to prove oneself still a vigorous man—these are some of the problems that produce stresses and strains on the heart."

The fears of middle age compound themselves; they take the pleasure out of sex and therefore make it immensely more strenuous. A man doesn't want to "make a fool of himself." He is determined to succeed at any cost. If he happens also to be trying to succeed with someone not his wife, the regrets he may have only serve to increase the load on his heart. Nevertheless, he keeps on "even if it kills me." There is a real danger that it will, if he feels that way.

Perhaps if this man knew what sexual excitement could do to his heart, he could save his own life. Men who know are more likely to adjust themselves to middle age and cut down their chances of getting heart trouble. Still, heart disease does come to even the most well-adjusted fellows.

This brings up *Blessing Number Two*. The tests of Bartlett and Bohr and others present us with the *maximum sexual challenge to a man's heart*. That is, one can whistle at the terrific heart strain demonstrated by the able young couples of Bartlett and Bohr's experiments and still not give up sexual activity altogether. In the first place, the oldest participant in those tests was thirty, but most heart patients are middle-aged. Second, the novelty of the experimental conditions probably heightened the excitement and thus upped the findings. So, for example, if these couples showed a pulse rate of 170, it is reasonable to assume that this rate is near the top. A heart patient, on the other hand, is not out to break their record; somewhere between the normal 72 and that figure of 170 he's going to find a modest point at which he can safely have his sex and his heart disease, too.

Exceeding that point may be dangerous. Most husbands and wives who have faced the problem successfully have trained themselves to find satisfaction at a lower level, in what Dr. John F. Oliven calls "moderate indulgence in sedate coitus." Dr. Oliven, a psychiatrist, is the author of the highly regarded *Sexual Hygiene and Pathology*, a guide for physicians in dealing with patients' sex problems.

Sedate coitus may strike many men as a contradictory phrase. But Dr. Oliven describes it sensibly:

"Sedate coitus is marital intercourse in the presence of a good, affectionate relationship, with the healthy spouse willing to co-operate in all measures which the patient's health makes advisable."

Moderate indulgence, says Dr. Oliven, is sexual activity practiced with the least frequency necessary to fulfill the physical and emotional needs of both spouses. "Although one may rather arbitrarily set an average figure of one to two times a week, frequencies as high as five times a week probably do not, per se, constitute harmful excess in couples accustomed to, and genuinely and mutually desirous of, this rate."

To make sedate coitus even less strenuous, Dr. Oliven adds these practical precautions:

a. Arrange sexual relations for a time of day when the act can be preceded and followed by rest or sleep. The end of the day when a man's energy reserve is low may be a poor time, unless he can take a nap first. Morning is probably the best time if the patient doesn't have to get up immediately afterward to go to work.

b. Do not indulge in sexual activity on a full stomach, while wearing constricting garments, or under unusual conditions of atmospheric heat, cold or humidity.

c. Choose comfortable and relaxed positions and avoid interruption.

Every patient and his spouse, of course, should discuss their sexual relations thoroughly with the physician and get a detailed, individual appraisal of the sexual regime which will best suit both man and wife.

Physicians have increasingly followed the lead of specialists such as Dr. Paul Dudley White and Dr. Arthur Master, who were among the first to suggest that a man with heart disease did not have to give up all that made life enjoyable for him. "Today the designation 'chest pain' or 'coronary disease' is no longer a stigma," Dr. Master said recently. "Its presence rightly generates caution but not panic."

Most patients can go on leading normal, active lives. This, of course, includes a normal sex life, too. Many patients who are able to go to work and perform ordinary activities are told by their doctors that they can safely have sex relations. Very often, the decision is left to the patient. If he has no discomfort, intercourse is allowed; if the disease is in the acute stage, sex will probably be the last thing in the world he thinks about anyhow. In the usual "coronary insufficiency," as distinct from coronary occlusion, there is no actual blocking of the heart arteries. The source of the trouble is not a clot but an inability of the coronary artery to dilate properly, which produces an insufficiency of nourishment following exertion. As long as exertion doesn't exceed the supply of nourishment, many doctors see no particular danger in accelerating the pulse rate for a short period of intercourse. If the heart is not getting enough blood, it will sound the alarm in the form of an intense pain—"it feels like being stabbed while drowning," one patient said.

About 10 per cent of heart patients experience such a pain during intercourse because of their arteries' inability to dilate properly. This can be relieved and a better flow of blood to the heart can be assured during the effort of intercourse with the help of such drugs as glyceryl trinitrate or nitroglycerine. A tablet of either of these drugs, dissolved under the tongue just before intercourse, helps avoid the pain that might otherwise make intercourse impossible. (It should be emphasized that no one should take either of these drugs except on a doctor's prescription.)

Of such are made the blessings of medical science to the unhappy possessor of a weak heart, provided that the individual involved is essentially well adjusted.

But what about men who *aren't* well adjusted?

At Temple University, Dr. Weiss has found that a majority of heart patients tended to be fearful and dependent long after the acute stage of the illness had passed. This complicated the heart patient's convalescence and his sexual adjustment; it was also very tough on the patient's wife.

Naturally, sex works best in a man when it is most spontaneous. The more he worries about it, the harder it is for him to perform. The man who approaches love-making with the thought, *I hope nothing is going to happen to me,* may find that he cannot carry through. For a man who is worried about his heart, there may be dread in the anticipation of the act.

During intercourse, a man can't help communicating his sex anxieties to his wife. If he's afraid, chances are she'll be afraid, too—and the fear that her sexual gratification may kill her husband is likely to make any woman frigid. Yet her failure to respond freely to him only increases his frustration and adds to the burden on his heart.

"Marriage is a lock-and-key proposition," says Dr. Weiss. "You cannot understand a man except in relation to his wife."

Here are two cases in point which recently were related to me by doctors.

A few months after one husband recovered sufficiently from a heart attack to resume sexual intercourse, his wife was compelled to seek help from his doctor. "I feel like a murderer," she said and told how she stayed awake night after night, tortured by longing and dreams of infidelity. Her husband had never been a great lover, but before his attack she had at least been able, by taking the initiative, to get regular satisfaction. Nowadays, he would say, very hesitantly, "Well, if you think we ought to take the risk. . . ." His martyred tone implied, "If anything happens, you know who's to blame." The woman was on the verge of a nervous breakdown. And, needlessly, heart disease had ruined what had once been a tolerable marriage.

In another case—and a more typical one—the male heart patient became more demanding of his wife than ever before, and strictly on his own terms. "He always had to have his own way," the distressed wife told a doctor friend of mine. "Our whole married existence was that way, but at least in sex I had the right to say no. Now he insists I put myself at his disposal. If I refuse, he says, 'You heard what the doctor said about my blood pressure. If you rile me up, it'll be the death of me.'"

"Is it any wonder," the doctor remarked, "that in the midst of the love act the wife of such a man may find herself thinking guiltily, 'I hope it kills him.' And sooner or later, the husband himself will receive the emotional wages for the job that he and his heart disease have been doing on his wife."

In case after case, doctors are confronted with such emotional complications in the lives of heart patients. Each time he considers the advisability of sex for his patient, the doctor must ask himself: *What does intercourse mean to this man?*

The motives behind sexual intercourse give the doctor some measure of the strain that sex, or the lack of it, will place on the patient's heart. Doing work you enjoy obviously takes less out of you than doing work you detest; a man can feel rested and satisfied after working in his garden, tired and irritable after working on his income tax. It's the same way with sex.

"You take a heart patient," a Chicago specialist said to me, "who's always thought of sex as something of a chore. Well, now that he has an excuse, maybe now he'll come around to it once or twice a month, maybe less. On the other hand, there's the kind of patient I had referred to me just the other day. When I asked about sex, he said, 'Oh, sure, ever since my attack I've cut way down.' When I asked him how often that was, he hesitated. Then his wife spoke up for him. 'He means we're down to only once a day now. It used to be ten or twelve a week.'"

The doctor continued:

"Sex is never just plain sex. You discover that Patient X has deep-seated doubts about his masculinity. For him, sex is a way of assuring himself, 'I'm a man after all.' Patient Y has suppressed feelings of hatred toward his wife and intercourse is his way of attacking her. For patient Z, sex is a form of religion. Intercourse is a ritual that makes him feel one with the universe. For such men, the strain of abstinence would be greater than the strain of intercourse. Thus, sexual activity becomes important to the very survival of the patient."

OTHERS' EMOTIONS COUNT, TOO

With all this talk of emotions, it should not be forgotten that the doctor himself is subject to them. Quite often, his advice is influenced to some degree by his own private attitude toward sex. If it is not very important in his own life, he is more likely to rule it out for his heart patients—"just to be on the safe side." Advocates of more freely active lives for heart patients contend that such private attitudes account for many of the restrictions still placed on some heart patients' sexual activities.

There is a more practical reason: the doctor who advises his patient to go ahead and enjoy life always runs the risk of being embarrassed when a patient drops dead in the bedroom.

One final word needs to be said, whether or not the heart patient is well adjusted, emotional, troubled or just damned unhappy to be motoring in second gear on a superhighway. After a heart attack, a man's biggest asset is a tactful and considerate wife. If she can allay his anxieties and let him know he is still a man, many of the problems will soon melt away. As you may know, the secret of having such a wife is to be a considerate and tactful husband. Being a heart patient doesn't exempt a man from the amenities of sex, nor does it mean that he must assume a passive role.

"In a happy marriage," says Dr. Weiss, "a heart attack, like any other emergency, is apt to bring a man and a woman closer. In a shaky relationship, it usually drives them further apart."

Love will find a way. Being able to love at all suggests sufficient adjustment to life to be able to temper impetuosity in love-making and still derive satisfaction from it.

It's a risk, but there are some things worse than death.

FOR MEN ONLY

If there is a male counterpart to what the old wives used to call "female trouble," this is the trio: hernia, prostate trouble and gout. Hernia, which most of us call "rupture," hits men in a canal unknown to female anatomy. The prostate gland is also missing from Adam's rib. And if the cause of gout can be laid to no such exclusively male bit of anatomy, its preference for the male sex puts it nonetheless in the category of "male complaint." To the point of these three man's maladies, then, some man-to-man talk:

HERNIA, THE MAN CRIPPLER

Hernia, which many of us call "rupture," is crippling more men today than any other physical infirmity except heart disease and arthritis. Equal only to the spread of this disability is the ignorance about it. Of the millions who have hernias, practically none knows anything about his disability, why he has it or how to cure it; many don't even know they have it.

Even when not dangerous to life, hernia is a crippler. It interferes with a man's efficiency at work, or may incapacitate him entirely. With modern surgery ready to help, there is rarely a reason for anyone to continue suffering from hernia; yet many herniacs seem to prefer discomfort and unemployment to a safe cure and a normal life.

Last year in this country about 3,500 men died of strangulated hernia; nearly 375,000 hernia operations were performed on men (making it second only to the removal of tonsils or adenoids as the reason for male surgery), but an estimated 4,500,000-plus American males were walking around with hernias down to here, untreated. A lot of them were wearing trusses (at an annual cost of $7,200,000), which helped their physical condition not at all. On a world-wide estimate of between 150,000,000 to 300,000,000 herniacs, three out of every four of these sufferers are men.

It is estimated that at least two-thirds of all hernias are caused or aggravated by strain—too much, too steady or too sudden. The greatest incidence is found among athletes, glass blowers, gardeners, coal heavers, longshoremen, tailors, musicians (wind instrument), blacksmiths, masons and plumbers. In one group of herniacs in the Henry Ford Hospital in Detroit, 82 per cent had been engaged in heavy lifting. Only 17 per cent of the group worked sitting down.

Massive or chronic attacks of coughing or sneezing may bring on a hernia in a predisposed person. One man who had been passed by Army doctors after careful examination on a Tuesday, sneezed hard on Wednesday and found he had a hernia. More typical is the case of Mr. X.

X was brought up on a farm in the Midwest. He is thirty-four years old, over six feet tall and strong; and he still thinks of himself as an "outdoors" type, although he has done nothing more active than week-end fishing since he got out of the Army in 1945. A few weeks ago he set out with a friend for some small-mouth bass in a backwoods lake, where a farmer had a boat they could borrow. Only trouble was that the boat, a large, flatbottomed scow, was resting about a hundred yards from the lake. Nothing to do but carry it. X and his buddy both reached for the scow at the same time, gave a hearty heave and raised it in their arms. X suddenly "felt something give" in his stomach. There was a slight pain and nothing more.

They put the boat in the water and spent the day happily fishing. That night, X noticed a slight feeling of weakness around his groin. The next day after taking a shower he saw an unfamiliar lump on his groin. He pressed it. It was soft, but when he took his fingers away, the lump returned to its former position. It didn't disappear, although when he lay down he could press it back into place.

X was a little ashamed to tell anyone about it, but he thought he ought to go see a doctor. He did. The doctor told him he had a hernia.

"You mean I'm ruptured?" X asked.

"That's the common word for it," the doctor said, then went on to explain that a hernia is not, in itself, a rupture, but a sac of tissue protruding from one of the body cavities. There are hernias of the navel, the back and the side; but when a man gets a hernia ninety-six times out of one hundred he gets it where X got his—in his groin. This is called, the doctor told X, an *inguinal* hernia.

When they are visible, inguinal hernias look like lumps or bulges, but màny small ones can be detected only by a physician. They appear most often at the apex of the diagonal line that marks the joining of the thigh with the trunk; or in the scrotum. They are more apt to appear on the right side than the left; and they frequently come in pairs, although not necessarily simultaneously.

What About Operations?

X's doctor advised an operation, and soon.

"Isn't it dangerous?" X wanted to know.

"No," said the doctor, "not nearly as dangerous as walking around with that lump. What's more, you'll never be able to live a normal life until you have it done; it will almost certainly affect your reations with your wife, if only because of your own feeling of embarrassment. And the longer you put it off, the less successful the operation's likely to be." X heeded his physician's advice; a surgeon was selected, and the operation performed.

X found out that any hernia can, like his, be cured surgically if the operation is done soon enough. Most hernias are easily reducible (can be pushed back in) when they first occur. At this stage no dangerous complications develop and they are most easily cured. Disregarded long enough, they are bound to get worse. They never (except in infants less than a year old) get better spontaneously. And, as his doctor had indicated, the younger you are, the more assurance you have of a good surgical repair; and the less time and cost involved.

The operation for hernia is as safe as internal surgery can be. It is almost never fatal and 95 per cent of hernia operations cure the affliction permanently by repairing the weakness that caused the trouble. Patients in the other 5 per cent of cases may have to try a second time; but they are usually cured in the return operation. Recurrence of hernia may be the patient's fault (he waited too long before being operated on; he wasn't in good enough physical condition), or the surgeon's. So the man with hernia is advised to waste no time and to get himself as healthy as possible before the operation and to select a surgeon who knows his business, i.e. who has seen ward service in a large hospital.

If you must get hernia, you're better off having it today than you would have been fifteen years ago. Your cure will be more rapid—you'll spend an average of only 9.1 days in the hospital as against 15 days in 1944—and more permanent. Your convalescence will last only three or four weeks (provided you do no heavy labor); it used to take months.

Hernia is a peculiarly human affliction. Four-legged animals don't get it; people do because we insist upon standing on our hind legs. This posture puts a heavy strain on, among other places, our lower abdominal wall, whence most hernias spring.

Male people get many more hernias than female people because of different anatomy and pattern of growth. The primary cause is the descent of the testicles, described by one physician as the "most important voyage in history." In the fetus, the testicles are situated just in front of the kidneys. They begin traveling downward three months after conception, pushing various tissues, including the peritoneum, in front of them. (Visualize shoving two golf balls through a thin, partially inflated balloon.) The tissue forms temporary passageways that are supposed to close after the testicles reach the scrotum. In many men, these passageways remain open, leaving one or two sacs into which any of the abdominal organs may protrude.

Then, too, all men (and *only* men) have the inguinal canal, a passageway by which the spermatic cord penetrates the abdominal wall. This is a permanent "weak spot" through which a hernia may force itself. And, in addition, men do most of the heavy work, thereby putting extra pressure on an area already considerably weakened by the descent of the testicles.

The Trouble with Trusses

It is a fact that many more men with hernias depend on trusses than on surgery; and no truss has *ever* cured a hernia in a grown man. A truss will, while it is being worn, hold a reducible hernia in, but it will also, over a period of time, weaken the surrounding tissues and thereby enlarge the hernial sac. One physician says bluntly: "Perhaps no class of patient has been more imposed on than those suffering from a hernial disability, because most trusses are not fitted by the attending doctor." Lay truss-fitters in drug and surgical supply stores, some of whom have had as much as five days of training on the use of trusses in hernia cases, think they do a pretty good job of truss-fitting. A wise man who has hernia and needs a truss (because, perhaps, he won't take time to be operated on immediately) will have the fitting supervised by a qualified physician, a man who has spent years studying anatomy in school, in hospitals and in his day-to-day practice.

An ill-fitting truss is not only useless but downright dangerous: it may allow strangulation of the hernia. And trusses should not be used at all in the following kinds of hernia—many of which only a physician is trained to detect: old hernias; femoral hernias; undescended testicles; incarcerated, inflamed or strangulated hernias; irreducible hernias. For example:

A man in New Orleans recently visited a doctor. "My hernia is bothering me, Doc," he said. He then stripped down to a leather harness that he was wearing around his waist.

"You've been wearing this contraption for over three years, I should say," the doctor said, and pointed to a bronze mark on the man's skin that was approximately the shape of the truss pad. "You wouldn't get that in less than three years and you'll have it for the rest of your life."

"Is that bad?" the man asked.

"No," the doctor said, "but the truss is. How did you buy it?"

"By mail," the patient answered. "I just order a new one every year or so."

"It may possibly have fitted you," the doctor replied, "when you first bought it, but it doesn't any more." He pointed to the lump, larger than the truss pad, which protruded from the man's groin. "What finally made you come to me?"

"It hurts," the patient said, "it throbs and I've been feeling kind of sick."

The doctor examined him carefully and said, "You'll have to get to a hospital in a hurry. Your truss has injured your hernia so that now it is absolutely necessary to have an immediate operation."

"Will I need to wear a truss afterward?" the man wanted to know.

"You can throw it away today—in fact, I'm telling you not to wear it again," the doctor replied.

The man underwent a successful operation and is now better and, best of all, he doesn't have to wear the harness that kept him strapped in for so many years.

Some men try to have their hernias cured without surgery by the injection method. This treatment consists of a series of hypodermic injections—from fifteen to thirty—of an irritant liquid into the inguinal canal. The irritation is supposed to cause internal scar tissue (adhesions), which it does, and to close up the opening by which the hernia has descended. Meanwhile, the hernia is held back by a truss that must be worn day and night during treatment. The advantages claimed for this method by doctors who give injections are low cost and avoidance of hospitalization.

Many surgeons dispute the use of injection, and on various grounds. It is a "blind" procedure, they say, in that injections are given by hypodermic and the organs and blood vessels inside the hernia or in the inguinal region may be injured by the needle, and often are. The patient may be made sexually sterile if the scar tissue constricts the *vas deferens* (carrier of the sperm) or its blood vessels. In the event of recurrent hernia (which surgeons say is frequent in the injection treatment) and surgery becomes necessary, so much scar tissue is formed inside the area that the surgeon's efforts are rendered difficult, ineffective or impossible. The low cost of the injection method is questionable since simple arithmetic shows (number of treatments at ten dollars each) that it may cost more than surgery-and-hospitalization.

Improper treatment or lack of treatment of hernias can be fatal, as in the case of a young (twenty-year-old) man who was attending an Eastern university not long ago on a scholarship requiring him to play football. He managed to conceal his hernia from the coach and the squad physician and played in the first three games of the season. His position was right halfback on the attack, fullback on defense. In one deceptive offensive play, he was called on to carry the ball off tackle without interference. Performing this assignment inside his opponents' twenty-yard line, he was tackled heavily. He held onto the ball until the referee blew his whistle, then lay writhing on the ground.

Although no one knew it, the full weight of the opposing tackler's body had been taken directly on the halfback's hernia, which meant that part of his intestines had received a direct injury—for, at that spot, they were covered only by the thickness of his skin and a few distended layers of tissue, plus his uniform.

The trainer gave him the usual treatment to relieve the pain of a groin kick, something every football fan has seen a hundred times. In a few minutes, the player was able to hobble around and, because of his skill, was left in the game.

He played through the second half, fighting pain with every step, and thanked his stars when the game finally ended and he could stretch out in the dressing room.

"Come on," his fellow players told him. "Get out of that uniform and meet us at the victory dinner."

"I can't," he said, "I've got to catch up on some reading."

When the team left, he removed his harness. He noticed that the familiar lump on his groin had turned black and blue, and was throbbing. He went out for a light meal and returned to his dormitory room. A few hours later he was sick and, when his roommate came in at midnight, he was writhing in pain. He refused medical treatment, however, and spent a restless night in his room. Next day he was taken to the local hospital, his condition diagnosed as acute strangulated hernia. An operation was attempted immediately, but gangrene and peritonitis had already set in. A few hours later the boy was dead.

"He didn't give himself a chance," the surgeon reported. "He should never have played football with a hernia and, if he had, he should have gone to a doctor immediately after he was injured. By the time we got the case at the hospital, his body was so thoroughly infected from gangrene and the perforated bowel that we couldn't save his life."

The death of the young football player is, admittedly, exceptional. Hernia is not one of our big killers, like heart disease or cancer. There are, however, dangerous hernias, the disability is widespread, and they all need immediate medical attention.

Strangulated hernias are the most dangerous. They occur when the neck of the hernia contracts, shutting off the blood supply. In its final stages, strangulation closely resembles peritonitis; gangrene may occur within a few hours. It is a real emergency and requires immediate surgery. A man whose hernia has been strangulated for twenty-four hours has only a 70 per cent chance to live; and his odds go down fast with every succeeding hour of neglect.

Other dangerous hernias are:

1. *Irreducible* (can't be pushed back)—usually the result of long neglect. Caused by the entry of some organ that cannot be squeezed back through the ring.

2. *Inflamed*—painful, generally with other symptoms—caused by a blow or the pressure of a truss.

3. *Incarcerated* (obstructed)—the bowel inside the hernia is blocked up. Fecal matter cannot move through. Very painful, and very dangerous; in fact, lethal if not treated immediately.

To sum up, there is no reason for any male in the United States to be crippled any longer by hernia. The operation is safe and cures permanently in 95 per cent of all cases. It is not expensive, either, and people who have health insurance (hospitalization and surgical) can usually get it done at little cost to themselves.

Remember, the longer you put off surgical correction, the worse your hernia will get and the more dangerous it may become.

PROSTATE TROUBLE

Doctors call it, among themselves, trouble in the plumbing department. It's an overgrowth of tissue which interferes with urination, and it occurs in 50 per cent of all men over fifty, 60 per cent of all men over sixty, 70 per cent of all men over seventy. Prostate trouble is no fun, but if a man knows enough to recognize its early symptoms, it can be "fixed." Here are the facts:

The prostate gland, no bigger than a horse chestnut, lies in a strategic position in the male body. Like a noose around the bladder's neck, it is in a position to choke off the outflow of urine if it alters its size. Since human life is impossible without the elimination of waste, this gland can be as menacing as a handful of machine gunners guarding a narrow mountain pass.

Your "Plumbing"

The male urinary system starts with two kidneys and two pencil-slim tubes called the ureters which lead out of them. These tubes enter into the urinary bladder, which is like an inverted grocery sack, and the bladder in turn empties out through another narrow tube called the urethra. The urethra extends from the bladder through the encircling prostate and after traversing the length of the penis reaches the outside of the body.

By far the most complex portions of the urinary tract are the kidneys. Each is about four or five inches long, and bean shaped. They lie obliquely with the concavity from which the ureter emerges, placed toward the spine. They are behind the abdominal organs in the small of the back, at about the level of the lowest ribs. They are secured in a bed of fat, which tends to keep them from sagging downward.

It required many years of the most exacting research, much of it done on huge frogs, to understand how these organs work. Kidney tissue is composed of countless miscroscopic filtering units called glomeruli, through which the blood circulates, and the molecules of waste and unneeded substance filter out. These molecules then pass through tiny tubules which have the power of selecting certain chemicals to be reabsorbed, thus conserving substances such as protein, which the body needs.

Medical men study the efficiency of the kidneys by observing substances in the urine and their relation to the chemistry of the blood. Albumin in the urine, for example, may mean that the filtering tubules of the kidney have been damaged by fever or disease, permitting good protein to be lost. When certain waste substances that are normally found in the urine disappear or diminish in quantity, the filtering process may be faulty and waste may be accumulating in excess in the blood.

The ureters, two muscular tubes about the caliber of a goose quill, extend from the pelvis of the kidney to the bladder. They are about twelve inches long and run downward diagonally from back to front. They enter the bladder wall obliquely at the base, posteriorly. This oblique angle through the muscular layers of the bladder wall makes an ingenious closure of the ureter's orifice when the bladder is distended, and effectively prevents any reverse flow of urine. The muscle of the ureter has a slow rhythmic contraction of its own which sends the drops of urine flowing onward in waves.

The bladder serves as a storage tank, collecting the urine so that it can be evacuated at chosen intervals. All day and all night urine is formed in the kidneys and at the rate of one or two drops a minute rolls out of the pelvis of each kidney to trickle slowly down the ureters to the bladder. There it is prevented from immediate escape by the corklike action of a system of sphincter muscles which close the exit channel. These sphincters are under both voluntary and involuntary control—Nature intended us to be capable of housebreaking and yet ready for all emergencies. When the bladder is full, a nervous stimulus leads to the relaxation of the cork-action sphincters. The urine is evacuated through the urethra by the squeezing action of the muscular walls of the bladder, which forcibly expresses the urine.

The bladder normally holds about a teacupful with comfort. When full, its walls are smooth and thin. When empty, they are thick and ridged into heavy folds. In the posterior lower portion is an important landmark called the "trigone." It is a triangular area, the lateral points formed by the tiny openings of the entering ureters, and the apex by the orifice of the urethra.

Until 1876 the diagnosis of bladder and kidney ailments was largely a matter of guesswork. In that year a noted German urologist, aided by mechanics and lensmakers, invented what has become known as a cystoscope—an apparatus for viewing the inside of the bladder. (The word "cyst" means pouch or bladder.) The instrument, gradually improved through the years, is a slender metal shaft equipped with lenses and a diminutive electric-light bulb. It is inserted through the urethra into the bladder, making it possible to inspect the lining of the bladder and the trigone, to note the type of urine entering it from each ureter. It is even possible to nip off small samples of tissue or tumor for microscopic study. The cystoscope is the urologist's mainstay, and a study of urinary-tract trouble is seldom complete without a cystoscopic examination.

The last eight or nine inches of the urinary tract are formed by the urethra, which carries the urine from the bladder to the outside. It is encircled by the prostate for an inch or so, then traverses the length of the penis, functioning not only as the outlet for urine, but also as the channel for the passage of seminal fluid and spermatozoa during sexual intercourse. Pencil slim, it is a tough membranous tube, subject to obstruction in its first portion by enlargement of the prostate and in its remaining length liable to damage if infection of a venereal nature is incurred.

This mapping of the urinary tract is important in the understanding of prostate disease. The prostate itself is hardly worth the trouble it sometimes causes. It evolves from the tissue of the urethra and forms, roughly, two lateral lobes and a smaller median lobe or bar. It is encapsulated, and in an operation can usually be shelled out like an outsized pea popping out of a pod. It is composed of a mesh of secreting glandular tissue bound together by smooth muscle and fibrous tissue, and its job is to manufacture a mucous secretion which forms part of the ejaculate during sexual intercourse.

As the years creep by Father Time puts his icy finger on the weak spots in a man's structure. After about fifty years have passed he begins to point to the prostate gland, though a number of ailments can hit the prostate gland at any time of life. Various kinds of infection may develop; abscesses, cysts, stone formation, and various growths may afflict the gland. But the common ailment that concerns us is a simple overgrowth of tissue which may involve any or all portions of the gland. The enlargement in itself would be unimportant if the prostate gland were not in a position to slow or obstruct the passage of urine by small change in size. That alone is the danger of simple, everyday prostatic enlargement.

When the prostate enlarges it sets in motion a whole chain of events based on simple hydraulic principles. First, the urethra, encircled by the prostate, is narrowed. The outflow of urine is impeded. The bladder fills, then swells; its walls become thinner. In complete obstruction, the bladder may expand until the walls are paper-thin, with no muscle tone, and it becomes a solid, visible, bulging mass in the front of the abdomen, sometimes extending like a pregnant womb as high as the navel.

Fortunately, most obstruction develops gradually, and the bladder walls work harder and harder in an effort to squeeze the urine through the narrowed channel. Just as a biceps muscle in a boy's baseball arm will grow with use, so the muscular bladder walls grow thicker and tougher. As a result, the bladder changes its smooth globular shape, and comes to look like an irregular cave with recesses and alcoves vaulted by muscle strands that have grown into heavy cords in their effort to empty the bladder against the obstruction of the swollen prostate.

At this point urine collects in the alcoves and pockets bulging between cords of overgrown muscle, and the bladder is never completely emptied. Stasis results and infection follows, just as the backwash of a river becomes murky and full of vegetation. The actual capacity of the bladder may be increased so it can hold more urine, but the walls can no longer contract evenly to empty all the pockets. The unlucky owner then has a continual sense of incomplete emptying—a disagreeable feeling. He may find himself able to get rid of only a few teaspoonfuls at a time, which means real trouble in the "plumbing department."

Unfortunately, the trouble does not stop there. Damage to the bladder walls makes it difficult to keep the openings of the ureters shut tight. There is back pressure and blocking of the outflow of urine back up to the kidneys, with gradual stretching and distortion of all the structures. Sooner or later this pressure and distortion so injures the kidney tissue that function is impaired and the kidney is no longer able to filter out waste products efficiently. Death by uremic poisoning follows, or used to. Nowadays it is an ignorant or foolish man who does not get surgical relief long before this fatal chain of events is set in motion.

Nobody knows why so many men of sixty and seventy should be plagued with enlargement of the prostate—"benign prostatic hypertrophy or hyperplasia" the doctors call it. In the animal world, a few horses and many dogs develop kindred trouble in their old age, though it never occurs in animals that have been castrated, which leads to the inference that male sex-hormone balance is in some way responsible. Men with prostatic enlargement have been treated with female sex hormone, a logical procedure, but the results have not been encouraging. Surgery remains the only effective treatment.

Sometimes prostatic enlargement develops so insidiously that a man may be unaware of his condition until it has advanced to a fairly serious stage. This is why all men over fifty are urged to have an annual physical examination. Enlargement, if present, can be easily discovered by rectal examination. The victim of prostatic enlargement usually experiences some difficulty with urination. Often the earliest symptom is the need to get up at night to urinate. From this mild symptom, the signs progress to real difficulty in urination—difficulty in starting the stream, dribbling, slowness of flow, inability to empty the bladder completely. The usual symptoms of infection are frequency, urgency, and discomfort on urination. Bloody urine and back pain may follow.

Victims of prostatic enlargement were offered little help until the beginning of the twentieth century, when a young Texan named Hugh Young was appointed to the chair of urology at Johns Hopkins. When offered the post, Young remarked that he didn't know anything about urology; he was told that nobody in the world knew much about it, and that he had the ability to learn. Working from this start, Dr. Young developed the specialty of urology, inventing and improving many instruments used in urological surgery and devising several excellent operations for the relief of prostatic trouble.

The Treatment

Because the difficulties produced in prostate enlargement are mechanical, the treatment is of necessity surgical—removal of the obstructing portion of the gland. The surgery is almost always successful, and the various operations are named according to the way they approach the gland. One of the earliest, devised by Dr. Young, is the "suprapubic prostatectomy," in which the prostate is removed through the abdominal wall and bladder. The "perineal prostatectomy" approaches through an incision between the rectum and the scrotum. One of the most ingenious methods, also perfected by Dr. Young, is the so-called "punch operation." In this technique, under local block anesthetic, a hollow shaft with a sliding, sharp-edged punch is passed up through the urethra into the bladder, cutting out a channel through the prostate as an apple corer cuts out the stem and seeds of an apple. This operation, now done with greatly improved instruments which cut and cauterize by electric current, is called the "transurethral resection."

There is no need for the layman to be concerned with the merits of the various methods, because each operation must be adapted to the needs of the individual patient. Such surgery should only be undertaken by men especially trained and accredited as urological specialists. The effect of such surgery, beyond the relief of obstruction, may be different for each patient and each type of operation. Under some conditions, sexual potency is altered, which is unfortunate but highly preferable to death by uremic poisoning. Dr. Hugh Young wrote a delightful autobiography in which he tells amusing anecdotes of the eminent men—business tycoons, admirals and senators—on whom he operated for the relief of prostate trouble. Their gratitude was amazing. Diamond Jim Brady, on whom Dr. Young did the "punch operation," was so grateful that he gave Johns Hopkins a hospital devoted to urological diseases, now known as the Brady Urological Institute. Tremendous strides have been made in recent years, not only by the improvement of techniques and instruments, but also by the use of sulfa, penicillin, and the newer antibiotic drugs. These drugs make it safer to operate on men of extremely advanced years, and many a man of eighty or thereabouts owes them his daily comfort, and quite possibly his survival.

Odd little gland, the prostate! Unimportant in itself, it holds a key position. By increasing its size the breadth of a pencil it can upset the smooth tenor of any man's days.

When Robert Ruark came down with gout, he summed up the ill-informed layman's attitude toward his suffering this way: "Gout," he wrote, "seems to come somewhere between the pratfall and the custard pie in the face, in American humor."

Frank Coniff's boss, William Randolph Hearst, Jr., told the columnist that he wasn't rich enough to have gout. "On your pay," Hearst told Coniff, "what you've got is a sore foot."

And if there is a gout patient anywhere who has not been accused of gluttony, lechery or drunkenness, that man is luckier than he knows. Most gout sufferers say that corny jokes about their ailment are almost more unbearable than their physical pain.

Actually, gout is far from funny. More than 350,000 people in the United States have gout, and 95 per cent of them are men: it is a rare disease in women. Gout hits the poor as well as the rich, teetotalers as well as men who drink port, vegetarians as well as lovers of rare roast beef. There have also been authenticated cases of gout among six-year-old children and other virgins. Gout, in short, is not the price of intemperance in food, drink or sexual activity.

It is not an old man's disease, either. It strikes, usually, between the ages of thirty and fifty. Although many men over fifty have gout, they generally have had it for a long time.

What *is* gout, exactly? Doctors call it a "metabolic disturbance"—which places it in the same group of diseases as diabetes. At some stage in the complicated chemical activity of the body, there is an imbalance which results in an excess of uric acid in the blood. By itself, this does not mean that a man has gout. But it is probably the prerequisite without which no one can get the disease. This makes gout, incidentally, a special disease of men and apes among mammals, since other mammals are able to oxidize their urate.

A man with gout will have, usually, in addition to high-serum urate, some of the following characteristics: a family history of gouty arthritis (50 per cent of gouty men have gouty fathers); one or more acute attacks of joint pain; evidence of some kidney disturbance; and his gouty attacks will be relieved by the drug colchicine.

This last fact is one of the most interesting things about gout. Doctors actually don't know what "causes" the disease (the above symptoms are not causes), but they do have the chemicals to relieve the unbearable pain of attacks. The drugs most widely and effectively used are colchicine and aspirin; however, ACTH shows some promise.

Since colchicine helps no other disease (it is being experimented with as a cancer cure), the man who is relieved by taking the drug must have gout. Doctors do not have the slightest idea of how colchicine works, but they know that it does work on the large majority of gout patients. It is not the pleasantest drug in the world to take. In gout attacks, doctors prescribe colchicine in amounts that cause gastric upsets. Later, the dose is diminished one tablet at a time, until a dosage is found that will relieve the gout without, if possible, upsetting the patient's stomach.

Aspirin is used in large quantities by gouty patients. Like colchicine, aspirin has a pain-killing property, but, in addition, if taken in large doses it helps the patient get rid of his excess of uric acid; so it cuts some of the ground from under the disease. Some gout sufferers have to take aspirin in such massive doses that they are mildly poisoned by this comparatively safe drug. Science has been working on the problem and has come up with a new substance that may give much more help than aspirin, and with none of its side effects. The new drug is p-(di-n-propyl sulfamyl)-benzoic acid and is manufactured under the name of Benemid by Sharp & Dohme.

With such aids readily available, proper treatment of gout needs only correct diagnosis. The layman is liable to confuse gout with rheumatism, arthritis, even bunions. An occasional doctor might relate the symptoms to an injury or an infection. But any medical student ought to be able to diagnose gout: it's a classic.

Symptoms

It usually begins with numbness or pain, usually in the big toe or some other part of the foot but often in a finger, the wrist, the ankle or some other part of the body. Early painful attacks are known as "acute gouty arthritis."

One of the special features of the disease is the long, symptomless period between attacks. This gap, which is called "intercritical gout (Stage 2)," does not indicate that the patient is cured. Though there is no pain, the crystals of sodium biurate—a salt of uric acid—are being deposited in soft tissues, cartilages, tendons, and joints until eventually (but not invariably) the patient may get "chronic gouty arthritis (Stage 3)." The younger the patient is when he gets his first acute attack, the more likely he is to develop chronic gout.

In the chronic stage, the deposits of urate crystals—called *tophi*—are most likely to be noticed first as a lump in the lobe of the ear. They frequently deposit in and around fingers and toes, and cause unsightly swellings; sometimes open sores. They may form as "gravel" under the skin, or as kidney stones, which are easily passed out of the body.

Even though there seem to be no effective "miracle drugs" for treating the final stage of the disease, the victim of chronic gout need no longer resign himself to a life of immobility and pain. Proper treatment and diet enable him to lead a normal life.

That word "arthritis" strikes such terror in men's hearts that it might be a good idea to pause, here, for a few facts. The word means, simply, inflammation of a joint. Such inflammation injures the joint structure, but the injury can take many different forms. Rheumatic fever causes temporary swelling of the soft tissues of the joints. Syphilis and tuberculosis destroy the bone itself. Osteoarthritis, the disease of old age that causes gnarled hands, damages the cartilages; spurs develop on the bones, making the afflicted joints look big and knobby. Rheumatoid arthritis, the dread variety of the disease, damages the synovial membranes (tiny balloons between the pads of cartilage that are found at the adjoining ends of any two moving bones) so that the joint space becomes fused and rigid. Bursitis, an inflammation that often results from an accident, is characterized by a filling up, with fluid or with lumps of chemicals that "salt out" of the fluid, in one of the saclike cavities that pad the surface of bones.

Gout is related to all these in that it affects joint structure; the victim's faulty uric-acid metabolism deposits urate crystals sometimes in the cartilage, sometimes in the soft-tissue structure, sometimes even in the bone itself. But it is not the crippler you probably visualize when you hear the word "arthritis."

"Acute gouty arthritis" is the first of three stages that gout usually works through. The progression may take from twelve to twenty years.

Diet's Role

Since, as we said earlier, nobody knows the cause of gout, there is no cure for the disease. The drugs we have discussed help to control symptoms; and diet may be used for the same purpose.

From what science has learned through the use of the isotope N^{15} we know that it is impossible to control the formation of uric acid in the body. However, the largest source of uric acid is in foods with a large amount of the protein known as purine. Eating such foods as liver, kidney, and sardines and anchovies—all high with purine content—definitely increases the amount of urinary uric acid.

There is some reason to believe, therefore, that a low purine diet will help some gout sufferers. Dr. John H. Talbott, well-known authority on the disease, advises that each case has to be treated individually and that the patient must co-operate in avoiding the foods or beverages that seem to bring on attacks. Dr. Alexander B. Gutman, also a specialist, believes that a low-purine diet may be of more aid to chronic cases than acute ones, but he prescribes a low-purine, low-protein diet for all gout patients.

There is, of course, no truth to the popular idea that gout is caused by a combination of roast beef and port wine. Red meats do have a high purine content, but many gout victims can eat them with impunity. On the other hand, one man gets an attack almost every time he eats asparagus; another gets gout pains after drinking milk. One truck driver who experienced constant acute attacks took his problem to Johns Hopkins. The doctors there advised him that the constant pressure of his gouty foot on the brake pedal was bringing on the attacks. They advised him to get another kind of job—and he hasn't had an attack since he switched.

But to get back to the diet problem; here is one man's record. For nine months he stayed in a hospital on a low-purine diet. During this period, he had twenty-one attacks of gout and spent thirty-nine days in bed.

The same man went home and ate red meat every day and drank a moderate amount of beer and hard liquor. In the next fourteen months he had only seven attacks, spent seven days in bed. In other words, he spent nearly ten times as many days in bed when he was taking care of himself as when he wasn't. Still, Dr. Talbott believes that overindulgence in any alcoholic beverage may bring on attacks—although some patients seem able to drink more Scotch than rye, or vice versa. Talbott says that drinking should be regulated "by temperance rather than abstinence." Another doctor notices an increase of gout attacks following such periods of overindulgence in food and drink as birthdays, weddings, Thanksgiving, and New Year's Eve; also, after conventions, lodge meetings, and hunting and fishing trips.

Dr. Talbott says. "I am confident that some day a cure will be found for the disease and have never felt otherwise. I have been optimistic ever since I became interested in this malady more than twenty years ago. . . . I believe that an effective form of therapy may not be far away. This effective form of therapy will restore the altered metabolism of uric acid in the body or alter the excretion of uric acid by the kidneys so that for all essential purposes a person has a normal physiology in regard to this substance. Just as a patient with diabetes isn't cured while undergoing treatment with insulin, nevertheless many of the processes are restored to the normal level."

5. CANCER

In an exclusive men's shoe store on New York's Madison Avenue recently, a salesman was fitting a man with a pair of bluchers. He noticed that his customer seemed a little hoarse, and he thought he knew why. For a lot of reasons, the salesman was shy about asking any questions, but finally curiosity took hold.

"Sir," he asked, "is there something wrong with your throat?"

"No," replied the customer, "but there used to be. I had a cancer in it, once."

"I thought so," the salesman said.

"Is my voice that bad?" the customer asked.

"Oh, no," the salesman said. "I'd never have known you had your larynx removed if I hadn't been around hospitals a lot and heard others."

"You seem familiar with cancer of the larynx," the customer said. "Has someone you know well had one, too?"

"Not exactly. I too had cancer, but mine was in the cecum. That's part of the gut. They took about eighteen inches out—let me see, it'll be fourteen years next month."

"Mine's eight years, touch wood," the customer said. "Name's White, Willard C. White. I teach other guys who've had their larynxes removed to talk by using the esophagus, at the National Hospital for Speech Disorders, here in New York."

The incident is worth reporting, but not because it is unusual for two cured cancer patients to meet, or because one of them does rehabilitation work for other patients. There are an estimated one million cured patients in this country today, many of whom had cancer years ago. A third of them are men, and many, like Mr. White or John Gilmore of Hartford, Connecticut, devote themselves to helping people who now have the disease.

The meeting between the salesman and White is significant because the two men (a) knew they had had cancer and (b) were not afraid to admit it.

THE ENEMY—FEAR

It is certainly no news that most cancer can be cured. Yet, many a man treats cancer as if it were a combination of syphilis and smallpox. He is afraid to find out if he has it, and he is afraid to admit that he has it or to do anything about it once his fears are confirmed.

In New York City today, for instance, there is a man walking around with a cancer that is going to kill him because he refuses treatment. He is fifty-seven years old. In a recent hospital examination, the doctor felt a small nodule in the patient's prostate gland. A smear test showed cancer cells under the microscope and the doctor advised an immediate operation. The patient refused. The doctor argued. The patient still refused. The doctor argued some more and the patient said, "All right, I'll think it over," and walked out of the clinic. He hasn't returned since; and, even though his own physician has added his appeals to those of the hospital, the man refuses the operation.

The reason more cancer cases are not discovered and treated earlier is not always the patients' fault, however. One of the big problems in cancer today is that many older doctors went to medical school when almost every cancer was considered incurable; and some still hold this idea. To remedy this, the medical profession and the American Cancer Society are getting the older men to come back to schools and hospitals for refresher courses on the disease. Even up-to-date physicians have to work hard to keep abreast of the advances in their profession.

More and more doctors are becoming aware of the new progress in cancer diagnosis and cure; and more and more laymen are learning the value of periodic examination. One of them, a former governor of an Eastern state, a gentleman in his middle sixties, had just returned from Washington where he had been visiting an old friend, an Army colonel, who was dying of cancer of the rectum. "Poor George," the governor was saying in his club, "he's such a nice guy, too."

He was overheard by a doctor, who couldn't let the opportunity go by. "Have *you* ever had an examination for cancer?" he asked.

"Me?" the former governor said. "I haven't a thing wrong with me except . . . well, I'm a little constipated."

"There's nothing to it," the doctor said. "I'll set up a date for you."

The patient was shocked to discover that he had the same disease as his Army friend. But he got his diagnosis early enough so that treatment was possible. He had an operation, recovered, and is now a hearty seventy-one and enjoying the company of his latest grandchild. He has joined the group of intelligent men who have had the fortitude to have themselves properly checked and to follow through on what they found.

It's the only way to outwit our second (next to heart disease) biggest killer, which will destroy 265,000 men and women in this country this year. Science will save about 150,000. But science could save—on the basis of facts known now, on the basis of treatments available today—*at least another 75,000, and maybe more, if the disease were diagnosed and proper treatment begun soon enough*.

Men do not contract cancer as early as women, generally speaking. But year for year, from forty on, men get as many cancers as women, although not in the same places. Some male cancers occur in strictly male places, such as the prostate gland, the penis and testicles. Men suffer much more from stomach cancers than do women and men have a great many more cancers of the mouth, larynx, lung, bronchus (part of the windpipe), skin, brain, and digestive and urinary tracts. In contrast, they hardly ever get cancer of the breast, a common site for cancer in women.

Each of these cancers is really a different disease, but none of them is new. Prehistoric man suffered from cancers. The ancient Egyptians knew and treated cancers with excision and arsenic, and other early civilizations used similar methods. Cancers occur mostly in older people, and since the life span is longer today than ever, the medical problem has increased accordingly. In 1911 a U.S. citizen could look forward to 51.49 years of life; a baby born in 1956 may expect to live 69.6 years (66.7 if he's a boy, 73 if a girl!). Since cancers occur mostly between the ages of forty and sixty, it is obvious why we have more of them now.

All cancers have one basis in common: wild, uncontrolled cell growth. Nobody knows *why*, for sure; but a lot has been learned about how the disease operates. That is why almost every type of cancer can be treated successfully; and there are a million people who have had cancer, who are alive and well, to demonstrate that fact.

There were enough of them, for instance, in the town of Andalusia, Alabama, to get together for a sizable banquet not so long ago—a banquet at which they made plans to raise money for fighting cancer by research, education, and building new detection and treatment centers. In small they represent what goes on in the rest of the country. Altogether, Americans have raised enough money (about $75,000,000 last year from private and government sources) and built enough hospitals and clinics and consultation services (662, as of 1957) to make this country by far the safest for cancer sufferers. Our national cancer cure rate is over 33 per cent: one in three is being saved today.

THE INCREASE IN LUNG CANCER

One of the current problems in the field of cancer is in the sharp rise in carcinoma (cancer) of the lung, an almost exclusively male problem.

Two of the reasons behind this increase are the antibiotics and sulfanimides. These germ killers have dropped the pneumonia death rate and cleared up inflammations around lung cancers, allowing much more accurate diagnosis. Other factors are increased public awareness of the disease and a more prompt recognition of its symptoms. Nevertheless, these factors also affect other kinds of cancer, none of which shows the same steep climb as lung malignancies.

What is the cause? Is it smoking? We live in an atmosphere charged with proof and counter-proof; we read frightening statistics one day, reassuring figures the next. At the Sloan-Kettering Institute there work men who are so convinced on this point that they would snatch cigarettes from the fingers of perfect strangers on the street. Elsewhere, some eminent scientists say that they will "wait and see," while others deliver diatribes on the meaninglessness of statistics. In the end, probably each of us will believe as he wants to believe, balancing whatever benefits we think we get from cigarettes off against the threat they may or may not hold for us as individuals. It's too soon for the *moderate* smoker to be alarmed any more than it pleases him to be.

At any rate, surgical procedures—the only way lung cancer can be cured—are constantly being improved since 1933, when Dr. Evarts Graham, a surgeon in St. Louis, Missouri, showed that it was possible to remove an entire human lung and save the patient.

Since that time, thousands of these operations have been successfully performed on men whose chances of life, before 1933, would have been precisely zero.

Take a look at one man who has had the operation. He was a sheet-metal worker, forty-six years old, living in an Eastern city, when he began to experience coughing, pain in breathing, spitting up blood and other symptoms which indicated the possibility of lung cancer. His doctor diagnosed his case, but wasn't sure of his diagnosis, so the man was sent to a hospital for examination.

Careful X-ray analysis showed the presence of a mass of tissue in the right lung; and the cancerous state of the tissue was confirmed by the Papanicolaou smear test, a microscopic examination of cells in the patient's sputum. Cancer cells were detected and the patient was asked to submit to an operation removing the lung.

"Will it stop me from working?" he wanted to know.

"No," the doctor replied.

"Is the operation dangerous?"

"Not very."

"What will happen if I refuse?"

"It will kill you."

"Then what are we talking about?" the man said. "I want to live, so I agree to the surgery."

The operation was performed in 1943 and the man was able to go back to work within a few months. Since that time he has moved to Florida; but he continues to keep in close touch with his physician by mail, and he still gets regular examinations. He knows the doctors saved his life and, although considered cured, he is aware that cancer occasionally, although rarely, may strike a second time fifteen or twenty years later. If it does, he wants to know about it soon enough so science can do him some good.

This is the tune that medical men play over and over: annual examinations, annual examinations, annual examinations. Doctors tell you not to neglect the Seven Danger Signals and not to wait for their appearance, but to get examined even if you feel fine.

THE DANGER SIGNALS

The Seven Danger Signals, as everybody knows by now, are:
1. Any sore that does not heal.
2. A lump or thickening in any part of the body.
3. Unusual bleeding or discharge.
4. Any change in a wart or mole.
5. Persistent indigestion or difficulty in swallowing.
6. Persistent hoarseness or cough.
7. Any change in normal bowel habits.

A TYPICAL EXAM

In the interest of science and fair play, *Esquire* reporter Walter Ross decided to find out what a cancer-clinic examination was like. So, with the American Cancer Society's help, an appointment was made to go through the Strang Cancer Prevention Clinic, in New York's Memorial Center, as a patient. Mr. Ross reports:

"When I arrived at the clinic I was led to a waiting room where several other people were seated. They soon called my name and ushered me into a little room where a girl (a medical technician) stuck a needle in my finger and took some of my blood to study the quantity and character of its cells.

"I was then taken into another room. A girl in a white coat said, 'Take off your coat,' and stood me in front of an X-ray machine. She told me to breathe deeply and hold it, and press up against the machine. In fifteen seconds I was told to put my coat on and go to the room where the new examinees come to keep their appointments.

"A few minutes later my name was called again and I was taken into the men's examining room. A nurse gave me a kind of nightgown that comes down to the knees and ties in front. She told me to remove my clothes in one of the curtained dressing cubicles, and put on the gown.

"I put on the gown and a nurse recorded my height and weight and arranged for a specimen of my urine.

"Pretty soon a doctor ushered me into one of the examining rooms and pulled the curtain. He asked me if my mother and father were still living, if anybody in my family had cancer, whether I had any brothers or sisters, and so on. Then he asked me to remove my robe and sit on the end of the table. He tested my reflexes, told me I was tense, and listened to my heart and lungs; he looked into my ears, examined my tongue and peered into my larynx, and took my blood pressure. Then he asked me to lie back and he probed me for lumps and bumps of the skin, thyroid, thymus, chest, stomach, abdomen, and testicles. Finally, he examined my rectum, using a narrow tube called a proctoscope which enabled him to see the lower bowel (the most common site of tumors in men).

"The whole thing took less than ninety minutes. At the end of that time the doctor—a young man who plans to make cancer study his life work—said he had found nothing wrong."

The Strang Clinic was established in 1940 by the late Dr. Elise L'Esperance. Since 1950 it has been under the direction of Dr. Emerson Day.

In 1958, 23,431 men and women went through the clinic, of whom 6,716 were new examinees and the remainder had been through once or more in previous years. Six out of a thousand men were found to have cancer, eight out of a thousand women. It doesn't take much imagination to suspect how the vast majority of the examinees felt when they got their reports!

DETECTING PRECANCEROUS CONDITIONS

Examinations do more than discover cancers—they uncover precancerous conditions which can be corrected before cancers form. Doctors are not entirely agreed on what constitutes a precancerous condition, but many of them advise immediate removal of any moles or birthmarks on the palms of the hand or between the fingers; on the feet (any part of the foot that fits inside the shoe) or on the scrotal sac. Some pigmented lesions (mole or birthmark) that are rubbed or pressed constantly may turn malignant.

A precancerous condition of the mouth is what doctors call leukoplakia—which may be a white spot on the lip or a thickening and whitening of patches of mucous membrane of the mouth. Leukoplakia can result from syphilis, bad oral hygiene, ill-fitting dentures, a Vitamin-B deficiency, excessive use of tobacco or alcohol; or from no apparent cause. No matter what its origin, it should never be ignored. It can be treated and stopped under a doctor's care before cancer gets started.

Men with duodenal ulcers almost never have cancer of that area. But gastric (stomach) ulcers, particularly of the greater curvature of the stomach, have to be "proved innocent or they are assumed guilty." Gastric ulcers that do not respond rapidly to treatment may be not ulcers but cancers, and further tests are immediately indicated. On the other hand, men with a long history of gastric ulcers probably do *not* have cancer.

It is impossible to locate stomach cancers without careful examination by X-ray and microscope, which is the reason this disease is so insidious. Men are apt to overlook indigestion, or to treat it with home remedies; a generally tired feeling doesn't tell them anything; loss of appetite is disregarded. But to a doctor with a "high index of suspicion," which every cancer detective must possess, these possible symptoms require examination, although most of the time they are not cancer.

Precancerous conditions do not necessarily become true cancers; they just mean that a better than average incidence of cancer is found among people who have the condition. Some things are known to be extremely dangerous, like the handling of radium and X-ray.

There are quite a few other things that have a more than passing relationship to cancer. Cancer of the scrotum was first identified as "chimney-sweep's cancer" because it was found so often among those workers. Contact with other irritant chemicals apparently leads to the skin cancers found among workers in gasoline-cracking plants, tar distilleries, shale oil refineries, gasworks and cotton factories. Men who work in aniline dye plants without proper safeguards frequently get cancer of the bladder.

The place you live in and the life you lead may have some effect on your cancer chances. Australia has an unusually clear atmosphere and Australians suffer five times as many skin cancers as do Britons. Medicos think that overexposure to ultraviolet rays of the sun may have something to do with it. Skin cancers are more frequent among the out-of-door type, such as farmers and sailors; in fact, there is five times as much skin cancer among U.S. Navy men as among the rest of U.S. males.

Boys with undescended testicles should have the condition attended to before puberty. In grown men, undescended testicles should be removed. For one thing, they are useless (internal body heat, two degrees higher than that of the scrotum, destroys their function) and, for another, they occasionally develop cancers.

It is probably a good idea to be circumcised, the younger the better. Jews, who are circumcised soon after birth, hardly ever develop cancer of the penis. Mohammedans, circumcised around the age of ten, develop it a little oftener. Cancer of the penis is found most frequently among uncircumcised adults.

There is no evidence whatever that there is any relationship between frequency of intercourse and incidence of cancer of the prostate or of any male sex organ.

Many men have trouble with their prostate glands as they get older, but this, in itself, is not a cause of cancer. The thing to worry about is detecting prostate cancer soon enough. Like the other hidden cancers, it can only be found by frequent examinations, especially of men over forty-five (it is most common after sixty).

The trouble is, most men wait until they get severe back and leg pains before they go to a doctor to discover that a simple prostatic cancer has metastasized (spread to new areas) into cancer of the leg and pelvic bones. Then it is too late for a cure but, by removing the testicles and/or giving injections of stilbestrol, many patients are kept comfortable for years. While 80 per cent of untreated cases die within forty months, many of the treated patients are still alive after five years. But this is obviously only a stopgap; the thing to do is find prostate cancer early and the only way that can be done is by having semiannual rectal examinations.

Surgery, even when it cures the cancer, may be tough on the patient. A thirty-nine-year-old policeman who had undergone removal of his prostate was talking to his doctor the other day.

"Gee, Doc," he said, "I'm kind of embarrassed."

"What about?" the doctor asked.

"Well," he said, then stopped, blushing. "It's hard to talk about it. I'm not even forty yet, and I can't have relations with my wife. Why is that?"

The doctor decided that the patient was man enough to stand the truth. "I removed your prostate," he said, "as I told you. What I didn't tell you at the time—because you didn't ask and we don't like to frighten people—is that you had cancer, so we had to remove your seminal vesicles and cut some nerves as well. The result is that you are unable to have sexual intercourse. It was the only way to save your life."

"Gee, Doc," the policeman said, "I wish you'd told me this before. I never realized."

"Well, was it worth it?" the doctor asked, knowing it was important for the patient to face this important psychological problem.

"Of course it was worth it. I've got a wife and family to take care of, and a job to do. Of course it was worth it. I'd rather be alive than dead. Wouldn't you?"

PROGRESS IN TREATMENT

There are two established methods of fighting cancer; irradiation (X-ray, radium, betatron) and surgery. All others are experimental, but several of them offer hope for the future.

Three new methods of fighting cancer are under study but no conclusive results have been achieved. (1) Science is trying to find substances that will starve cancer cells without affecting normal cells. (2) The search is continuing for substances that will kill cancers without harming normal tissue. (3) The new radioactive isotopes, outgrowth of atomic research, are being used to track down cancers within the body, and in some instances for treatment of cancer.

Cancer-detection methods are also being improved. The Papanicolaou smear test is being found more applicable and a new blood test may be in the offing.

Surgery is being used more radically. One extreme procedure, devised by Dr. Alexander Brunschwig for pelvic cancer, removes the entire contents of the pelvic cavity, eliminating many deep-rooted cancers of the cervix, rectum, etc. As a result, some cancers which were formerly inoperable are now being treated.

There are some who feel that, given enough money, our scientists could find the cause and cure for cancer within a reasonable time. Look what happened when they went to work on the atom. One doctor summed it up recently when he said, "There are enough lines of research, enough trained men to lick cancer. All we have to do is pay them to do that and nothing else, and to provide them the facilities to work with. They'll do it, and it probably won't cost as much as the atom bomb."

HERE ARE ANSWERS TO 33 OF THE MOST FREQUENTLY ASKED CANCER QUESTIONS

1. What causes cancer?

The essential cause is unknown. Many factors are involved, but the most common is some form of chronic or prolonged irritation. This may be of several kinds, as chemical, thermal (heat), or mechanical, as friction.

2. Is cancer caused by a germ?

There is no definite scientific evidence that cancer in human beings is caused by a germ.

3. Is cancer contagious or infectious?

As cancer is not due to a germ, it is neither contagious nor infectious. There is no record in medical literature of physicians or nurses having got cancer from patients despite the most intimate contact with them. A person can no more "catch" cancer from another than he can "catch" the color of his eyes.

4. How does cancer spread through the body?

In three ways. (1) Cancer cells grow through the walls of blood vessels and are carried by the blood stream to distant parts of the body. (2) They enter the lymphatic stream in a similar manner and are carried to near-by lymph glands. (3) Cancer cells grow directly from one tissue into another.

5. Does cancer come from a single bruise?

CANCER

A type of bone cancer may rarely result from a single severe injury. It is believed that a single injury to soft tissue, such as the breast, will not cause cancer to develop.

6. *What is the relation of food to cancer?*

In certain individuals, vitamin-B deficiency may result in changes in certain tissues, particularly of the mouth and lips which may ultimately become cancerous. In general, however, so far as is known, no food or combination of foods has any influence on the cause or cure of cancer.

7. *Will irregularity in eating cause cancer of the stomach?*

There is no scientific evidence that it will, since cancer of the stomach occurs in people who eat regularly the most healthful foods.

8. *Does eating hot foods cause cancer?*

There is little evidence that the temperature of food is an important factor in the development of cancer.

9. *Does the use of alcohol bear any relation to cancer of the stomach?*

Not so far as is known. Alcohol may have an unfavorable effect on stomach tissues of some persons, but no more so than other substances taken into the stomach with food or drink.

10. *Is cancer hereditary in human beings?*

There are probably inherited tendencies to form cancer of different types. Since, however, the method of inheriting such tendencies is obscure and undoubtedly complex, the presence of cancer in one or both parents should be merely a cause of greater alertness in looking for and recognizing suspicious conditions on the part of the individual. The facts do not justify fear.

11. *Do corns ever become cancerous?*

Cancer may occur in any tissue of the body, but since a corn consists entirely of nonvital cells it could not, in itself, develop cancer.

12. *Do freckles ever turn into cancer?*

Simple freckles do not. However, flat moles containing certain pigment of a bluish-black color and looking like dark freckles, may become cancers and should be checked periodically.

13. *Do hemorrhoids turn into cancer?*

No. Hemorrhoids are enlarged veins in the rectal wall. Cancer is occasionally found in the tissue above the hemorrhoids, so "bleeding piles" should be examined carefully to determine whether cancer is present.

14. *Can one's mental condition influence the course of cancer?*

Not so far as is known. Cancer is a disease of body cells. One's mental condition has no effect on the course of the disease since this malignant change is apparently due to physical processes.

15. *Can a tuberculous person have a cancer?*

He can.

16. *Is pain an early symptom of cancer?*

No, except in a cancer of bone or nerve tissue. Pain is usually a late symptom and when it comes the growth is often far advanced.

17. *How long is it safe to wait after suspicious symptoms appear before consulting a physician?*

Any delay is dangerous. Go at once to a doctor and ask for a thorough examination.

18. *Why are periodic examinations necessary?*

The earlier a cancer is treated the greater the chance of a cure. Through periodic examinations cancer may be detected in its early stages, before the individual has noticed any sign or symptom in himself.

19. *Does blood in the urine indicate cancer?*

It may, but it may also be caused by other conditions. A careful examination is essential to rule it out.

20. *Is it true that cancer generally develops among people in poor health?*

There is no known relation between the status of one's health and the development of cancer.

21. *Are all hospitals equipped to diagnose and treat all kinds of cancer?*

No, but many are. To be adequately equipped for this purpose a hospital must have an operating room; a laboratory for the microscopic diagnosis of tissue; X-ray equipment suitable for diagnosis and for treatment; and must own or have access to a sufficient quantity of radium. To make this equipment effective there must be physicians trained in its use.

22. *Is cancer more frequent among Negroes than among whites?*

Proportionately fewer cancer deaths are reported among Negroes than among whites, but this perhaps is due to poor reporting of the disease.

23. *Are X-ray treatments good for all kinds of cancer?*

No, treatment depends on type and location of the growth. Some cancers will not respond to X-ray or radium treatment, but must be treated by surgery or other means, as certain hormones or isotopes.

24. *Do surgical or radiation treatments spread cancer?*

No. In fact, such treatments tend to limit the spread of cancer.

25. *Is cancer curable only in the early stages?*

Yes, in the large majority of cases. At times, however, cures have been obtained after the cancers have been present for a long time.

26. *How long will an untreated cancer patient live?*

This will differ with each individual and the location and type of cancer.

27. Is there any chemical that destroys cancerous tissue?

There is some evidence that a few chemical substances such as the nitrogen mustards (chemicals related to the poisonous mustard gas) partially destroy cancerous tissues in some forms of cancer and leukemia. These chemicals are not cures, but may alleviate suffering and may prolong life.

28. Can cancer result from sexual intercourse?

No. There is no known relation between cancer and sexual activity on the part of the male or female.

29. Is cancer of the prostate common?

Yes, cancer of the prostate is one of the most common forms of cancer in older men. Men should be on guard against this form of cancer especially as they approach sixty. A thorough physical examination, *including rectal examination,* is the only way to discover this hidden cancer early enough for cure.

30. At what age do cancer deaths occur most frequently?

Age	Males (for 1956)
Under 5	1,047
5-14	1,252
15-24	1,081
25-34	2,107
35-44	5,378
45-54	15,474
55-64	32,704
65-74	40,249
75 & over	31,435

31. How can I go about locating the cancer-detection center nearest my home?

By inquiring from your family physician, the local unit of the American Cancer Society, or from your city or county health department.

32. Can a physician examine a patient thoroughly for cancer in his office or is it necessary to go to a hospital?

An office examination should be sufficient unless, by questioning or from his findings in his office, your doctor feels you should go to the hospital for a more complete examination, such as by X-ray and blood tests.

33. How can I tell a quack from a reputable physician?

If a person advertises or guarantees a cure, he may be classed as a quack. No reputable, ethical physician will do either of these things.

Everybody needs sunshine, or the Vitamin D which comes through the action of certain of the sun's rays upon the skin. But some people get all the Vitamin D they need in a hurry, while others have to soak up a lot of sun for the same effect. The difference is in the thickness and pigmentation of their skins.

Negroes, Orientals, peoples from the Mediterranean area and others who, from generation to generation, have adapted themselves to steady sunning, need not give a second thought to skin cancer. But the thin-skinned, blue-eyed peoples of the world should be wary of the sun. They are the ones who risk skin cancer when they go against the basic nature of their complexions.

If you tan easily, without burning and peeling, more power to you. But if you burn, watch out. Your burn turns to blisters, and whether the blisters are large enough to be visible or not, the outer layer of blistered skin dries and peels and removes the very protection the skin worked overtime for. Then no matter how fast the skin works to build new layers, the top exposed layer burns, blisters and peels; the protective thickness never increases. Then are the seeds of skin cancer sown. They may be sown in the teens and make no appearance until the thirties or forties.

Cancer is the result of the skin cells' battle to survive unusual or unfavorable conditions. Unfortunately, the survival of these cells in adapting to the unfavorable wave lengths of sunshine can have bad results. These altered cells, beginning to grow under conditions that weaken surrounding tissue, gain vigor and size and acquire a survival value that becomes greater than the surrounding cells.

Eventually, their presence can be seen as flat or elevated, sandpapery alterations of the skin's surface. They may be pinhead in size at first, but they grow. These growths are not cancer themselves. But, untended, they frequently become the breeding beds of the disease. These growths seldom hurt or are tender. They can be easily overlooked. They usually do not itch, but if they are scratched the granular surface flakes off. Sometimes this flaking discloses a slightly moist, shiny surface, or the removal of the flakes may leave a smooth pink area which promptly produces more flakes or scales.

Diagnosed in time and treated by a properly qualified physician, skin cancer can be cured, and without the terrors of pain or disfigurement. But prevention is always the best "cure," so if you are a burner, not a tanner, take sensible precautions when you go out into the sun. Protect all exposed skin with a recommended sun lotion or cream. Go very slow indeed during the first few days of a vacation away from your home base (where, presumably, you know how to judge the intensity of the sun's rays). Check the surface of your skin after exposure to the sun, and if anything unusual does develop see a doctor. Most important, if you're not of the skin type that develops a lifeguard tan quickly and easily, *respect* that fact. Respect the sun: one man's tan is another man's poison.

PART II HOW TO CHANGE THE MESSAGE ON THE WALL
—THE ART OF KEEPING FIT

Ah, but there's an answer to all that dreary data we've been setting before you, and the answer is in your hands.

The answer to many of the maladies that lie in wait for the modern male is, purely and simply, keeping yourself in shape.

Keeping fit is not as hard as you might think. It doesn't have to be a Big Project. You don't have to turn your life upside down. You have only to develop, gradually, a few good habits of living. Habits of eating and sleeping, working and playing. You may not have to give up your bad habits— you may find, in fact, that you get more fun from them when they're offset, a little, by good habits in other areas. And one thing is certain: you'll get more fun out of life in general when you feel and look your best.

Keeping fit is almost as easy as making up your mind to it, and you're already halfway there if you've read the handwriting on the wall (Part I). You know, now, that the health you're inclined to take for granted is not inviolable. You know what you're up against, in the mortality tables and in the wear and tear of everyday life. To the degree that you're impressed —and perhaps a little bit scared—by what can happen to your body, you're now ahead of the game. You're ahead by the knowledge that good health is not a matter of mere chance. You're ahead, we hope, by a resolve:

You're not going to die young. You're not going to slide into old age before your time. You're not going to run your physical machine into the ground. You're going to start taking care of yourself, and right now.

How?

Here's how. . . .

6. START BY TAKING STOCK

Get ready . . . get set . . . get a checkup.

If you can see your fortieth birthday, coming or going, it's time you began taking yourself to a good doctor, at least once a year, for a thoroughgoing physical examination. Even if you "never felt better in your life," you should have an expert's O.K. before embarking on the kind of physical fitness program we're urging you toward. And—let's just face it—if you're getting on toward forty the chances are that you *have* felt better in your life.

There's nothing wrong with being forty, nothing at all. It is not the beginning of the end any more than it is the beginning of real living, but it *is* a kind of halfway mark, appropriate for stock taking. And it is very often the time when a man is working hardest, under greatest pressure, with least time to "waste" on doctor appointments. Such a man needs a good prod, to make him take time out for a checkup. If turning forty is not enough of a psychic shock to serve as the prod, perhaps these simple facts are:

These changes appear to be fundamental to the aging process:

1. The cells composing the tissues of older bodies are not capable of imbibing as much water as those of younger individuals. This makes them less elastic, less resilient, and less able to recover from fatigue and injury than the cells of younger tissues.
2. The active cells of the body—those composing gland and muscle —become fewer and are replaced by inactive connective tissue.
3. The metabolism rate—that is, the rate at which food is converted into energy—becomes slower as we grow older.

. . . Nothing to get excited about, but something to make a *few* allowances for. If you're going on forty, your attack on life should probably be a bit different from what it was when you were twenty, say, or thirty. You may not have to start taking it easy, exactly, but you had better start taking yourself in for an annual checkup.

IT'S GOOD BUSINESS

If you are an executive in an enlightened company, you may find that it's part of your job to have a good diagnostic going-over once a year—on company time, at company expense. Some firms send their key men to the Greenbrier Hotel in White Sulphur Springs, West Virginia, where a three-day checkup can be combined with golf, rest, a change of scene. It's good business, such companies believe, to keep their top men healthy.

Insurance companies like the Metropolitan found this out long ago. With a few exceptions—notably Goodyear, Dennison and Standard Oil (New Jersey)—industrial companies have discovered it only recently.

"Usually," says Dr. James P. Baker, head of the Greenbrier Clinic, "they wait until they lose a key man before they start executive health checkups. But times are changing. We get letters all the time from companies that want to know about giving their executives diagnostic examinations. More than fifty companies use our clinic alone."

One company, which had not had an executive death but was concerned about its key men, picked one member of top management, told him he was a guinea pig, paid all his expenses to Greenbrier and sat back to await the report. (Company examinations are usually confidential between the executive and the doctor, but this was a special case.) The man dutifully went through the clinic, although he told his wife it was all damned nonsense, he'd never felt better in his life (except for those nagging lower-back pains, probably a muscle strain). The doctors of Greenbrier put him through the usual routine and discovered a well-advanced case of cancer of the prostate. It was, unfortunately, inoperable; it had been detected too late.

The fact that this supposedly healthy man had an incurable illness so shocked his superiors that they immediately instituted a program of annual examinations for all executives above the grade of department head. The company now sends these executives to Greenbrier every year.

The Greenbrier executive's exam starts on the first morning with a long talk with one of four trained internists (specialists in internal medicine) on the clinic staff. This is the key to the examination, for during the talk—which always reveals much more than the patient realizes—the internist learns about the patient's medical history, his personality, his job and his relations with his wife and children.

Then the actual testing begins. Doctors examine the executive's eyes, ears, nose and throat, listen to his heart and lungs, take his blood pressure. His abdomen is palpated, his prostate and lower bowel are examined with a proctoscope. An EKG (electrocardiogram) tracing is made of his heartbeat, both at rest and after he has run up and down a flight of small steps going nowhere. Specimens of blood and urine are taken for laboratory examination during the afternoon. If the patient shows signs of sinus trouble or arthritis, special X-rays are taken. Altogether, the first day's examination covers about four hours. For the rest of the day the patient is on his own.

The executive is asked not to eat breakfast the second day so that his blood will be in perfect condition for accurate chemical studies. A meal would throw the sugar content out of line, for example, and the diabetes test would not be reliable.

Basal metabolism—the rate at which the body burns oxygen—is tested with a breathing apparatus to reveal the functioning of the thyroid. If there are any symptoms of digestive trouble the patient gets either a barium meal or a barium enema, and careful X-rays are taken of the stomach or the colon.

Out of the first 2,178 executives and wives to come through the Greenbrier Clinic, 2,011 had one disease or another, and sometimes there was more than one to a customer. The medical conditions ranged from obesity (at least 10 per cent or more overweight—the dangerous stage) through heart disease, ulcer, diabetes, high blood pressure and the rest.

These percentages are duplicated in the Life Extension Examiners, a New York City diagnostic service specializing since 1914 in examinations of executives. More than three hundred large corporations have contracts with the Examiners. For $125 per man per year each executive gets the business-man's special top-to-toe, inside-outside, cradle-to-now examination that takes sixteen hours spread over three days. Recently, the Examiners made a study of a thousand supposedly healthy executive-patients and found that 888 had something wrong with them and 600 required the attention of a physician.

NUMBER ONE PROBLEM: FAT

Obesity is the most common problem, and one of the most dangerous. Life-insurance companies charge extra premiums for overweight adults. Not long ago Life Extension Examiners studied 2,400 electrocardiograph tracings of men whose average age was 47.8 years. More than half of them showed some borderline changes and one out of ten had a really serious heart condition. Fully half of those in the serious group were overweight, while only a quarter of the normal group carried extra poundage.

At two of these clinics for executives, the Vincent Astor Diagnostic Service at New York Hospital and the Benjamin Franklin Clinic in Philadelphia, the patient's history is carefully studied as a key to his health. Both clinics use questionnaires based on 160 yes-no queries, and doctors in both believe that the answers to these questionnaires, plus what patients say in the interviews that precede physical examinations, give many important clues.

One man, for example, came to the Vincent Astor people because his wife complained about his wheezing in bed. "But," he added, "I don't wheeze when I stand up." With that one sentence, the patient told the doctor more than he could have learned in a week of tests. In fact, the chest X-rays were completely negative—but the doctors knew that a unilateral wheeze was strong indication of an obstruction in the area of the wheeze and investigation showed that this man had a bronchial cancer. They suggested an operation to the man's physician (Vincent Astor does not operate). The man's left lung was removed three years ago and he has been living a full and happy life ever since.

One Ben Franklin examination showed that a forty-two-year-old captain of industry, who felt just fine, was giving house room to a lot of small bugs with the big name of endamoeba-histolytica. These germs were infecting the man's intestinal tract and would soon have caused ulcers, bleeding, diarrhea and serious weight loss. And he would almost certainly have passed them on to his wife and two children. Detecting the disease saved the whole family a load of grief, and the man was easily cured with one of the new antibiotics.

Sometimes the discovery of a disease can even help a man in his work. One top General Motors executive, for example, owes his promotion and a five-thousand-dollar raise to his examination. He had been run-down, his work had suffered and his morale had gone into a nose dive when he was passed over for promotion. Luckily, his checkup came soon after and told him what was wrong: a peptic ulcer.

In less than a year he had licked the ulcer and his work had improved to such an extent that he was leapfrogged into one of the top jobs in his division.

LIVING UP TO THE FINDINGS

What has made executive examinations so successful is the willingness of the executive to take the steps necessary to get himself cured. General Motors doctors say that 59 per cent of G-M executives examined in the clinics have made some important change in their living habits.

G-M knows the results of these examinations because the executives talk about them. The examinations are completely voluntary, and their results are given by the clinics only to the executive and/or his personal physician. Even though G-M and General Electric and the other companies pay the bills, they do not see the results. The clinic sometimes reports to the company's medical department, but even here the information is confidential. A man who wishes to keep his condition secret from his boss (and most men do) has no trouble on this score.

The confidential and voluntary nature of executive exams is maintained even by the companies who have their own examination units, such as Standard Oil (New Jersey) and Consolidated Edison of New York. In both, the records of individual examinations are seen only by the medical department and the executive himself.

Dr. Anthony Lanza, head of the New York University-Bellevue Institute of Industrial Medicine, says that it makes no difference whether the examination is given inside or outside the company, or in the office of an executive's family doctor. "The important things are," says Dr. Lanza, "how good is the doctor and how thorough is the examination."

The men who run in-company exams think they have an edge in detecting trouble and curing it because they know their patients on a day-in, day-out basis and see the job situations which create dangerous tensions. "A good half of the problems we see here," Dr. Robert Collier Page, Standard Oil (N.J.) Medical Director, says, "are not disease in the old sense, but symptoms of diseases that are starting, caused by maladjustment, insecurity, overwork or a bad home life. And our experience is typical."

Dr. Page finds that the worst problem is the man who brings home a brief case crammed with papers and burns the midnight oil over them. Eventually his twenty-four-hour day gets him down. He suffers "intermittent attacks of constipation or diarrhea; he burps and regurgitates; his piles begin to trouble him; his homework lacks perfection in performance; he begins to eat too much; and is apt to imbibe too freely. . . . If he's lucky enough not to succumb to an acute coronary attack, malignancy or an unforeseen accident, chances are he'll become eligible for retirement on medical grounds at the age of fifty-eight or sixty." In other words, if he doesn't die young, he will be an old man several years before his time.

No business is any better than its management, and the cost of medical examinations is trifling in the total cost of running even a small company. "Everybody knows the price of a machine," says Arch Patton, McKinsey & Company's executive compensation expert, "but nobody knows how much an executive is worth in a lump sum. If executives were traded like ball players, there'd be some way of finding out. Follow it further—because everybody knows how much a ball player is worth, nobody ever questions how much a club spends not only on diagnosing but on actually curing their players. One thing we do know: a good executive becomes more and more valuable as he gets older. It's just common sense for a company to spend a few hundred dollars each year to see that a top man stays healthy."

Other companies are more specific as to the value of executive examinations. The head of an instrument company says that four of his executives are alive today only because they had thorough examinations and followed through on doctors' recommendations; the president of a steel company said he was sure the clinics had saved the lives of several of his assistants.

Moreover, the life-and-death cases are only part of the story. Dozens of companies are now receiving more efficient work from sounder top-management groups and the executives themselves are healthier and happier. Even those who came through the examinations with an unmarked record feel that they gained by the experience. "After all," one of them says, "everybody's got a little worry in him. It's always nice to know you're healthy."

7. NEXT: FIVE CUSTOM-MADE DIETS

Once a checkup has shown you in what areas your health could stand a bit of improvement, and once you know for certain what limitations a doctor might possibly set on your corrective program, you're ready to map out your plan for keeping fit.

And chances are that, if you're in that age bracket where you just "haven't time" to think about your*self,* you'll have to start by taking off a few pounds.

By the time they reach forty, a large percentage of men are overweight. If your normal is 150 pounds, and you weigh 175, that means the strain on all your vital organs—heart, lungs, liver, etc.—is increased by about 16 per cent. That's why fat is fatal to longevity; for every pound of overweight, the mortality rate increases about 1 percent.

For a long time after forty, your appetite is going to be just as good as it always was; and that's too bad, because your food requirements have been getting smaller since you were thirty. Both kind and quantity of food desired are largely a matter of habit.

All of us become accustomed to eating large quantities of rich foods (carbohydrate and fat) in childhood, when we need a high energy-producing diet; and most of us go right on eating a football player's diet after forty, when frequently our most strenuous exercise is hoisting our feet up onto our desks. That's why waistlines slowly lengthen after thirty.

At forty, we should begin to change our eating habits. More protein (lean meat, beans, cheese, milk, eggs), more vitamin-containing vegetables and fruits (except things like potatoes and avocado pears) but less fat (cream, pork, butter, fried foods) and less carbohydrate (pastry, candy, jellies, preserves, etc.)

It takes courage to give up the things you like and eat things you don't. You can change your eating habits and your desires; and it doesn't take long. After only a few months' perseverance you'll really *want*, for the most part, the things that are good for you. We said, "for the most part"; you may prefer chocolate custard pie to spinach, but you can teach yourself to prefer string beans to potatoes—and that's something.

The facts of modern life, we'll admit, make it hard for a man who wants to change his eating habits. The commuter train leaves before you feel like eating much of a breakfast. The coffee break at the office comes complete with a hunk of pastry. The business prospect who sits across the lunch table from you "needs" two martinis before he can soften up enough to hear you out, and as you bolt down a big lunch you're chewing over your sales talk more than your food. You get back to the office limp and logy, but twenty people called while you were out and your headache can only get worse through the afternoon. The evening's cocktail party, or the camaraderie in the bar car, improves nothing. Dinner is apt to be late, heavy and stultifying. The miracle is that you can fight your way out of bed the next morning, to go through the whole ghastly process yet again.

With the facts of your daily life stacked up against you, then, you have to be pretty darned determined before you can get your weight back to where it belongs. Here are five ways to do it.

Determination is the main ingredient in our first diet (below). The diet consists in counting your calories, that's all—in eating no more than you need in any given day.

Diet No. 2, page 99, is a refinement of the first diet. It, too, is calorie conscious, but it gives you a little help on figuring out what and where to cut your intake.

Diet No. 3, page 100, puts you onto another plane. In contrast to the slow and easy results of the first two diets, this "Feast Without Famine" can melt off as many as twenty pounds in two weeks.

Diet No. 4, page 102, requires a fresh gastronomical point of view—hard to learn (impossible for some men) but full of lifelong rewards for those who adopt it.

Diet No. 5, page 104, designed for the bachelor who would rather have his tête-à-têtes over alcohol and oysters than over milk and molasses, gives you two weeks of elegant eating. It compromises on quantity, not quality, so it can be followed in first-rate restaurants. It promises to shear you of five to seven pounds in two weeks, even if you're benedict rather than bachelor.

There are, of course, hundreds of diets, some good, some dangerous, but few are specifically concerned with the problems of today's metropolitan executive. These are. If you are confronted with the virtual necessity of lunching out in good restaurants, drinking sociably, often dining or partying for the sake of business, these diets will help you do what does not come naturally: get your weight where it belongs, and keep it there!

DIET NO. 1—FOR CALORIE COUNTERS

A man's caloric intake ought to be about 20 calories per pound per day, less if he takes no exercise. Your ideal weight multiplied by 20 is the number of calories needed each day to maintain that weight. To lose weight, about 3 ounces of fat per day, subtract 750 calories per day from the ideal.

NEXT: FIVE CUSTOM-MADE DIETS

ESQUIRE'S CALORIE CHART

BEVERAGES:

Cocoa (1 cup) .. 150 c
Coffee (with
  cream) .... 25 c
  (with cr. & sug.) 55 c
Tea (plain) 0
Buttermilk (8 oz.) 85 c
Milk (8 oz.) .. 165 c
  (Skimmed)... 80 c
Ginger Ale (8 oz.) 80 c
Ale (8 oz.) .... 100 c
Beer .... 100 c
Sweet cocktails ..250 c
Dry cocktails .. 90 c
Highball ...... 150 c
Liqueur ...... 80-100 c
Whiskey (jigger) 110-150 c
Sweet wine
  (glass) ...... 130 c
Dry wine ...... 95 c

BREAD:

Raisin (1 slice) . 100 c
Rye .... 70 c
White .... 65 c
Whole Wheat .. 75 c
Biscuit (1 lg.) .. 100 c
English muffin .. 130 c
Saltines
  (1 double) .. 40 c
Danish pastry .. 120 c

CAKES, COOKIES:

Chocolate layer
  (slice) ...... 400 c
Sponge .... 115 c
Pound .... 115 c
Marble (slice) .. 150 c
Fruit shortcake
  (with whipped
  cream) ...... 300 c
Cheese .... 350 c
Brownie ...... 140 c
Toll house cookie
  (each) ...... 125 c
Chocolate cookie 125 c
Oatmeal ...... 110 c
Fig bar .... 110 c
Almond
  macaroon .... 110 c

CANDY:

Chocolate bar ..240-295 c
Bon Bon ...... 50 c
Chocolate mint . 50-100 c
Candied fruit .. 30 c

Fudge .... 100 c
Gumdrop ...... 35 c
Peanut brittle .. 50-75 c

SAUCES, STUFFINGS:

Butter (1 sq.).. 50 c
Clear gravy (2 t.)
  .... 100 c
Creamed gravy
  (2 t.) ...... 100 c
Cream sauce
  (2 t.) .... 150 c
Poultry stuffing
  (2 t.) ...... 75 c

CHEESES:

Cheddar (cube). 100 c
Camembert .... 100 c
Cottage (1 tbsp.) 25 c
Limburger .... 150 c
Roquefort .... 200 c
Swiss (slice) .. 100 c

DISHES:

Baked Beans
  (½ cup) .... 150 c
Chop suey
  (½ cup) .... 250 c
Chow mein
  (½ cup) .... 150 c
Macaroni & Cheese
  (¾ cup) .... 200 c
Stuffed pepper .. 175 c
Spaghetti with to-
  mato sauce (¾
  cup) .... 200 c
Corned beef hash
  (½ cup) .... 100 c
Chili con carne
  (½ cup) .... 250 c

DRIED, CANNED FRUIT, JUICES:

Dried apricots
  (5) .... 100 c
Dried dates (4) 100 c
Dried figs (2) .. 100 c
Dried prunes (4) 100 c
Applesauce
  (½ cup) .... 85 c
Canned apricots
  (5) .... 150 c
Canned berries
  (½ cup) .... 100 c
Canned figs (3) 150 c

Canned pears
  (3 halves) .. 100 c
Canned peaches
  (2 halves).. 100 c
Canned plums
  (4) .... 100 c
Apple juice
  (4 oz.) ...... 60 c
Grapefruit juice
  (1 cup) .... 100 c
Orange juice
  (½ cup) ...... 65 c
  (1 cup) .... 130 c
Pineapple juice
  (½ cup) .... 65 c
Prune juice
  (1 cup) .... 200 c
Tomato juice
  (½ cup) .... 25 c
Vegetable juice
  (½ cup) .... 35 c
Sauerkraut juice
  (½ cup) .... 20 c

FLAVORINGS:

Catsup (1 t.) .. 25 c
Chili sauce (1 t.) 25 c
Hollandaise
  (1 t.) ...... 100 c
Mustard (1 t.).. 10 c
Horseradish (1 t.) 5 c
Worcestershire
  (1 t.) ...... 10 c
Currant jelly
  (1 t.) ...... 50 c
Pickles (1 sm.) .. 10 c
Olives (6 m.) .. 50 c
Sugar (1 tsp.) .. 18 c
Cream (1 tsp.) .. 20 c
Lemon (1 med.) . 35 c
  juice (t.) ... 5 c
Butter (1 t.) .. 100 c
Oleomargarine
  (1 t.) ...... 100 c
Syrup (1 t.) .... 70 c
Marmalade (1 t.) 100 c

FRESH FRUITS:

Grapes (1 cup) 100 c
Half grapefruit . 85 c
Lime (juice)
  (1 t.) ...... 10 c
Orange .... 80 c
Peach .... 50 c
Apple .... 100 c
Cherries (20) .. 100 c
Cantaloupe (½) . 50 c

ESQUIRE'S CALORIE CHART

Plums (4) ..... 100 c
Pear .... 65 c
Pineapple (1
   slice) .... 50 c
Watermelon
   (1 slice) .... 100 c
Tangerine .... 35 c

ICE CREAM:
Vanilla (½ cup) . 200 c
Chocolate (and
   others) (½ cup)
   .... 250 c
Sherbet (½ cup) 110 c
Sundae (½ cup) . 400 c
Chocolate milk
   shake .... 385 c
Chocolate malted 460 c
Ice cream soda. . 350 c

CEREALS, PANCAKES:
Corn flakes
   (cup) ...... 80-100 c
Rice Krispies .. 50 c
Shredded wheat 100 c
Grits .... 125 c
Oatmeal ...... 133 c
Cooked wheat
   cereals ..... 100 c
Pancake ...... 75 c
Waffle .... 225 c
French toast ... 105 c

DRESSINGS (SALAD)
French (1 t.) .. 75 c
Mayonnaise
   (1 t.) ...... 100 c
Thousand Island
   (1 t.) ...... 100 c
Russian Dressing
   (1 t.) ...... 75 c

SANDWICHES:
   (no dressing)
Bacon & tomato 300 c
Cheese .... 270 c
Cheeseburger .. 360 c
Cheese & Olive . 350 c
Chicken salad . 245 c
Sliced chicken .. 275 c
Corned beef .... 250 c
Egg salad ...... 300 c
Hot dog ...... 180 c
Ham .... 270 c
Ham & cheese .. 380 c
Hamburger .... 250 c
Liverwurst .... 210 c

Pastrami ...... 350 c
Peanut butter .. 200 c
Roast beef .... 250 c
Roast pork .... 320 c
Salami .... 275 c
Salmon .... 200 c
Tongue .... 200 c
Tuna .... 350 c
Denver
   (Western) .. 325 c

NUTS:
Almonds (15) .. 100 c
Brazil (2) ..... 100 c
Cashew (4)... 100 c
Chestnuts (7) .. 100 c
Peanuts (18) .. 100 c
Pecans (6) .... 100 c
Walnuts (8) .. 100 c

PIES, PUDDINGS:
Apple (1 portion)
   .... 330 c
Banana cream
   (⅙ of pie) .. 250 c
Berry (⅙ of pie) 330 c
Chocolate
   (⅙ of pie) .. 350 c
Coconut custard
   (⅙ of pie) .. 300 c
Lemon meringue
   (⅙ of pie) .. 300 c
Mincemeat (⅙ of
   pie) .... 340 c
Pumpkin (⅙ of
   pie) .... 265 c
Nesselrode (⅙ of
   pie) .... 265 o
Brown Betty
   (½ cup) .... 150 c
Bread pudding
   (½ cup) .... 150 c
Custard (½ cup) 140 c
Caramel (½ cup) 150 c
Chocolate pudding
   (½ cup) .... 200 c
Jell-o (1 cup) .. 75 c
Tapioca (½ cup) 125 c
Rice (½ cup) .. 150 c

POULTRY, EGGS:
Roast chicken
   (3 slices).... 300 c
Chicken fricassee
   (1 leg) ...... 200 c
Broiled chicken
   (½ med.) .... 100 c

Fried chicken
   (1 leg) ...... 150 c
Roast duck
   (1 pc.) ..... 300 c
Roast goose
   (1 pc.) ..... 300 c
Squab (1 sm.). 200 c
Roast turkey
   (1 sl.) ...... 100 c
Boiled egg
   (medium) .. 70 c
Fried egg ...... 110 c
Poached egg ... 70 c
Scrambled egg .. 125 c

SEA FOOD:
Broiled fish
   (lean) ...... 100 c
Broiled fish (fat) 200 c
Lobster (½) .... 125 c
Oysters (⅓ cup) 65 c
Clams (6) .... 100 c
Fried oysters (2) 60 c
Fried clams
   (10 av.) .... 250 c
Fried scallops
   (6 lg.) ...... 300 c
Boiled shrimps
   (10) .... 75 c
Fried shrimps
   (10) .... 175 c
Herring (marinated,
   cream sauce) 300 c

MEATS:
Beef
   Corned (1 sl.) 100 o
   Dried (2 sl.).. 50 c
   Roast rib (1
      sl.) .... 275 c
   Pot roast (1
      sl.) .... 275 c
   Hamburger
      (1 patty) .. 150 c
Sirloin (1 pc.) 100 c
Bacon (4 slices) 100 c
Frankfurter .... 150 c
Baked ham
   (slice) ...... 325 c
Meat ball ...... 150 c
Meat loaf (1 sl.) 150 c
Kidney (3 oz.).. 120 c
Lamb chop .... 100 c
Lamb roast
   (1 sl.) ..... 100 c
Liver and bacon 200 c

NEXT: FIVE CUSTOM-MADE DIETS

ESQUIRE'S CALORIE CHART

Meat stew (1
cup) .... 250 c
Pork chop ..... 200 c
Pork roast (1 sl.) 300 c
Sausages (2 av.) 190 c
Pork spareribs
(4 ribs) ..... 150 c
Veal cutlet .... 185 c
Veal roast (1 sl.) 150 c
Sweetbreads (2) 240 c

SALADS:

Cream cheese &
pineapple .... 200 c
Chicken ...... 250 c
Cole slaw ...... 65 c
Egg .... 125 c
Fruit (½ cup) .. 150 c
Lettuce, tomato 35 c
Lobster .... 175 c
Crabmeat ..... 320 c
Salmon .... 200 c
Waldorf ...... 185 c
Cucumber
(& tomato) .. 40 c

SOUPS, APPETIZERS:

Fruit cocktail
(½ cup) .... 100 c

Bean soup
(1 cup) .... 200 c
Beef broth
(1 cup) ..... 30 c
Bouillon (1 cup) 25 c
Chicken broth
(1 cup) .... 50 c
Jellied consomme
(1 cup) .... 20 c
Lentil (1 cup) . 200 c
Cream of mushroom
(1 cup) .... 270 c
Onion (1 cup) . 150 c
Pea (1 cup) .. 160 c
Vichysoisse
(1 cup) .... 275 c
Tomato (creamed)
(1 cup) .... 230 c
Vegetable
(1 cup) .... 100 c

VEGETABLES:
(no butter or sauce)

Asparagus
(8 stalks) ... 18 c
Green lima beans
(½ cup) .... 100 c
Wax beans
(1 cup) .... 25 c

Beets (½ cup) .. 45 c
Broccoli (1 cup) 42 c
Cooked cabbage
(1 cup) ..... 40 c
Carrots (½ cup) . 25 c
Celery (6 stalks) 15 c
Corn on the cob
(1 ear) ..... 75 c
Endive (5 pcs.) 60 c
Mushrooms
(1 cup) .... 25 c
Onions, stewed
(½ cup) .... 50 c
Fresh peas
(½ cup) .... 65 c
Baked potato .. 100 c
French fried potato
(4 pc.) ...... 80 c
Fried potato
(4 sl.) ...... 80 c
Scalloped potato
(½ cup) .... 150 c
Baked sweet potato
(1 sm.) .... 185 c
Sauerkraut
(1 cup) .... 40 c
Squash (½ cup) . 50 c
Spinach (1 cup) 40 c
Tomato (1) ... 35 c
Turnip (½ cup) . 25 c

For instance . . .

Here is a week of menus that are well balanced nutritionally, well figured calorically, and yet, as you will see, not without a few pleasures of the palate. If you're the man who can more cheerfully give up cake than cocktails, see your calorie counter and substitute at will. . . .

BREAKFAST	LUNCH	DINNER
	Monday	
Orange juice	Split pea soup	Broiled lamb chops,
1 cup oatmeal with 1	Grilled cheese sand-	mint jelly
tsp. brown sugar	wich	Small whole baked
1 egg	Cole slaw salad with	potato
1 slice whole-wheat	oil, vinegar and	Brussels sprouts
toast with butter or	pinch of sugar	Celery and carrot
margarine and jam	dressing	sticks
Milk, coffee or Postum	Apple Brown Betty	Jell-o fruit cup
	with lemon sauce	Milk, tea or coffee
	Milk, tea or coffee	

ESQUIRE'S THE ART OF KEEPING FIT

BREAKFAST	LUNCH	DINNER

Tuesday

Grapefruit juice 2 small shredded wheat cereal biscuits with 1 tsp. brown sugar and sliced dried figs 1 poached egg 1 slice enriched bread with butter or margarine Milk, coffee or Postum	Cup of vegetable soup Spaghetti Tossed green salad with oil dressing 1 slice French bread (garlicked) Vanilla ice cream Milk, tea or coffee	Pan-broiled or oven-broiled liver (calf or beef) Baked acorn squash with brown sugar or baked sweet potato Chopped spinach Orange Jell-o salad with grated carrots Baked apple with cream Milk, tea or coffee

Wednesday

Orange juice Whole-grain cooked cereal with brown sugar and raisins Scrambled eggs 1 slice whole-wheat toast with butter and honey Milk, coffee or Postum	Tuna fish salad Ring of cantaloupe filled with fresh fruit Celery curls and ripe olives Whole-wheat muffins Tapioca custard Milk, tea or coffee	Cup of chicken broth Filet mignon Buttered parsley potatoes Green string beans Lettuce wedge with Russian dressing Peppermint ice cream with chocolate sauce Milk, tea or coffee

Thursday

Pineapple juice Corn flakes with 1 tbsp. wheat germ and brown sugar 1 egg with 2 slices crisp bacon Whole-wheat muffins with butter or margarine and blackberry jam Milk, coffee or Postum	Baked meat loaf Fresh corn on the cob Sliced tomato Dried fruit compote Milk, iced tea or coffee	Apricot juice Shoulder pot roast Potatoes cooked and browned with pot liquor Buttered broccoli Wooden salad bowl: crisp lettuce, tomato wedges, cucumber slices, parsley, served with Russian dressing Orange sherbet Milk, tea or coffee

NEXT: FIVE CUSTOM-MADE DIETS

BREAKFAST	LUNCH	DINNER
	Friday	
Orange slices with 1 tsp. powdered sugar	Clear consommé	Tomato juice
Cream of Wheat with brown sugar	Cheese soufflé	Rocky Mountain trout with tartar sauce
Soft boiled eggs	Tossed green salad with mild French dressing	Small whole baked potato
1 slice whole-wheat bread with butter and honey	Canned sliced peaches with small slice chocolate cake	Buttered peas
Milk, coffee or Postum made with milk	Milk, tea or coffee	Relish platter: carrot sticks, celery curls, radish roses, fresh onions, pepper rings, pickled beets, ripe olives
		Tart apple pie
		Milk, tea or coffee
	Saturday	
Stewed prunes or prune juice	Cup of creamed mushroom soup	Broiled sirloin steak
Bran flakes topped with sliced bananas	Cottage cheese with fruit salad (fresh or canned)	Corn on the cob
1 egg	Raisin spice cake with lemon sauce	Asparagus
1 slice dark rye toast spread lightly with jam and butter	Milk, tea or coffee	Tomato and cucumber slices with shredded lettuce with French dressing
Milk or coffee		Vanilla ice cream with frozen red raspberry topping
		Milk, minted tea or coffee
	Sunday	
Half grapefruit broiled with brown sugar	Creamed cheese flavored with grated onions served with Wheat Thins or Triscuits	Apple float (1 heaping tbsp. orange sherbet in 4-oz. glass of chilled apple juice)
2 buckwheat cakes (made with milk and eggs) served with hot thin syrup	Relish platter of carrot sticks, celery, radishes, olives, bread and butter pickles	Broiled chicken
Crisp bacon	Angel food cake	Mashed potatoes
Soft dried prunes (uncooked)	Milk, tea or coffee	French string beans
Milk, coffee or Postum		Candlelight salad (½ banana into slice of pineapple)
		Small slice of blueberry pie
		Milk, tea or coffee

DIET NO. 2—THE SLOW AND EASY WAY

If you'd like to continue eating about as usual, and if you're in no hurry to slim into a size smaller suit, try this:

First, find out how many calories you now average. For a month, eat and drink exactly the way you have been eating and drinking lately, but keep a precise list of *everything* you consume: every drink, every roll, every second or extra-large helping. At the end of thirty days, you'll be able to see some sort of pattern.

Suppose, for instance, that your usual breakfast consists of juice, two eggs, one slice of toast, coffee. For lunch you have a cocktail, an entrée (chopped beef, roast lamb or chef's salad, say), a couple of slices of buttered bread or rolls, fruit for dessert, coffee. For dinner a couple of cocktails, an entrée (perhaps a larger serving than at lunch or with an extra vegetable), some bread and butter, a dessert, coffee.

That's not a particularly Henry VIII sort of diet, but if it has gradually been putting weight on you it has to be cut. Studying your month-long inventory, you see that by giving up one egg (75 calories) at breakfast, one buttered roll (140 calories) at lunch and one cocktail (150 calories) or the bread (225 calories) at dinner, you may prune at least 300 or 400 calories a day out of your routine and still keep the *status* of your eating and drinking *quo*.

Probably those few-hundred-minus calories are all you need to start the scale going down instead of up. Results will be slow to show—months at least; perhaps a year or more. But you are eating as you please, having tilted the caloric balance slightly in the opposite direction.

And maybe the ease of this process will persuade you to lop off a few more calories next month, and a few more the month after that, for a more impressive showing.

As you know, a man gains weight because he eats and drinks up more calories than his body burns. Just how many calories your body normally needs depends on height, frame, metabolism and type of activity. A man thirty-five years old, five feet ten inches tall, of medium bone structure and engaged mostly in sedentary pursuits, works off 2,700 calories a day. His desirable weight: 162 pounds.

Suppose he weighs 175. He'll be expending another 50 calories or so in carrying around that extra 13 pounds, a total of 2,750 calories burned up each day. To lose weight he must cut his intake of calories below that level.

There are 3,500 calories in a pound of excess fat. If our sample man puts himself on a rigid diet of 1,500 calories a day, he will smoke off his flabbiness

NEXT: FIVE CUSTOM-MADE DIETS   **99**

at a rapid rate—1,250 calories a day, 8,750 (2½ pounds of fat) a week, or 15 pounds in six weeks.

But if he's not in that much of a hurry, and not that *ready* for the unpleasant business of real dieting, he can eat 2,500 calories a day and still see results: 250 calories a day taken out of his excess poundage, about a pound of fat shed every two weeks.

This method is slow, you see, but it *is* easy. If you've had little or no luck with "crash" diets, or if you tend to put your extra weight back on the minute you stop following a rigid diet, ease into the weight business with this Diet No. 2.

DIET NO. 3—FEAST WITHOUT FAMINE

Though gradual regimens are usually preferred, many men are impatient with long-term programs and want things done in a hurry. Though they did not get stout in a hurry, they can slim down in two weeks—provided they follow this diet *to the letter.*

The diet has a chemical as well as a caloric effect on the system, so it will not be successful if you make any substitutions or omissions.

Some hospitals use this diet as a treatment for obesity, sometimes as a preoperative measure. It is safe for the majority of people but perilous for a few. High in protein and in cholesterol (a chemical involved in thickening the blood-vessel tubing—see page 7), it is *not* recommended for anyone afflicted with kidney trouble, high blood pressure or arteriosclerosis. It should be started only with a doctor's approval.

Got your O.K.? Got your nerve up? Here, then, a few advance instructions:

Eat everything and change nothing. Unless an amount is specified, quantity is not important—eat all you want. On this diet you can keep your innards fairly full; it's not a famine.

Take vegetables without butter, salad without oil.

Take your coffee black and sugarless. Drink nothing else except water. You're on the wagon, for the duration.

Avoid the fatty parts of meat.

Have the eggs any way you like them—poached, soft- or hard-boiled, scrambled, omeleted, coddled or even fried—but use only very small amounts of fat and salt.

Now, here's the Feast Without Famine diet. It is a sensationally fast pound-shedder, but it supplies you with enough to eat so you need never feel hungry. And there are some toothsome high spots to relieve the rigors of the plains.

BREAKFAST	LUNCH	DINNER

MONDAY

Grapefruit	Tomatoes	Combination salad
2 eggs	2 eggs	2 eggs
Coffee	Coffee	1 slice dry toast
		Grapefruit

TUESDAY

Grapefruit	Grapefruit	Steak
2 eggs	2 eggs	Tomatoes, lettuce, celery, olives, cucumbers
Coffee		Coffee

WEDNESDAY

Grapefruit	Spinach	Cabbage
2 eggs	2 eggs	Cottage cheese
Coffee	Coffee	2 eggs
		1 slice dry toast

THURSDAY

Grapefruit	Spinach	Cabbage
2 eggs	2 eggs	Cottage cheese
Coffee	Coffee	2 eggs
		1 slice dry toast

FRIDAY

Grapefruit	Spinach	Fish
2 eggs	2 eggs	Combination salad
Coffee	Coffee	1 slice dry toast
		Grapefruit
		Coffee

SATURDAY

Grapefruit	Fruit salad	Steak
2 eggs		Celery, cucumbers, tomatoes
Coffee		Coffee

NEXT: FIVE CUSTOM-MADE DIETS

BREAKFAST	LUNCHEON - DINNER	SUPPER
Grapefruit	Vegetable soup	Cold chicken
2 eggs	Chicken	Tomatoes
Coffee	Tomatoes,	Grapefruit
	cabbage	
	carrots	
	celery	
	Grapefruit	
	Coffee	

Repeat the same diet for the second week.

Fourteen days of this may melt off twenty or more pounds if you are grossly overweight, ten or fifteen if you're only moderately so. That's triumphant dieting. But if you revert to the same sort of fodder that laid it on in the first place, it could be just a swing around another curve of the vicious cycle. So you'll have to watch yourself—or acquire new ideas about eating.

DIET NO. 4—THE SLIM GOURMET WAY

One reason many men get fat is because they are not interested in food. They go to the table hungry, wolf down whatever happens to be there, especially the starches and fats that provide an illusion of filling, and 800 to 1,500 calories are taken aboard without any conscious pleasure or discernment. At least that was the self-discovery of Martin Lederman, a management consultant by profession and a world traveller and gourmet by preference, who for twenty-five years suffered through seventeen diets, lost four hundred pounds and regained every one of them before learning that simply by concentrating on the taste of each bite of food, each sip of wine, he derived infinitely more enjoyment from his meals and was content, even satiated, with much less quantity than he had previously considered necessary to still his hunger. Lederman has detailed his experiences and theories in a book (*The Slim Gourmet,* Simon & Schuster) which should be edifying also for those who are interested in making the most out of a meal.

By taking all your senses to the table, says *The Slim Gourmet,* you can develop your taste so that you are keenly and appreciatively aware of the savor, flavor, aroma and consistency of the food. Thus, "If we eat a frankfurter for its taste, with conscious pleasure, we know we have eaten a frankfurter and are satisfied. But if we do not consciously enjoy the first, we eat another and another, until we are stuffed." Also, by refining your taste-consciousness, you probably will come to prefer foods in their natural condition, cooked or raw, and eschew the rich sauces and gravies that so many home cooks and restaurant chefs seem to think are integrals of fine dining.

The Slim Gourmet, of course, is ever widening his food vocabulary. He soon knows that there are dozens of varieties of steaks, shrimps, beans, asparagus and oranges coming into the market as the seasons progress. It is part of his pleasure to distinguish among them, to taste and relish the difference between a Bartlett pear and a Kieffer, for example, or a Winter Nelis and a Poire d'Anjou. Unlike the Plump Glutton who goes to the grocery time after time with virtually the same list, the Slim Gourmet regards the supermarket, with its modern methods of distributing, freezing, and storing foods, as a wonderland of excitements and anticipatory delights. Where the Plump Glutton gives a restaurant menu a cursory glance, then orders the same meal he has eaten there a dozen times before, the Slim Gourmet reads the *carte* with unreserved attention and frequently orders experimentally.

By cultivating the pleasures of taste and thereby eating less of more kinds of food (including now and then candy, soufflés, hot cakes, and other high-calorie items, providing they are really enjoyed and needed psychologically), it is possible for an executive to lose his second chin and middle tire permanently and at the same time add new dimensions of entertainment to his life. This sample menu will give you an idea of how the Slim Gourmet eats while reducing:

BREAKFAST	Calories	DINNER	Calories
China tea	0	Fresh asparagus with	
1 slice buttered toast	120	smoked calf's tongue	250
Fruit salad	70	Cantaloupe with bourbon	100
	——	Coffee with cream and	
	190	sugar	70
		Almond coffee cake	200
LUNCH			——
½ glass milk	85		620
½ cold lobster	100		
Tossed green salad with		AFTER DINNER	
egg whites and pearl		1 glass red wine	70
onions	100	Wedge of Camembert	110
1 roll	80	1 slice pumpernickel	80
	——		——
	365		260
		Day's calories total	1,435

NEXT: FIVE CUSTOM-MADE DIETS

DIET NO. 5—THE BACHELOR'S DIET

This diet has a gourmet flavor, too, and it has an eye on the temptations of the menu card in a good restaurant. But it takes you down to 1,400-1,500 calories a day, and that can shear you of five to seven pounds within the prescribed two week period. The diet is approved by Dr. Robert S. Goodhart of the National Vitamin Foundation. It will also win the approval of the most discerning and adventurous gastronome.

Ground rules: If you're the kind of dieter who craves "pacifiers" between meals, reach for the celery, carrot sticks or radishes. Choose your cocktails from the plain list; leave the sugary drinks, with the creamy desserts, to the ladies. Have a nightcap every day, but make it either a glass (8 ounces) of skim milk or a plain yogurt (85-120 calories).

Here we go, on a two-week vacation from that overstuffed feeling:

BRUNCH	AFTERNOON SNACK	DINNER
	SUNDAY (first day)	
Bloody Mary; one egg scrambled in pat butter, on slice wheat toast, topped with tablespoon caviar; *café au lait* with half cup skim milk. (400 calories)	Glass (8 ounces) beer; thin slice Swiss cheese on slice wheat bread spread with mustard. (280 calories)	Drink (your choice); half cup veal paprika (or veal Stroganoff) with half cup Brussels sprouts; half cup fresh fruit cocktail flavored with teaspoon brandy; plain coffee or tea. (535 calories)

BREAKFAST	LUNCH	DINNER
	MONDAY	
Half cup fresh orange juice (or half grapefruit); shredded wheat biscuit in half cup skim milk, teaspoon sugar; *café au lait* with half cup skim milk. (255 calories)	Drink (your choice); two slices leg of lamb (or one broiled lean lamb chop) with teaspoon mint jelly, cup wax beans; half cantaloupe filled with one-fourth cup cottage cheese; plain coffee or tea. (455 calories)	Drink (your choice); broiled medium-sized lobster with two tablespoons tartar sauce (or chili sauce); Caesar salad with two slices melba toast; half cup red raspberries; plain coffee or tea. (495 calories)

BREAKFAST	LUNCH	DINNER

TUESDAY

Half cup fresh orange juice (or half grapefruit); one soft-cooked egg on slice buttered wheat toast; *café au lait* with half cup skim milk. (275 calories)

Drink (your choice); broiled salmon (or swordfish) steak with lemon wedge, broiled tomato; small wedge Camembert cheese with three fresh apricots (or half cup canned halves—drained); plain coffee or tea. (465 calories)

Drink (your choice); two slices veal scaloppine (or one sautéed veal chop) with four large sautéed mushroom caps, half cup sliced cucumber salad; wedge of honeydew melon; plain coffee or tea. (515 calories)

WEDNESDAY

Half cup fresh orange juice (or half grapefruit); cup bran flakes in half cup skim milk, teaspoon sugar; *café au lait* with half cup skim milk. (270 calories)

Drink (your choice); one leg and thigh chicken cacciatore with two tablespoons sauce (or half cup chicken curry), cup spinach; half cup cubed fresh pineapple topped with fourth cup cottage cheese; plain coffee or tea. (515 calories)

Drink (your choice); twelve mussels marinière (or sautéed oysters) with tossed green salad, thin slice French bread; half cup sliced fresh peaches (or half cup drained canned slices) topped with teaspoon sour cream; plain coffee or tea. (420 calories)

THURSDAY

Half cup fresh orange juice (or half grapefruit); one-egg parsley omelet, cooked in pat butter, on slice wheat toast; *café au lait* with half cup skim milk. (275 calories)

Drink (your choice); sautéed filet of sole (or flounder) amandine with lemon wedge, half cup sliced carrots; fourth cup raspberry sherbet; plain coffee or tea. (390 calories)

Drink (your choice); broiled minute steak (or three slices flank steak) with six asparagus spears, sliced tomato with teaspoon French dressing; half cup strawberries flavored with a teaspoon Kirsch; plain coffee or tea. (510 calories)

NEXT: FIVE CUSTOM-MADE DIETS

BREAKFAST	LUNCH	DINNER
	FRIDAY	

BREAKFAST

Half cup fresh orange juice (or half grapefruit); cup corn flakes in half cup skim milk, teaspoon sugar; *café au lait* with half cup skim milk. (250 calories)

LUNCH

FRIDAY

Drink (your choice); ten frogs' legs Provençale (or half roast pheasant) with tossed green salad, two slices melba toast; half cup blueberries topped with fourth cup cottage cheese; plain coffee or tea. (480 calories)

DINNER

Drink (your choice); one Knackwurst (or two slices sauerbraten with tablespoon sauce), half cup sauerkraut, half baked potato; two canned pear halves flavored with teaspoon crème de menthe; plain coffee or tea. (470 calories)

BRUNCH

Half cup fresh orange juice (or half grapefruit); one egg, poached in water, on slice buttered wheat toast; *café au lait* with half cup skim milk. (275 calories)

AFTERNOON SNACK

SATURDAY

Drink (your choice); tablespoon *pâté de foie gras* on slice wheat toast; medium-size apple. (290 calories)

DINNER

Drink (your choice); small broiled ham steak with slice canned pineapple, fourth cup mashed potatoes, tossed green salad; half cantaloupe; plain coffee or tea. (700 calories)

SUNDAY

Screwdriver; one egg baked in whole tomato, with slice buttered wheat toast; *café au lait* with half cup skim milk. (380 calories)

Glass (8 ounces) beer; slice boiled ham on slice wheat bread spread with mustard; four carrot sticks. (370 calories)

Drink (your choice); baked brook trout with fourth cup mixed vegetable stuffing, half cup diced beets; small bunch grapes with small slice Brie cheese, one slice melba toast; plain coffee or tea. (370 calories)

BREAKFAST	LUNCH	DINNER

MONDAY

Half cup fresh orange juice (or half grapefruit); cup corn flakes in half cup skim milk, teaspoon sugar; *café au lait* with half cup skim milk. (250 calories)

Drink (your choice); small roast duck (or goose) leg and thigh with tablespoon orange sauce, half cup puréed turnips; wedge honeydew melon; plain coffee or tea. (385 calories)

Drink (your choice); six oysters Rockefeller with half cup cauliflower topped with teaspoon hollandaise, thin slice French bread; broiled half grapefruit; plain coffee or tea. (580 calories)

TUESDAY

Half cup fresh orange juice (or half grapefruit); one egg baked on slice buttered wheat toast; *café au lait* with half cup skim milk. (275 calories)

Drink (your choice); fourth avocado (or whole medium-size artichoke) filled with half cup lobster (or crab) meat, topped with teaspoon Italian dressing, two melba toast; half cantaloupe filled with fourth cup cottage cheese; plain coffee or tea. (430 calories)

Drink (your choice); Salisbury steak (or slice broiled calves' liver) with half cup sliced carrots; half cup gooseberries; plain coffee or tea. (500 calories)

WEDNESDAY

Half cup fresh orange juice (or half grapefruit); s h r e d d e d wheat biscuit in half cup skim milk, teaspoon sugar; *café au lait* with half cup skim milk. (255 calories)

Drink (your choice); fourth cup Welsh rarebit on slice toast with one strip crisp bacon, broiled tomato; half cup fruit gelatin; plain coffee or tea. (465 calories)

Drink (your choice); six broiled jumbo shrimp with endive, sliced egg salad topped with teaspoon Roquefort dressing, two melba toast; sliced orange flavored with teaspoon a p r i c o t brandy; plain coffee or tea. (545 calories)

NEXT: FIVE CUSTOM-MADE DIETS

BREAKFAST	LUNCH	DINNER

THURSDAY

BREAKFAST	LUNCH	DINNER
Half cup fresh orange juice (or half grapefruit); one egg, scrambled in pat butter, on slice wheat toast; *café au lait* with half cup skim milk. (275 calories)	Drink (your choice); sautéed calves' brain (or twelve *escargots* in garlic butter) with cup chopped broccoli; small baked apple; plain coffee or tea. (490 calories)	Drink (your choice); two slices roast turkey (or chicken) with teaspoon cranberry sauce, six asparagus spears; fresh nectarine; plain coffee or tea. (480 calories)

FRIDAY

Half cup fresh orange juice (or half grapefruit); cup bran flakes in half cup skim milk, teaspoon sugar; *café au lait* with skim milk. (270 calories)	Drink (your choice); half cup spaghetti topped with fourth cup marinara sauce, tossed green salad; small serving zabaglione; coffee or tea. (475 calories)	Drink (your choice); Shish Kebab (four cubes lamb or beef, two small onions, one wedge tomato) with fourth cup saffron (or plain) rice; one large fresh plum; plain coffee or tea. (540 calories)

BRUNCH	AFTERNOON SNACK	DINNER

SATURDAY

BRUNCH	AFTERNOON SNACK	DINNER
Half cup fresh orange juice (or half grapefruit); one egg, poached in tablespoon catsup on slice buttered wheat toast; *café au lait* with half cup skim milk. (290 calories)	Drink (your choice); whole green pepper filled with fourth cup crab meat, topped with teaspoon mayonnaise, slice wheat toast. (350 calories)	Drink (your choice); baked Cornish game hen stuffed with fourth cup wild rice; half cup carrots and peas; half slice watermelon; plain coffee or tea. (585 calories)

And here's the market list for breakfasts, week-end snacks and nightcaps. Liquors not included.

small jar caviar
can *pâté de foie gras*
small can crab meat
small can tomato juice
2 cans beer
6 quarts skim milk (or 14 plain
 yogurts and 2½ quarts skim milk)
¼ pound butter
8 eggs
sliced boiled ham
sliced Swiss cheese
small loaf wheat bread

corn flakes, bran flakes, shredded
 wheat biscuits
26 juice oranges (or 6 grapefruit
 and 2 oranges)
apple
lemon
green pepper, carrots, parsley
salt, pepper, mustard, catsup,
Worcestershire and Tabasco sauce
sugar, coffee
mayonnaise

NEXT: FIVE CUSTOM-MADE DIETS

8. AND THEN? EXERCISE, AND HOW TO
   EASE INTO IT

Take a deep breath, now; this is going to hurt. We are about to print a bad word . . .

Exercise.

There is no getting away from it, although men continue to try. They joke about exercise, in a variety of moods:

SARDONIC: "I get my exercise serving as a pallbearer to my friends who exercised."

SATIRIC: "How do I keep fit, sir? I rest quietly three hours before each meal and three hours after, and never wind the wrist watch more than twice a day."

COY: "Whenever I feel like exercising I lie down until the feeling passes."

SLY: "The best thing to exercise is discretion."

FAT MAN: "It cost me a lot to put it on and I'd like to keep it."

We have made our own sorry jokes on the subject. But in the end—or, more especially, in the sagging middle—most of us eventually come around to agreeing that brisk physical activity is an adjunct to health and a trim appearance.

A few men are blessed with a sensationally efficient metabolism. Their exercise consists of lifting forks, bending elbows and working zippers. Yet they retain, right into their doddering years, the same tidy outlines they carried as striplings. For the rest of us, among whom the ravages of time or just plain visceral entertainment has produced a doughy thickness in middle or anterior regions, some organized form of exercise becomes a necessity.

Why a necessity? Get a side view of yourself, stripped, in a mirror. If you say anything resembling "Jeez, do I look like that?" you have your answer. Diet, and probably *only* diet, can take off pounds. Exercise, and probably *only* exercise, can take out the resulting sag.

Why organized? To defeat inertia, man's natural state when it comes down to the question of exercise. One knee bend this morning is worth more than three sets of tennis *mañana*. Exercise will always be *mañana* unless you organize it.

The purpose of the following pages is to help you organize your exercise so painlessly you'll hardly know it's happened. We're going to ease you into the kind of daily exercise you need in order to keep trim, firm, young-looking. With any luck at all, we'll have you doing setting-up exercises as automatically as you now brush your teeth or shave your face.

For an easy start we give you, first, a few simple posture exercises. They're almost too effortless to be labeled "exercise," but to urge you on we tell you what they'll do for your aching back (page 114).

Next, a set of exercises you can do as you swivel at your desk, reach for your hat, run for the train—exercises you can fit into your everyday activities, hardly noticing them except for their salutary effect (page 116).

Then, assuming that you are psychologically prepared for out-and-out exercise, a ten-day crash program of rhythmic exercises, to be gone at for thirty minutes a day. Now you're out in the open, exercising for real. The effects will be real, too.

Finally, for men who like both a stiff workout and the hard muscles that follow, a three-month course of bar bell exercises (page 121).

Go as far as you like—but get going!

EASY DOES IT

Even the man who is exhausted by the very idea of exercise should be able to read the following without getting overtired. He should, in fact, be able to do the exercises recommended, almost without noticing them. For these are posture exercises, minimum effort for maximum protection against backache. They won't transform you into an Apollo; they won't necessarily tighten your belt; and if your golf game is a little bit "off" this season, these exercises won't reduce your handicap. They *might* do all those things, it is true: your sagging midriff, like your huffing and puffing after exertion, may very well be due, at least in part, to the faulty way you sit and stand. But the most we can promise, if you read and follow the following, is that you will not soon join in the national chorus . . .

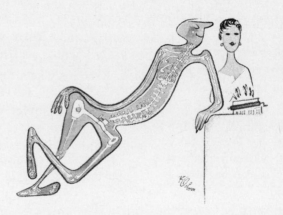

OH, MY ACHING BACK!

Dr. Bess M. Mensendieck, author of *The Look Better, Feel Better, Mensendieck System of Functional Exercises* and other books, has said:

There are two facts every man should know: (1) No matter how big and strong he is, his back can cause him trouble all his life if he abuses it; (2)

there are certain simple exercises and ordinary precautions that will enable him to avoid such unpleasant complications.

Every man should have an understanding of the structure of his lower back, but unless he has actually stood undressed before a front- and rear-view mirror combination he has never seen how his own back looks—the appearance of the muscles and the make-up of the back in general.

The pelvis, which the layman calls his hips, is that most important bony structure on which the whole weight of the trunk rests. This imposition of considerable weight, if wrongly placed, is the cause of the common complaint of backaches among businessmen. These backaches seem to be concentrated in that particular part of the pelvis where the hipbones on each side are joined to the sacrum. These joints are the all-important, mysterious sacroiliac joints. Every so often (and it is becoming more frequent) you hear a businessman saying that his "sacroiliac hurts." It is a vague, all-descriptive, all-inclusive term for trouble in the back, but very few men know enough about their physical make-up to know what they are referring to when they talk about their sacroiliac joints.

These joints are not fastened together as a firmly knit bony structure, but are bound together by tight bands of ligaments and tendons.

When the back muscles—which, by the way, are the biggest and strongest muscles in a man's body—and the buttock muscles get flabby and loose and spreading, the weight of the back through bad posture, excess avoirdupois and bad muscle habits throws a heavy strain on both sacroiliac joints. This strain, in degree to its severity, causes a slight loosening of the tendons and ligaments binding the sacroiliac joints together and results in an irritation and a chronic inflammation of the whole area. In some cases this area of irritation and pain is minor; in others it is more severe. Moreover in some extreme cases there is pressure on the sciatic nerve, causing the well-known sciatic pain down the back of the legs.

Nature has provided a bony ridge at the bottom of the pelvis which might well be called the "sitting bone." Yet our businessman in his comfortable position, sometimes with his feet on the desk or slouched way down until he's resting on his sacrum, no longer uses those two important sitting bones. Thus he is likely to rest his considerable weight on the back of the pelvis and on the end of his spine—the coccyx. As a result, the bones in his lower back are wrenched out of their normal, healthy position, and in time irritate the nerves in that region.

The signs of this back trouble are very insidious and gradual in their approach. The damage of the excess weight on the lower back area is, unfortunately, accomplished before we are aware of it. A man may be bending over to tie his shoelaces when he will be stabbed by an excruciating pain on one side or the other of his lower back. Sometimes, even, he finds it almost impossible to straighten up, move or bend after an attack of this sort. And when the pain fails to disappear he hopefully consults his doctor for some magic dressing or application that will alleviate the condition and let him assume his normal posture.

Unfortunately, there are no pills, no magic words, no braces that can cure this sacroiliac backache. Pathetically enough, once backaches start we know very little about how to stop them. Doctors will suggest diathermy (heat treatment), or braces, or supports, but no one knows any better than the medical practitioner that such measures are but the weakest kind of crutches.

The truth is, *the best way to cure a backache is to prevent it.* Too many men wholly ignore the simple rudiments of posture and exercise that could save them this endless pain and discomfort.

My whole life has been devoted to the subject of proper posture and muscle function. The system, which is called the Mensendieck System, is based on the proper superimposition of bodily masses, starting at the feet, placing one part upon another so that the body will be maintained in proper balance.

For the purpose of this discussion we will concentrate on the muscle functions of the back. In every man's back are two important muscles whose function it is to keep the spine and the trunk erect. These are known as the two *long back muscles,* one on either side of the spine. They are assisted in this activity by the *muscles of the buttocks.* If the back muscles and the buttock muscles are properly developed and utilized, the human back can achieve maximum comfort by helping to ease strain on the sacroiliac joints where most back trouble is found.

There are other sets of muscles involved, but let's avoid complicated discussion of the body structure. Instead, let us look at some simple exercises which, if you adhere to them, can save you from pain later on, or can help to relieve pain now if you are already a victim of your own back. (And you will forgive our adding that these exercises might make you feel generally better if you take the time to do them daily.)

Exercises to Prevent Backache

Are you ready? Strip and stand in front of a mirror. If you can manage it, try to place another mirror behind you so that you can see reflected in the front mirror the action of the muscles working along your back and buttocks. Note the simple action of the buttock muscles. Draw both buttocks firmly together. Observe the narrowing effect of your action. Then allow the buttocks to relax and note how they fall back into their original flabby position. Spend a few minutes every day in consciously contracting and releasing them, and before long your buttocks will become smaller, your hips slimmer, and the extra layers of fat on thighs and abdomen may begin to vanish.

Next let us pay attention to the position of our shoulder blades. Due to our bad habits of posture, the shoulder tips are allowed to drop forward, thus spreading the shoulder blades apart in the back. The way to correct this difficulty is *not* to yank the shoulders backward, but to concentrate on tightening the two muscles that are situated between the shoulder blades on either side of the upper spine, which are called the *trapezius muscles.* Your shoulder blades will assume their correct position and stay there if you order the trapezius muscles to do their function a few times a day.

Now for those back muscles. When they are flabby from disuse, or unevenly developed from the wrong kind of use, such as the uneven distribution of weight or the excessive use of one side, the spine may get out of line and some of the vertebrae may become displaced. When this happens, any one of a series of possible back ailments may result. Here, then, is a fine exercise for developing these muscles as well as for increasing the flexibility of the spine. Stand up straight with your feet about two inches apart. Squeeze the buttocks as tightly together as you can and keep them that way. Now, drawing in your abdomen at the same time (which you are likely to find a little difficult), bend forward from the lowest part of the back, remembering to keep your legs straight and your buttocks tight. You won't be able to touch the floor with your finger tips, but don't let that worry you. The purpose of this exercise is to provide sufficient spread for each vertebra and thus benefit the entire spine as well as the abdomen. Straighten slowly, starting from lowest part of back and keeping the buttocks as tight as possible. And then do the exercise over again.

Remember that these exercises are not meant to be indulged in once or twice a day and then forgotten. Whenever you stoop to tie your shoelaces or to pick up a golf ball, for example, try to keep your abdomen flat and your buttocks squeezed together. Also, when you're walking or standing, try to keep your shoulder blades in place. See to it that your weight is balanced completely and equally on both feet, and bend from the lowest part of your back. Too, every time you get up from a chair or sit down, use the buttock muscles to assist you without the use of the hands.

In arising, you squeeze your buttock muscles together just as you did when you were standing in front of a mirror. These muscles will give impetus and—together with thigh muscles—will lift you forward and up so that you can rise to your feet without the assistance of your hands. By the same token before the act of sitting down see that you are close enough to the chair so that by contracting the buttock muscles you can ease yourself into the seat without the use of your hands. Above all, walk—don't ride—whenever possible, and maintain a good, erect posture.

If you follow these few suggestions, the chances are you will never become one of those sad sacks whose favorite expression is, "Oh, my aching back!"

HOW TO EXERCISE WITHOUT REALLY TRYING

If you're too busy (or simply too lazy) to set aside a definite time and method of exercise, you can nonetheless manage to flex a few muscles as you go about your daily work. For instance . . .

. . . While driving your car, waiting for a bus, sitting at a conference table or even while lying in bed, let your stomach muscles go lax, then slowly tighten them, pulling your stomach in and up. Do this over and over and over again, ten or fifteen times at a crack, every time you get a chance, and those muscles will soon be able to hold your stomach flat without any comscious help from you.

. . . While standing around, anywhere—waiting in a line, talking at the water cooler—put your hands in your hip pockets and, while standing erect, slowly draw your buttocks together. You'll feel the muscles tighten beneath your hands. Slowly let go, again, and repeat the process as often as is convenient. No one will notice.

. . . When reaching for your telephone, *reach*. Put your telephone in the middle of your desk, just slightly out of range. Every time it rings, whip yourself into a good, straight sitting position (which of course you should, but don't, maintain all day long), then reach for the phone with both arms out straight, at shoulder height, hands dangling from wrists. Or put the phone in a side-stretch position, alternating the sides each day, and make yourself reach across your body, with your far hand, with a conscious swivel of your waistline. If you keep your arm or arms straight and your stomach in, your telephone bell can do almost as much for you as a set of bar bells.

. . . While dictating, talking or just sitting in your desk chair, form the habit of dropping your arms outside the chair's arms, now and then, and lifting them upward and back in a way that will square those rounded shoulders. You'll feel this in your chest and shoulders, but you won't have to *think* about it.

You could also put your "in" and "out" baskets on the floor, on either side of your chair, forcing yourself to do side bends (back straight, seat and feet flat) to reach them. Or you could pace the floor backward, on tiptoe. But someone might catch you at *those* nonexercises and ask you why you didn't go off to Vic Tanny's health emporium for a real workout, instead.

Said Mr. Tanny, who is Apollonic in mold, himself, despite his over-fifty age, designed the following series of exercises for *Esquire* readers who are glued to their swivel chairs. Somewhat more strenuous than the above suggestions, they are nonetheless sedentary. If you want to sit and stay fit, try these:

Bulge That Bony Bicep

Place hands palms upward on the bottom of your desk. Attempt to raise the desk from the floor. Chances are you'll be unable to do so, but if you try as hard as you can ten times in a row, your upper arms and forearms, as well as those back muscles that are supposed to give you a V-shaped torso, will begin to show the results of your efforts after just one week.

Flatten Your Abominable Abdomen

Lean back in your swivel chair and raise your legs until they are parallel to the floor. Ankles together, describe twelve-inch circles slowly twenty times in each direction. Guaranteed to lay waste to an over expansive waist.

The Diminishing Side Effects

Fill two brief or attaché cases with as many books as they'll hold. While sitting or standing, grasp one in each hand and, arms at forty-five-degree angles, bend the torso to each side until the floor is touched by the brief cases. This simple exercise is one of the most effective flab-firmers known to man.

Sweep Your Flabbiness Under the Shrug

You literally can knock this one off with a shrug because that is precisely what this exercise is. Place your hands behind your back, gripping one wrist tightly with the opposite hand. Raise and rotate your shoulders, trying to touch your ears with your shoulders on each rotation. Unless your ear lobes are especially droopy, you won't quite touch them, but the effort involved is great for transforming a sagging chest and shoulders into the ego-building façades they were meant to be.

The Sophisticated Approach to Touching Your Toes

This one is really a soft touch: prop your feet up on your desk—you may even cross them. Arms extended, touch your toes, then lean all the way back in your swivel chair. From that extended position, repeat this process fifty times. Your lower back will get a thorough going over from this one.

SET 'EM UP

Eventually, if not right now, you will come around to daily "setting-up" exercises. You will find that in the long run they are less trouble and more effective than all the substitutes you have ever promised yourself to try. Twenty minutes of setting-up exercises can do more to promote strenuous body activity than two hours of baseball. A round of golf may be more fun, but a short session on the bedroom floor (or at the health club, if you need that kind of discipline at the start) will give you more exercise where you need it most.

Sold? Well, anyway, give the idea a try.

As a starter, here is a ten-day "crash" program—easy enough for a fluffy fluff to breeze through; effective enough, as you will see, to give you a new feeling of well-being.

After the first grunting day or so, you will find that the exercises outlined here will take on a pattern of smooth, unhurried, leisurely movement. At least that is the co-ordinated rhythm you should try for.

Take the ten-day program slowly, one day's activity at a time, adding the exercises up as you go. Practice the routines for at least thirty minutes a day for their full benefit. Repeat each routine five to ten times at the beginning.

The most important single trick involved is to breathe deeply as you exercise: inhale slowly and deliberately along with each motion; exhale with each release; rest momentarily before continuing with the next gyration. Above all, take it easy: jerky motions rob you of energy, but slower, more rhythmic exercise helps to create energy.

Chances are that when you see (and feel) the very noticeable results of this ten-day crash program, you'll be ready to continue indefinitely.

TEN-DAY CRASH PROGRAM

First day—strengtheners for abdominal muscles, diaphragm and correct posture:

Lie flat on your back, on the floor. Point your toes, straighten your knees, put your arms at your sides. Inhale. Raise both legs slowly, keeping your knees straight. Exhale, and slowly lower your legs. Now raise and lower, first the right leg, then the left leg, breathing in and out.

Second day—abdominal firmers, back strengtheners and spinal stretchers:

In the same flat position, place your hands under your head and bend your knees. Bring your feet up close to your thighs. Inhale. Pull your knees down to your chest. Stretch your legs slowly upward, straighten and lower. Exhale.

Third day—thigh and hip strengtheners:

Sit on the floor, legs straight out, hands behind you, palms down and fingers pointing toward your buttocks. Point your toes. Place your weight on your hands and inhale. Lift your legs from the floor and bring your knees toward your chest. Keep the toes pointed and the head up. Now, head back, stretch your legs forward and up, exhaling. Slowly lower your legs to the original position.

Fourth day—for flexibility and slimming the hip joints and lower limbs:
In the same sitting position, legs out, roll your weight to your left hip. Supporting yourself with your hands (palms down) raise your top leg (the right, yes?) as high as you can. Now, bend that right knee, point your right toes, and touch your other knee with pointed toes. Grasp your right heel, now, with your right hand, and straighten your right knee. Repeat the entire action on the other side.

Fifth day—waistline slimming and trimming:
1. Rest your body on your buttocks, head back, legs raised. Keep your balance with your hands behind you, palms down. Roll your body to the right and exhale. Inhale, lift the left side of your body from the floor, resting all your weight on your right hip and thigh. (Bring your left hand to the floor on your right side.) Now roll left, raise the right side, and rest on the left hip and thigh. Resume your original position and repeat. During this exercise, be sure to keep your legs up off the floor, preferably at a forty-five-degree angle that will make your waistline work. 2. Lie on floor, face down. Raise torso and legs from floor, using your abdomen as your only point of contact with the floor. Now rock forward and back, your abdomen the fulcrum for your motion. Go flat again and repeat.

Sixth day—correct the waist, abdomen and spine:
Lie flat on the floor, toes pointed, arms overhead. Inhale. Rise slowly to a sitting position, keeping your heels flat on floor. Exhale. Arms straight out before your chest, fingers pointing toward ceiling, push palms and torso forward from the hips. Keep your shoulders straight.

Resume lying position; rise slowly to the sitting position. Spread your legs and touch the toes on your right foot with both hands. Repeat the entire action, alternating between right and left feet.

Seventh day—hip, thigh, calf and foot-and-ankle normalizers:
Inhale. Squat, feet apart, arms between your knees, palms flat on the floor. Put your weight on your hands and lift your heels from the floor. Exhale. Raise your head and stretch one leg back, straight out behind yourself, touching toe only to the floor. Return to the squat position and stretch out the other leg. Repeat, alternating legs—a kind of backward Cossack dance.

Eighth day—posture correctives for strengthening hips, legs and feet:

From the squat position, weight on your hands, shoot both legs out behind yourself at once, landing on your toes. (You're now in the same position you'd have achieved after a routine push-up, but getting there from a squat takes different muscles.) Return and repeat, body always off floor.

Ninth day—body rhythms for balance and co-ordination:

Rise from a squat position. Place your feet apart and arms overhead. Sway the body three times to the left, then three times to the right.

With your left hand raised and your right hand down, sway the body three times to the right, then three times to the left.

Step forward on one leg, bending that knee. Sway the body three times. Repeat entire action, reversing position to the other leg.

Tenth day—stretchers for new waistline slimmers and perfect carriage:

Stand erect with your feet together. Inhale slowly while raising your arms overhead. Step back with the right foot. Sway your body backward from the waist. Exhale and bend forward, keeping your back straight. Touch the toes of your left foot with both hands. Return to the standing position and repeat with the other foot.

ALL OUT FOR MUSCLES

Milo of Crotona, about 600 B.C., is the legendary father of self-developed strong men. He appears to have been a mathematical student who made himself the physical wonder of the antique world by an intelligent course of training. The classical joke about carrying a calf on his shoulders every day until it grew to be an ox indicates his method.

It still is the method. Take a hint from Milo. Work progressively. Start with easy exercises, using light weights, gradually increasing the number of times you repeat each exercise; then add poundage to the work you do.

At sports you are lucky if you can play once a week, over the year. A real conditioner must be something you can do at home. The answer is in bar bell work, a form of training that can make you look like a Greek statue. Once you can get under way, you may forget such halfway measures as diet and massage. You may eat and drink and lounge as much as you like, and your body will nonetheless become as streamlined as that of the Apollo Belvedere and as powerful as a steam winch.

Try this three months' muscle-building course and see it happen. The procedure is this: get yourself a bar bell with weights adjustable up to 100 pounds. They are not expensive. If you can't get it from a sporting goods dealer, you can make it or have it made. What you want is a bar—wood or pipe—an inch and a half in diameter and about four feet between the weights, which will be fastened at each end.

The chief point to be observed is that none of these exercises should be overstrenuous or overtiring. Exercise, like life and love, should be taken without excess. If any procedure seems tedious, lighten it. Don't exercise every day. Give your muscles time to recover.

With these words of sage advice well digested and a few pounds lifted from the floor every day, you are pretty well vaccinated against ill effects of indulgence in things you like best. Your waistline will take care of itself.

Bars away!

MUSCLE BUILDERS

A ninety-day progression of bar bell exercises. Do each exercise ten times at first, adding one exercise each period until you have worked up to twenty-five. Then add ten pounds and start again with ten repetitions, increasing movements and weights as desired. Starting weight varies.

1. The Warm-up

Bar loaded with thirty pounds. Stand legs apart. Pick up bar, bending knees, raise overhead and put bar back on floor.

2. Two-Hand Curl

This develops the biceps. Start with thirty pounds. Stand erect and, with arms close to sides, raise bar to shoulder height ten times.

3. Rocker-Beam Bend

Thirty pounds. Stand erect, legs apart. Put bar on shoulders behind neck. Holding firmly, bend as far to right as possible. Hold a few seconds, straighten up and bend to left.

4. Waist Reducer

Thirty pounds. Stand erect, legs apart, barbell held slightly below waist. Bend forward and swing bar to right and touch floor. Bar should be at right angle to starting position. Raise and repeat motion to left.

5. Dead Lift

For muscles of the lower back. Double the weight. Stand with legs apart, bend over, grasp bell and pull up to erect position, keeping knees stiff. Lower bell to within one inch of floor.

6. Two-Hand Military Press

For muscles of shoulder and back. Sixty pounds. Stand erect, heels together, barbell against chest with overhand grip. Slowly push bar to full arm length overhead. Lower to chest.

7. Shoulder Shrug

Sixty pounds. For the trapezius muscles. Stand erect, heels together, bar at arms' length, overhand grip. Shrug shoulders high as possible. Start with fifteen repetitions.

8. Deep Knee-Bend on Toes

For all-round body tone. Sixty pounds. Stand with legs apart. Bar on shoulders behind neck. Raise to tiptoe position, then squat to full knee-bend.

9. Boxer's Hop

Sixty pounds. Stand erect with bar on shoulders behind neck. Jump, landing with feet apart, then jump back to original position. Repeat rapidly.

10. Tiptoe Bracer

Load to full 100 pounds. For muscles of the calf, buttocks and arch. Stand erect, legs slightly spread, bar on shoulders behind neck. Rise to tiptoe position, bring heels slowly back to floor.

11. Straddle Lift

One hundred pounds. Stand astride the bar and grasp it with right hand in front of body, left hand behind body. Straighten and stand erect, not moving feet. Bend knees again until bar almost touches floor. Change hands.

12. Abdomen Builder

For muscles of stomach and lower abdomen. Sit on a stool or box. Hook feet under edge of bed—or something. Lean back, pick up barbell from floor. Holding it behind neck, raise to sitting position. This may be too hard at first. You may start with the bar unloaded for ten repetitions. Then twenty-five, then load bar with ten pounds. Increase as you can do it comfortably.

ANTIDOTE

. . . for those who are slightly fatigued from the exercise of making plans to exercise, these therapeutic thoughts from Dr. Logan Clendening . . .

Exercise is like education. They are both all right for the young, but they were never designed for the old. There is a definite moment in the life of man—but of that, later.

If a man is healthy, he doesn't need exercise, and if he isn't, it won't do him any good.

Does exercise make you live longer? Not if you walk in front of a truck on your way home from the gym. Does exercise keep you from having colds or infections? Not a bit. You can take a bushel of "stiff workouts"—I think that's the word—and walk into a pesthouse and if you've never been vaccinated you will have just as swell a case of smallpox as the flabbiest clerk. Maybe sweller.

You could go right down the line with this. Does it stave off kidney and heart disease, high blood pressure—all the bugaboos of middle age? You know better than that. You must have seen plenty of the boys who are determined to beat that game by keeping in trim, pop off at what would be a shocking age to a billiard marker.

But you say it makes you better able to endure more. More what? More exercise. Well, there you are—in a vicious circle. Here is where the analogy to education comes in again. As I understand it, the psychologists have decided that the old idea that learning Latin, for instance, was good for you because it trained your mind, is no longer true. It just trains you to learn more Latin. Whether this holds for the realm of the spirit or not, it certainly holds for the realm of the muscles. You play tennis and it trains you, but only to play more tennis. Of course you can train your heart and increase your wind, but stop a while and see how soon you lose it.

Of course, I don't mind if people take exercise. I make no criticisms or sneering remarks. But I hate to have 'em keep after me about taking exercise. And I don't want to go to athletic contests or feats of strength. There is no more painful sight than a class of businessmen exercising through the noon hour—the thin ones expecting to get fat, and the fat ones expecting to get thin. I don't belong to clubs where they allow that sort of thing to go on.

The exact moment in life when a man should give up regular exercise is marked by an event which is performed just as unconsciously and naturally as winding up your watch at night. It is the moment when you buy and have sent home a rowing machine. In spite of the fact that it is a complete waste of money it is a very sound investment.

You get the thing home and "Here," you say to yourself, "is something that is going to keep me in trim. There are lots of bad days around here when I can't play golf and besides my old foursome is pretty well broken up. Ed moved away, and Duncan has got arthritis and Charley is crazy about that new wife of his and spends pretty near every Saturday afternoon gardening with her. Now here is something practical that will take its place so that I can get my exercise, rain or shine, and every morning and every night before going to bed." So in a day or two it is all set up and along comes one of those fine, drizzly afternoons just made to sit in a big chair with not the slightest temptation to get out and be a strong man, but there is the rowing machine. You have bought it and now you are going to use it. So you sit down and row across Lake Geneva, and arise feeling as if every internal organ you have, had ruptured. Your face is red and remains in a scorched condition for hours. Your back and arms and the back of your legs are killing you.

That is the beginning of the end. Every time you look at the machine after that, you are filled with loathing. From then on you wait for nice days to take your exercise, and not much at that.

There are even times at this dreadful time of middle age when exercise is positively harmful. The theory is gaining ground in this renascent period of the three-bottle-men reputation, that an extra round of golf or a set of tennis will allow you to have one more highball or cocktail than usual. Now, experience will show that exercise provides no immunity from the action of alcohol either. Many an athlete has become good and plastered by relying on this "every-extra-hole-means-an-extra-highball theory."

Even the value of exercise as a means of reducing weight has been challenged by the work of a professor at the University of Michigan. When he starts to reduce a patient—and he takes only those weighing over three hundred pounds, I understand—he exacts an agreement from him to go into a hospital room and give him the key to it. All the food that the patient eats is inspected by him and every visitor is searched for smuggled goodies.

He recently showed the pictures of a patient who began treatment at 570 pounds. For three years he ate mostly lettuce and slaw, but he came down to 170. All the exercise he got was in the hospital room.

When you come to figure it out, the professor says, exercise doesn't use up so much weight. Climbing up to the top of Pike's Peak only requires about 2,000 calories and you could balance that by omitting bread, butter, meat and gravy, vegetable and dessert from your daily intake. A bout with the dumbbells is balanced by omitting two soda crackers from the menu.

My Uncle Johnnie, who was a distinguished classical scholar, used to illustrate it out of Homer. He subscribed to the theory of the natural strong man. He really was that kind of person himself. The only muscles he ever moved habitually were those of his jaw in eating, and occasionally the opening or closing of an eyelid. But he could lift a piano if he had to.

His illustration of the natural strong man was Ulysses and the bending of the bow. He drew a picture of the suitors after Penelope had agreed to marry the one who bent the bow of Odysseus. He pictured them working up their muscle in the gymnasium, and hiring trainers. He said for a while the lanes around Ithaca were impassable on account of the besweatered suitors taking their workouts and heaving large rocks around in a circle like a medicine ball.

And, after all, when the time came for the contest, none of them could bend the bow, but here came poor old tired Ulysses. He wasn't in condition at all. He was all worn out and he had been sleeping around anywhere and eating whatever came to hand. But even so, he bent the bow of Odysseus and the string twanged sweetly at his touch. It all came, said my Uncle Johnnie, from being a natural strong man and not wasting his time in gymnasiums.

9. AND NOW: RELAX!

Or, rather . . . relax. No capitals. No exclamation point. No nothing. Just (sssh) . . . r e l a x . . . .

If you can lean back, right this minute, close your eyes, and drop immediately into sleep . . . if you can wake up, five or ten minutes later, springy and refreshed . . . you're the one in a million who may skip this chapter. You already know the secrets, and the recuperative effects, of relaxation.

More likely, however, you are tensed up even as you read this. Your life is all capitals, all exclamation points. You work hard; you play hard; and if it ever occurs to you that you may be racing your engine too steadily, you console yourself with the thought that tension is a necessary part of modern living.

And so it is. Tension has its certain value for everyone, with the possible exception of a beachcomber. You can't "relax" yourself into a bigger job, a happier home life nor even, perhaps, into a better game of golf. You can't relax your efforts, and a certain amount of tension helps to keep you going ahead, strong.

But tension as a full-time state is a killer.

The results of chronic strain are at first imperceptible. Your body is like a new rubber band. Stretch the band within its limits, and it retains its resiliency when you release it. However, if you overstretch it (and often) it becomes limp. You say it has lost its zip.

So it is with your body. At first you can mistreat it repeatedly. You even wonder how it can take so much abuse without showing it! You are amazed that you can "eat nails" without having indigestion; that you can sleep four to five hours night after night and still be able to work; that you can smoke cigarettes end to end without even the discomfort of a heart skip; that you can go to bed a veritable "tank" of champagne cocktails or gin without having the expected morning-after hangover.

You are proud of your body; you begin to believe that you are different: a pale-faced, small-muscled sort of Tarzan.

But as in the old-time movies, "comes the dawn"—of sad realization. You learn, sooner or later, that although the "real you" is an indefinable spirit or soul, it is transported here and there by a machine (your body).

The machine needs proper fuel, as we have discussed in our section on diet. It needs the kind of everyday tuning up that we outlined in our chapters on exercise.

It also needs rest.

What kind of rest does your body need, and your mind? When and especially how are you going to manage it? These are the subjects at hand. Here you'll read about how to "go fishing" in the middle of your working day, through scientific muscular relaxation. Here you'll read a few odd prescriptions for relaxers, including a consolation prize for those who can't seem to quit smoking. Here you'll find everything you need to know, and do, about sleep. And here, right now, is the time to add a fourth plank to your new fitness platform. So far you've resolved, let us hope, to:

1. Take stock: get a checkup.

2. Get your weight where it belongs, and keep it there.

3. Make a place for exercise in your daily schedule.

Now, with however much determination you can manage to express through a slack jaw or a relaxed yawn, promise yourself you'll learn to . . .

4. R e l a x.

IT'S NO TRICK TO RELAX

It's a pretty generally accepted medical fact that people who know how to relax have a definite advantage over those who stay tense and wound up all the time.

Teddy Roosevelt was one of the gifted relaxers. On a campaign tour, T.R. could sink into a convenient seat in the campaign car and drop off to sleep immediately, oblivious of the continual racket around him. When the train began to slow for a stop, his private alarm clock would go off. Teddy would stir a little, and rub his eyes. By the time the wheels were complaining against the rails, he'd be in the aisle, heading for the rear platform. Yawning, looking as though he were still asleep, he'd reach the back door just as the train slid to a stop. Then, in a flash, as he heard the cheering of the crowd gathered outside, he would straighten up and come completely wide awake. Half a second before, he'd looked like a sleepwalker. Now he became the dynamic Teddy the voters loved—bellowing, waving his arms, shouting his famous "Bully!"

Roosevelt had learned one of the prize secrets of modern times. He could turn his energies on or off as casually as you turn a faucet. When he worked, he worked with all his might. When he relaxed, he could relax completely. Happily, anyone who really wants to can acquire the art of relaxation—which will improve his ability to work hard.

The people who can relax have developed a definite rhythm in their work. They go all out for a time, then step back and take things easy. They have a keenly developed sense of values. They keep the results of what they are doing constantly in mind and weigh them against the effort it's costing them. They don't just work for the sake of working. Even more important is their ability to relax their muscles in any part of their bodies. And finally, like Teddy Roosevelt, these individuals can go to sleep whenever they want to.

The cat-nappers probably have the most valuable approach to relaxation. They can take a quick snooze anywhere—on a bus, in the subway, relaxing in a chair behind their desks. It's amazing how often politicians have cultivated this ability. William Jennings Bryan, who not only ran for the Presidency three times, but worked the Chautauqua tent circuit during the boiling Midwestern summers for decades, used, sometimes, to schedule as many as seven speeches a day on his speaking tours. But Bryan could sandwich in a five-minute nap wherever he was—in the jolting seats of day coaches, in the back of a surrey rolling along a country road, on a pile of blankets in the back of the Chautauqua tents. After a few minutes, he was up and ready, with the golden voice that could carry for three blocks, with the appetite that left a dinner table looking as though a threshing crew had just departed.

Soldiers, too, have learned to cultivate cat-naps. Napoleon could catch up on his sleep anywhere, any time—even on horseback. Simon Bolivar Buckner, Jr., killed leading the Tenth Army on Okinawa, could turn his back on his staff gathered around his desk and take a sound five-minute nap. Even in the ranks, the art of cat-napping can be acquired. The private who hit the beach at Makin and killed the first six Japanese he had ever seen took a brief snooze in the midst of the fighting and woke up ready for more battle. Carlos Romulo, who learned rugged living on both Bataan and the American lecture circuit, once said, "I can sleep anywhere. When I go down to the station and have a five-minute wait for a train, I sit down on the bench and sleep for five minutes."

For years, Thomas Edison campaigned for the idea that human beings didn't need more than the four or five hours of sleep that *he* got every night. People marveled at Edison's stamina and drive. What most of them didn't know was that by taking frequent cat-naps during the day he was constantly recharging the dynamos of his energy.

Others have relied on a fixed nap during working hours. This fits in with the findings that you can work an eighteen-hour day if you make a complete break with work from time to time. Winston Churchill led Britain's war effort at an age when most executives are forcibly retired from U.S. businesses. He's a stanch advocate of the nap after lunch. Referring to his World War II activities, Churchill said, "I found I could add nearly two hours to my working effort by going to bed for an hour after luncheon."

The after-lunch rest has definite effects; it doesn't merely make you think you feel better. Tests were run off on students at Stephens College. Half a group was kept awake after lunch, the other half allowed to relax as they pleased, as long as they stayed quietly in their rooms. Results showed that the latter half got distinctly better grades in their studies than the former.

IF YOU CAN'T NAP . . .

But even if you don't have a chance for cat-napping or a quiet place to lie down after lunch, there are other ways to rest your mind. Walking has done the trick for such people as Bernard Baruch and Percy Grainger. Many a top-flight executive finds it restful to retire to his basement workshop at night, to fret over the vagaries of wood and metal instead of making split-second decisions on which his career might depend.

Hobbies of almost any sort help to relieve tension. Collectors soothe themselves by fingering their treasures and dreaming of new acquisitions. F.D.R. found solace in stamps. Henry Ford forgot production problems while he tracked down priceless American antiques.

Sports . . . reading . . . all these are fairly conventional ways of relaxing. But what works for one man does not necessarily work for another.

The whole problem is by no means simple. Ever since 1880 they've been talking about the speed of modern living in this country and trying to figure out some way in which people could relax, yet keep up the pace. Some of us apparently are fagged out already. According to studies made a few years back, only 52 per cent of us are capable of real all-out hard work. The rest of us haven't learned how to husband our energies well enough and have forgotten—if we ever knew—how to rest.

Frequent periods of rest, incidentally, are both a physical and a psychological necessity. Dr. Karl A. Menninger, noted psychiatrist, has made a scientific study of play. In his book, *Love Against Hate*, he says: "People who don't play are potentially dangerous. There seems to be a general idea that recreation is all right if one doesn't take it too seriously. My belief is that much the greater danger lies in not taking it seriously enough." He points out that for a few fortunate adults play becomes an indulgence, but that for others play is psychologically helpful because it helps you to return to that happy childhood state when you weren't tied down by routine and responsibilities; and enables you to work off aggressions (which cause so much harm otherwise) in harmless forms.

Over at Cambridge University, Professor F. C. Bartlett has discovered that there are two basic types of tiredness. The first kind comes when you get tired doing a routine job. The results are simple—you just don't produce as much. More dangerous is the kind of tiredness that hits executives, engineers, doctors, and statesmen. Here fatigue cuts down not on how much you do, but on how well you do it. When you suffer from this second kind of weariness, your sense of timing goes first. You decide to do the right thing, but you do it at the wrong time. Then, if you worry about your timing, you do the wrong thing at the right time. Furthermore, you may not even realize that you're doing badly.

Sleep is almost the core of the problem of relaxation. (See page 140 for everything you need to know about sleep.) But even those who "sleep like babies" need restful breaks during the day, as well.

One way that even the jumpiest of men can learn to relax is through scientific muscular relaxation, a system devised by Dr. Edmund Jacobson.

Dr. Jacobson tackles the problem on the basis of tenseness in your muscles, and he feels that proper relaxation demands that you make as many muscles as possible go limp. He calls his method progressive relaxation and says it can be learned just like driving a car or playing a musical instrument. The basic outline of his system starts you out lying flat on your back in a quiet room. (Lying on your side involves some muscle strain.) First you learn how to relax the major parts of your body. You do this with an arm, for example, by raising it up and feeling the tenseness in your muscles. Then you let the arm plop down on the bed beside you noting how different it feels when all the muscles are relaxed. You practice this way until you can relax an arm at will; then you go on to other groups of muscles.

Actually, as Dr. Jacobson sees it, relaxation isn't something that you do. It's something that happens when you stop doing something else. After you learn to relax groups of your muscles, you can practice wherever you are, sitting in a chair, reading, or even writing. What he's shooting at in this kind of partial relaxation—which he calls differential relaxation—is what the golf pro tells you to do. The pro who insists that you relax means you should keep relaxed all muscles not directly involved in walloping the ball. It's the mark of the beginner in any sport to tense all his muscles, thus causing them to work against one another.

Emotions can tense your muscles, too. Tests have shown that students who try too hard to solve problems unconsciously tense their muscles and consequently tire themselves out. Nervous tension is, in effect, muscular tension, for the nerves are no more than communication lines between the brain and the muscles or body organs. When tense, a nerve is holding a muscle in readiness for action. The muscles of the body, like a hair trigger, are set into action by the slightest physical motivation. Thus if you are startled when you are tense, you may leap out of your chair: you are, quite literally, "jumpy." If you remain in such a state for long enough, the tension can exhaust your nerves, stiffen your muscles and strain your heart. It can, quite literally, "jump" you into your grave. In the interest of plain survival, then, you *must* relax from time to time. And the best time to relax is, always, the time when you are most tense. The feat would be impossible but for a system you had learned at a time when you were better able to relax.

Dramatic results can be had from these very simple relaxation practices:

1. Turn off your thoughts and emotions for one minute on the hour and before and after important sessions, every day.

2. Nap for twenty minutes after lunch.

3. Make the room in which you relax quiet and dark.

4. If possible, lie down; otherwise, sit back in your chair, head on chest, feet on stool or desk.

5. Be conscious of "rhythm breathing." Inhale softly, effortlessly, deeply; then exhale easily, steadily. Make it long. Then relax, extending the exhale after the lungs are empty. The key to the whole process is to make your breathing a rhythmic, three-count action; inhale, exhale, and relax.

6. Concentrate on your breathing process, turning off all other thoughts.

7. Instruct yourself audibly, increasing power of concentration.

8. Shut out all stimuli. Once this skill is learned, you can practice a full program of rhythm breathing and relaxation of face, head, arms, shoulders, chest, abdomen, small of the back, legs, eyes, and throat, one by one.

AND NOW: RELAX!

This is self-induced muscular relaxation. This method, properly applied, will cease mental effort. It will stop thought and emotion.

The hard-driving businessman must possess this gift—to relax under fire. With mental strains lightened and emotional conflicts mellowed, you can ease the strain on your heart, prevent overexpenditure of nervous energy, and gain creative silence and composure in the midst of confusion.

You will feel better having taken advantage of these daily *vacations from tension.* Try it. There is no better way to spend your time.

Rx FOR RELAXATION—

CAUTION: USE ONLY AS DIRECTED

In the end, you're the one, and the only one, who can talk yourself into taking it easy. You're the one, and the only one, who knows what comes under the heading of relaxation for the unique individual who is *you.* But while you're mulling over the question, you might like to consider these points of view:

FROM DR. PETER J. STEINCROHN:

I think the trouble is that too many of us live our lives as if we have been given a thousand years here. Unconsciously we think that there will *always* be time *later* for the rewards and the fun. We forget that life is a one-way street.

Time, like money, is a commodity—and our most invaluable one. Money can be replenished; time *never* can. Rather than lose yourself in planning for the future, you should find yourself in the present. Be continually aware of this: a day lost is a day never regained; youth and middle age are rich in time; old age may be a pauper, no matter how much money it has in the bank.

Live up to the hilt. One of the essential ingredients of the happy life is the proper mixture of work and relaxation. If you master the trick (and you don't have to be a Phi Beta Kappa to do it), you will find that daily tension and strain will be the exceptions rather than the rule in your life.

Here are some practical antidotes for the common daily poisons of overwork, fatigue, tension, strain, and resulting discontent:

Don't be jealous of time lost from work. To live today fully you must be willing—and happy—to give of yourself to your wife, children, and friends.

Don't allow the hands of the clock to bedevil you. Start your day in a relaxed mood by rising one-half hour to one hour earlier. Enjoy your breakfast, have time to skim the paper, and depart for your work in leisurely manner. Leaving your home without inner strain you will approach your work in the same frame of mind.

Now for lunch—still unhurried and relaxed. Resolve not to "eat in" any more. Take your full hour or hour and a half. Don't eat alone. Make a luncheon date with your friends. If you can hold liquor, a martini is nice before lunch.

If you are fortunate enough to have a long lunch hour, there may be times when you can vary the procedure by going for a swim, or by bowling a string or two, or by continuing your discussion during a walk before you return to the job, or by settling for a nap.

Having finished your work downtown, don't look for more to take home with you. Try to get home early enough to get acquainted with your children.

Never sit right down to dinner; no matter how relaxed you have learned to become in your work, there is always some slight tension that needs to be broken. Take an ounce of whisky or a glass of beer—and stretch out with the paper. After half an hour of that you will be not only ready for dinner, but a pleasure for the wife and children to have around.

You will be amazed at how much time you have discovered for evenings with your family; for hobbies, for reading, for cards, music, or the theater. After such evenings you will rarely be troubled by the lack of a refreshing sleep.

Become a time-miser. Be thankful for the many years you have coming to you. *Less* of tension and *more* of living in the present are basic ingredients of contentment—and each is an efficient antidote against slow suicide.

FROM DR. J. B. RICE:

Drinking, smoking, cussing, gambling and other equally pleasant methods of relaxation may be doing you more good than harm. Don't swear off any vice lightly, but take an inventory first and decide, or let your doctor decide, whether it's hurting you or not. It may be just what you need.

Whole libraries have been written on the evil consequences of alcohol and tobacco. That their excessive use is harmful, or even disastrous, no one can deny. But one book, which appeared about the middle of the last century, to cite an extreme example, discourses at great length on the deleterious effects of tobacco on the chastity of young females. Had tobacco any such intriguing action, the spectacular rise in its use throughout the world would, likely enough, have been even more precipitous than it was.

Tobacco lessens jumpiness or nervous irritability by providing a brake on the emotional pendulum, keeping it from swinging too far in either direction.

For the high-strung man or woman who is continually beset from morning to night by petty irritations, disappointments and frustrations, the blessed relief of tobacco may be well worth all the disastrous physical effects blamed on it—even if they are real. Mankind's universal craving for something to sooth his jangling nerves actually represents a pressing psychologic need.

Despite popular belief to the contrary, alcohol is not a stimulant, but a relaxer. After a drink or two you feel like skipping rope with a telephone cord because the alcohol has relaxed certain mental and emotional brakes which were causing friction. Modern life, with all its cares, worries, frustrations and inhibitions, is like a car driven with the brakes on. A drink gives you the same relief (and sometimes the same gliding motion) that releasing the brakes gives your car.

The normal, happy human being never drinks to excess, not by virtue of self-control, but because he doesn't want to. A couple of drinks relax his inhibitions and lighten his cares. Only the neurotic needs escape so deeply that he drinks himself into unconsciousness. These sick people cannot drink moderately, not because of a craving for alcohol, but because of a craving for escape. That alcohol speeds them on their downward path to dereliction is undeniable. It is no cure for anything, any more than aspirin is; but its moderate use by the average man often prevents minor emotional disturbances from setting the stage for the entrance of a full-fledged mental ill.

But there are other vices than tobacco and alcohol that we should think twice about before suppressing. Even swearing helps relieve tension; but to be really effective a cuss word must be new enough or bad enough to comfort the swearer by mildly shocking himself or somebody else. As soon as it becomes accepted by polite society, an oath loses its healing properties. "Damn" now has no more therapeutic value than "piffle." However, a few of the good old four-letter words are still potent, especially if uttered in the presence of sweet little girls or dear old ladies.

A friend of mine, a very successful New York surgeon and a man of the highest intellectual attainments, is a racing addict. Every moment possible outside the operating room and his office is spent in the passionate study of racing forms. Every week end and holiday he can steal from his practice is spent at the race track. He manages to average a loss of about fifty dollars a week on the ponies, but he feels that it is money well spent.

All of us have the urge to take a chance; and most of us can indulge it. But a surgeon who takes chances soon has no patients—no living ones, at any rate. Gambling on the races gives this man the outlet he needs and makes it possible for him always to play it safe in the operating room. Many of his patients probably owe their lives and health to the bookies and the horses that keep him on an even psychologic keel.

This is an extreme case, but poker playing, betting and even crap-shooting east the lot of many people caught in the rat race of a humdrum existence. Both gambling and drinking have helped many men wreck their lives, but they were only the instruments of the destruction. The real cause lay in their own maladjusted personalities, which would probably have blown their tops eventually anyway. Although our vices cannot cure insanity nor even prevent it in most of those tottering on the verge of a psychosis, they do ease the strain of living in a cramped and uncertain world. From the standpoint of mental hygiene, it is quite possible that your bad habit is good for you. For psychiatrists are beginning to find out that halos fit angels better than men.

AND NOW, HEAR AL HIRSCHFELD ON "HOW I STOPPED SMOKING":

I have always smoked. It never occurred to me that life was possible without a pipe, cigar, hookah, cubeb or cornsilk, hand-rolled or manufactured cigarette projecting from the front of my face. And I always assumed that smoking, like pregnancy, was a matter of nature's capricious selection. One either was, or was not, a smoker; and that was that. But coughing was a different department. Coughing seemed an acquired habit. I could have sworn under oath that I used the cough as a social mannerism, in place of words, to cover acute cases of embarrassment. I am not referring to the common cold or virus type of cough; but to the controlled enforced jet genus, which usually accompanies a hearty laugh. They sort of go together socially. As a matter of fact, I established a considerable reputation as a raconteur based on nothing more than a well-timed combination of cough and laugh. Then, quite suddenly, the thing got out of control: my cough developed a life of its own.

There came a day when I could not stop coughing. My cough had felt its power, and with each passing year it became more arrogant. My family grew accustomed to Daddy's catarrh in the middle of the night; I accepted as normal the coughing fit which attacked me every morning the moment I got out of bed and stood upright; the hysterical stagger to the bathroom gasping for breath; the clutching at the sink for support while a face, the color of an eggplant—and just about as interesting—coughed back at me in the mirror. I consoled myself with the notion that none of us was getting any younger, serves me right for sleeping on my left side, that's the last time I go to bed sober: these and similar justifications made it possible for me to live in the same house with myself.

But this insane state of affairs could not last forever, and it changed completely about three months ago, when a short, unexpected, fast cough caught me off balance and threw me down a flight of stairs. While the doctor from the emergency ambulance was basting my calf I let go with a whopper that blew his glasses off and smashed them against the farthest wall. Retrieving the frames from the floor, he started to expostulate; then another blast stopped him short and spun his toupee around. The doctor threw up his arms in a lightning thrust to ward off another attack.

"Better take care of that cough, m'boy!" he said.

I assured him that I had tried every known cure, pill, opiate and cough medicine extant, that I had been coughing for years in every country and climate of the world, and that quite obviously there was nothing anyone could do about it.

"Ever try to give up smoking?" he said unsympathetically.

"Be easier to give up eating," I told him.

He was unimpressed. "Start tomorrow morning," he advised. "Set your alarm for ten o'clock, and no matter what happens don't take a cigarette until you hear the alarm ring; then smoke as you normally would for the rest of the day."

I promised him that I would try his system. "Keep it up for a week," he continued, "then increase the time one hour weekly. At the end of four weeks you'll suddenly discover that you've gone without a cigarette up till one o'clock in the afternoon. After that, it's easy sailing. Eat peppermints or chew gum to satisfy any temporary nervousness. The important thing is, don't cheat: remember—it's your life you're playing with."

It all sounded so crisp and easy I decided to give it a try. I have always been a sucker for reasonable advice. The only positive lesson I learned in art school was a piece of advice given me by my instructor: "Don't let the point of your pencil interfere with your artistic ability." And to this very day I cannot draw unless the point of my pencil is needle-sharp. Who knows, perhaps this strange doctor would have as profound an influence on my health as Mr. Shapiro—of the Vocational School for Boys—had on my art.

The following morning, at ten o'clock sharp, my alarm clock rang and woke me: I reached out of bed and lit a cigarette. "Why, shucks," thought I, filling my lungs with pure, rich nicotine and coal tar, "there's nothing to it."

The second morning was a trifle more difficult: I got up before the alarm went off. For some unaccountable reason, my cough blasted me out of bed at a quarter to ten. Those fifteen minutes before the alarm rang have become permanently recorded on my unbreakable memory. I took a shower, brushed my teeth, sang the complete score of *High Jinks,* looked at the clock, rang ME 7-1212 (my clock was absolutely right: five to ten), tried getting dressed, then undressed, then dressed again, picked up *War and Peace* and read it from cover to cover (still four and a half minutes to go), thought that if I live through the day I'll organize a Smokers Anonymous, re-examined Buckminster Fuller's theory of Dymaxion Energetic Geometry—and had just about discovered the flaw when the alarm rang. It was a sound such as stout Cortez may have heard at the Pacific. With trembling, bleeding fingers I lit my beard and cigarette at the same time.

Having mastered those fifteen minutes was the toughest assignment I had ever given myself; but now I am living proof that the thing can be done, and as easily as outlined in the doctor's recipe. Furthermore, it is all absolutely true. I have not coughed once in the past week, my appetite is unbelievably ravenous and my sense of smell has become so heightened that I can now distinguish the subtle aromatic distinction between different kinds of blotting paper. I have gained twenty-two pounds, and none of my clothes fit me any more. My doctor now tells me that I shall have to lose those extra pounds; too much strain on the heart.

There is no doubt about the matter: it is much easier to give up smoking than to give up eating. I can no longer work unless my drawing table is well stocked with platters of raw carrots, cut celery, peppermints and my daily ration of four or five packs of chewing gum. My mind, free of the nicotine drug, is clear, direct, literate: no more fuzzy abstractions, meaningless fantasies, speculative illusions. A cumulus cloud against a cerulean sky no longer challenges my interpretive powers; it automatically becomes a giant turkey on a blue plate. My abstract doodlings come out as careful academic drawings of little bloated pigs with apples stuffed in their mouths. In recent weeks I have taken to roaming the streets in the middle of the night looking for an open delicatessen. Neither rain, sleet nor hail can stop me when my stomach whispers in my ear, "Corned beef on rye." And the weather has been foul. I have had a succession of sniffles, colds, wheezes and sinus attacks. Most of all, the cough, stimulated now by germs, is threatening to return in glory.

I am convinced that I have grown a small blast furnace where my stomach used to be. Any kind of food, even the pills I take, is sufficient fuel to generate a hot-air system which circulates in my throat. I have become an ice-sucker as well as a gum-chewer and a peppermint-eater. The chewing gum and peppermints have successfully removed the thin veneer of porcelain from my teeth so that I can no longer even part my lips without severe pain. And as for my sense of smell . . . now there is one sense I think we could all happily do without. Take it from one who can smell not only all the kitchen odors, but the Airwick as well. I am afraid that if my sense of smell improves any more I shall have to leave the city. The stink is unbearable. Equipped with these heightened senses and a new pair of spectacles—

through which I cannot help seeing every hair follicle and pimple on a face a block away—I fail to see the advantage of preserving a lung or two at the expense of the stomach, heart, teeth and nervous system. As for me, I shall face the future with a stogie firmly clamped between my teeth and an unpredictable cough lurking in my throat. Happy and unafraid.

SLEEPING IS AN ART

Irving Berlin, an expert insomniac—*everybody* is an expert on some phase of sleep—who claims he hasn't slept well for thirty-two years, was vacationing in Bermuda a while ago with Irving Hoffman, the *Hollywood Reporter's* ubiquitous columnist. Berlin is a true insomniac: he goes to bed late, wakes up early and, like many who don't sleep well, believes insomnia to be a state of existence as important as, though distinct from, sleeping or waking.

One morning Hoffman noticed that his host looked more finely drawn than usual and asked Berlin if he had got any sleep.

"Yes, I slept," Berlin said bitterly, "but I *dreamed* that I didn't."

Berlin is so interested in sleep that he tiptoes around to everyone's bedroom as soon as he wakes up, asking, in what he fondly imagines to be a whisper, "Are you awake?" With this simple device, he has murdered more sleep than Macbeth. His old friends lock their doors when Berlin is in their homes.

Actually, it is not necessary for Berlin to ask, nor for anyone to be asked, about sleeping. Doctors and the Gallup poll have handled the matter already. From their reports we know that if you asked the 100,000,000 adult Americans how they slept last night, *any* night, about fifty per cent would tell you they slept well, fifty per cent would tell you they had trouble falling asleep, or woke up during the night, or woke up early and couldn't get back to sleep, or got up feeling tired. Some claim they never sleep badly, some that they never sleep at all—which cannot be literally true—but most of us are in-and-outers. And we worry about it. We shouldn't.

If you believe:

1. that a certain number of hours of sleep each night is necessary to your health;
2. that if you lose sleep for any reason over a night or two, you must make it up as soon as possible;
3. that insomnia is dangerous to health, either physical or mental, and may lead to insanity or death

. . . you're wrong. There is no set number of hours of sleep necessary to health—you sleep as much, usually, as your body needs. If you lose a night's sleep, your efficiency will not necessarily be impaired, your health will not be affected. Nor is persistent insomnia, unless due to physical or psychic ailment, dangerous to either your mind or your body.

Generally, old people sleep less than youngsters, men sleep less than women, and Americans sleep less than anybody. According to a Gallup poll 52 per cent of Americans suffer from some difficulty in getting to sleep. The same is true of only 41 per cent of Britons, 23 per cent of Danes and 15 of every hundred Norwegians. College graduates sleep more soundly than those with only a grammar-school education, and married people sleep better than single folk.

Insomnia as such is not a disease—the word is a loose term used to describe certain disorders of sleep. There are diseases in which people sleep too much, but none in which they never sleep. Everyone sleeps sometimes and no one has ever died of lack of sleep. The story that the Chinese used to put people to death by keeping them always awake has never been confirmed.

One man, convinced that sleep is "only a habit," stayed awake for 231 hours, almost ten straight days, punching a watchman's clock every ten minutes. Although he began to exhibit delusions of persecution after the fourth day, his physical health was good at the end of the marathon. His weight, pulse rate, blood pressure and basal metabolism were the same as when he started.

When Leo Durocher was managing the Giants, he once ordered the players *not* to go to bed the night before a game.

"I've done everything I can," Durocher told them. "Just forget about the training rules tonight. Go out, stay out, do whatever you like. There'll be no checkup. Just show up in time for tomorrow's game."

The jittery athletes did as they were ordered, came in the next day and beat the brains out of the opposition. And kept it up through the rest of the season to come from last place to third by the end of September.

Probably the most common causes of sleepless nights, for all adults, are worry about one's competence or efficiency, an exaggeration of personal shortcomings, a fear of failure.

Dr. John Millet, a psychiatrist, says that difficulty in sleeping is generally caused by anxiety, found most often in men with easily upset nervous systems. The more you worry, the less you sleep. Pretty soon you begin to worry about not sleeping. Then you've become an insomniac.

In such cases the patient transfers his worries about himself to his insomnia and, depending on his condition, needs psychiatric or other medical help to get back to his normal sleeping routine.

A typical neurotic insomniac was F. Scott Fitzgerald, who wrote a piece for *Esquire* in 1934 which still evokes the horrors of a man who wants to, must, but can't, sleep. ". . . If insomnia is going to be one of your naturals," Fitzgerald wrote in "Sleeping and Waking," "it begins to appear in the late thirties. Those seven precious hours of sleep suddenly break in two. There is, if one is lucky, the 'first sweet sleep of night' and the last deep sleep of morning, but between the two appears a sinister, ever-widening interval."

"In the dead of the night," Fitzgerald wrote, "I am only one of the dark millions riding forward in black buses toward the unknown.

"Conditioned by intense fatigue of mind and perverse alertness of the nervous system—like a broken-stringed bow upon a throbbing fiddle—I see the real horror develop over the roof-tops, and in the strident horns of night owl taxis and the shrill monody of revelers' arrival over the way. Horror and waste—

"—Waste and horror—what I might have been and done that is lost, spent, gone, dissipated, unrecapturable. I could have acted thus, refrained from this, been bold where I was timid, cautious where I was rash.

"I need not have hurt her like that.

"Nor said this to him.

"Nor broken myself trying to break what was unbreakable.

"The horror has come now like a storm—what if this night prefigured the night after death—what if all thereafter was an eternal quivering on the edge of an abyss, with everything base and vicious in oneself urging one forward and the baseness and viciousness of the world just ahead. No choice, no road, no hope—only the endless repetition of the sordid and the semi-tragic. Or to stand forever, perhaps, on the threshold of life unable to pass it and return to it. I am a ghost now as the clock strikes four.

"On the side of the bed I put my head in my hands. Then silence, silence— and suddenly—or so it seems in retrospect—suddenly I am asleep.

"Sleep—real sleep, the dear, the cherished one, the lullaby. So deep and warm the bed and the pillow enfolding me, letting me sink into peace, nothingness—my dreams now, after the catharsis of the dark hours, are of young and lovely people doing young, lovely things, the girls I knew once, with big brown eyes, real yellow hair:

> *In the fall of '16 in the cool of the afternoon*
> *I met Caroline under a white moon*
> *There was an orchestra—Bingo-Bango*
> *Playing for us to dance the tango*
> *And the people all clapped as we arose*
> *For her sweet face and my new clothes—*

"Life *was* like that after all; my spirit soars in the moment of its oblivion; then down, down deep into the pillow . . .

"'. . . Yes, Essie, yes.—oh, my God, all right, I'll take the call myself.'

"Irresistible, iridescent—here is Aurora—here is another day."

For most of us insomnia is neither so terrible nor so beautiful. For some of us it may be simply relieved.

Its cause may be physical rather than neurotic. If you have persistent insomnia, see a doctor to find out whether unrecognized illness might be interfering with your sleep.

Sleeplessness may be due to frustration, ordinary or sexual. There is little question that unsatisfactory sex relations are as sleep-destroying as none at all.

For example take the annual vacation of a family in which the husband suffered from impotence to a degree which interfered with his wife's enjoyment of sex. For two weeks they stayed at an expensive dude ranch in the Nevada mountains where the company was congenial, the food excellent and the beds soft. At the end of two sexless weeks they returned to Chicago. A friend met the wife on the street and commented on her hollow-eyed appearance.

"We had a terrible time," the wife complained. "The mountain air is no good for sleeping. I got no rest at all—I'll never go back there again!"

Another woman who had been having unsatisfactory sexual relations with her husband for years, and had insomnia as a result, went to Nevada to get a divorce—stayed at the same dude ranch—and began to sleep like a top. "That mountain air," she told a friend, "is just perfect for sleeping."

As a human activity around which mankind has draped its assorted emotions, and as the only sure retreat from politics, taxes, television and bill collectors, sleep gets more than its share of attention from commercial enterprise. Pajama manufacturers have a vested interest in your sleep. Sheet manufacturers work around the clock to keep your nights smooth. Mattress makers import wool, horsehair, hoghair, kapok, rubber and other materials for cushions for your rest.

One progressive sheet maker, The Springs Cotton Mills, has devised a bed with foam-rubber springs, a pulsating mattress, antiallergy pillows, static-proof sheets and an electrically heated bedspread. According to the company, the entire bed is air conditioned, has automatic fire protection, television, home movies, an oxygen mask, an electric razor, an electric vibrator, a compass and an intercom. "For those who like sport in bed," the Springs people add, "there is a slot machine and a folding canasta board."

AND NOW: RELAX! **143**

They're kidding, but not a few thoughtful men have gone to considerable lengths to redesign their bedrooms. Designer Nat Karson turned his bed into a studio, complete with headboard shelves for his drawing tools, a hospital-type rolling table that puts a drawing board across his knees, perfect lighting and all the comfort and convenience features he could think of. Object: to work in bed. Anyone who has begun to worry about sleep might well get into bed with the idea of working and see what happens. In the usual bedroom, with bad bed, bad lighting, inadequate curtains, flapping shades, primitive ventilation and a walk across the room for the ash tray, nothing will happen, not even work. But in a big and comfortable bed, in a room decorated with soothing care, who knows?

According to some insomniacs, the only way to sleep is alone. Clark Hunter Bradford, writing in *Esquire,* put the case for solitary confinement at bedtime this way:

"I have not been feeling too peppy for the last decade or two.

"Clever doctors diagnose my tiredness as a form of fatigue, brought on by exhaustion. But the real trouble behind my poor physical condition is that I have been foolish enough to go around sleeping with people.

"It is time for a clear-thinking man of courage and genius to decry the ridiculous, indeed perilous, habit of sleeping with others.

"I am not against the opposite sex—rather let me say some of my most inspiring moments have been spent against the opposite sex—but sleeping is a delicious and delicate operation which can only be safely and enjoyably accomplished when one is thoroughly alone.

"The gentlest companion is capable of accidentally inflicting brutal punishment, given a lethargic state of mind and a darkened room.

"In making a final decision each one must be his own master, and if there are imbeciles who insist on sleeping in company, that is a matter for his own conscience and psychiatrist.

"But I for one am tired of saying politely, 'Would you please remove your knee from my jugular vein?' to an invisible, sexless, insensible monster lurking in the dark at my side.

"In the future I intend to be pleasant but firm. I will lock the windows and close and bolt the doors securely. Then, before stringing high-voltage wires around my bed, I shall bid a cheery 'Good night' to my friends through the keyhole."

But another writer, Whitney Bolton, dismissed the twin-bed or cleft-pallet school of sleeping with a single sentence: "You have narrowed your existence and snarled your psyche."

Single, double or king-sized in your sleep habits, you may now and then be tempted by some of the gadgets put forward to woo sleep. They include relaxing bath salts, records that lull you into drowsiness, earplugs, eye-shades, electric blankets (for controlled warmth without weight), air conditioners, snore suppressors for your mate, specially shaped pillows, dark-lighted note pads you can jot genius ideas upon without really waking up, and more.

To each his own—except for sleeping pills. Sleep-inducing drugs should be taken regularly only under the attention of a doctor. There are some supposedly soporific drugs on the market which can be obtained without a prescription, but even a "harmless" drug should not be taken steadily; though not harmful in small or sporadic doses, it may do real injury as a regular practice. And, remember, any drug you rely on to get to sleep becomes a habit.

If broken sleep is caused by indigestion, however, an alkali such as sodium bicarbonate may sometimes relieve symptoms and send you back to sweet repose. But no one should attempt to dose himself for persistent indigestion.

Since falling asleep is a conditioned reaction, you can help yourself by following a set routine. For an hour before going to bed, do nothing exciting or stimulating. John Kieran's system is simple: "I read until I get drowsy," he says, "and then I go to bed. If I don't sleep, I don't fight it. I figure my body isn't sleepy. I just get up and read some more."

Listen to the radio, or what you will—but nothing stimulating. If you sleep in a single bed, make sure it's at least thirty-nine inches wide. Follow a definite pattern of undressing, brushing your teeth, drinking water (or warm milk or Ovaltine or beer or whisky). Or try the formula that Paul Gallico picked up from an old Kentucky colonel who had plenty of worries but managed to sleep anyhow. Asked for his recipe, he replied, "Well, sir, when I figure it's about time to rest my bones, I pour about two, three fingers of my best whisky and drink it. Then I go upstairs, and when I think I'm going to sleep badly, I pour out another few fingers of the same whisky. And drink it. Then I get undressed and put on my nightshirt and get into my bed. Just to prevent anything from making me restless, I take a small drink of whisky. If I don't fall asleep right away, I figure I better keep my worries from bothering me; and, just to occupy myself, I have a drink of whisky. By this time, if I don't sleep at all I don't give a damn, I'm having so much fun!'"

FOURTEEN FACTS ABOUT SLEEP

1. You move in your sleep; too little movement leaves your muscles stiff, too much movement means you're not resting.
2. You sleep in waves, heavy and light.
3. One hour of sleep before midnight is *not* worth two after midnight.
4. Insomnia may be due to: climate, occupation, mode of living, neighborhood, ill-fitting pajamas, uncomfortable mattress or bedclothing, full stomach, abuse of coffee, worry, fear, fever, sexual abstinence, many more.
5. Average time to fall asleep: thirty minutes.
6. One cup of coffee at night probably won't keep you awake; three cups almost certainly will.
7. Alcohol in any form is conducive to sleep.
8. In sleep: blood pressure usually falls, heartbeat may slow down or speed up, brain does not stop working.
9. Generally, the longer you sleep, the better you rest.
10. If you miss a night's sleep, it won't hurt you.
11. You don't have to make up missed sleep the next night.
12. There is no necessary number of hours of sleep. It's an individual matter.
13. No one ever died of insomnia.
14. If you can't sleep, don't worry; if insomnia persists, see your family physician or a psychiatrist.

THE THREE TYPES OF INSOMNIA AND WHAT TO DO ABOUT THEM

1. *Delayed Sleep*
   Usual Causes: Tension, worry, overtiredness.
   Try: Steady bedtime routine—regular bedtime hour, warm bath, hot drink (or alcoholic nightcap), relaxing exercises, pillow rolled up under back of neck.
   Lie down, close eyes.

Lie perfectly still—it's difficult to do this and stay awake.

Relax to the point where your limbs fall of their own weight.

Don't: Move around to find a comfortable position. The more you move, the more awake you become.

Count sheep. Any conscious mental effort is the same as physical movement: keeps you awake.

Worry about missing sleep.

Also: Check your bedroom for too much noise and light (try mask, earplugs); your pajamas, mattress, sheets, blankets.

2. *Broken Sleep*

   Usual Cause: Upset stomach.

   Try: Some antacid prescription when you wake up.

   Don't: Dose yourself. If insomnia persists, see a doctor.

3. *Early Wakening*

   Usual Cause: Old age. Men and women over sixty often can get along on three to four hours of continuous sleep a night. But they go to bed at an early hour.

   Try: Going to bed later, or getting up when you wake up. Don't lie there and fret because you can't sleep.

   BUT, IN ANY CASE, DON'T WORRY ABOUT YOUR INSOMNIA.

PART III RELAX INTO A NEW SPORT!

Now this *part of your new fitness program, this part at* least, *is going to be pure fun. Absolutely. Guaranteed. For fun is the whole point of it.*

This part of your fitness program consists simply in picking out a new sport for yourself—and then throwing yourself into it.

Why a new *sport? Just for the fun of it. There is nothing like a new interest to put the zip back into a man, or to keep it there. And if the "new interest" happens to take him out of himself, mayhap also to take him out into the fresh air and sunshine, so much the better.*

What's wrong with your old sports? Nothing, probably. Keep on with them, by all means, if they're right for you. They're right if they're fun, if they're frequent, if you pursue them because you want to (not because it's good business, not because "everybody does," and not because of what your wife says about "togetherness," either.) They're right if you haven't outgrown them, the way a forty-five-year-old week-end athlete has, whether he cares to admit it or not, outgrown tennis. Keep on with your old sports, by all means, if they're right for you. . . .

. . . But take up a new sport, now, too—something you've never tried, maybe never even thought of trying. Take it up for fun, for the diversion it can give you, and never mind about breaking its records. As Henry McLemore says in his delightful article on page 152, "Anyone who is old enough to read is too old to start becoming a champion." So don't expect too much of your performance. Anything worth doing is worth doing badly. Get off your dignity; get onto a new sport.

If you were to choose your new sport the way a geneticist would choose the mother of your children, you'd look for a sport that gave you:

> *A very real and refreshing change of pace from the type of activity that is your regular routine. (For the man who works all day in a noisy plant, not the added racket of bowling but the soothing silence of a trout stream . . . for the man whose livelihood demands meticulous care, painstaking precision, not billiards but possibly bobsledding!)*

> *A chance to make up for what you may lack in youth and energy with skill, finesse, experience. (Golf, hunting, fishing, trap-shooting, sailing: none of those requires a continuous expenditure of large amounts of energy as does, say, basketball; and all of them reward practice and study.)*

> *A way to let off steam. (Your way is not necessarily the next fellow's: he needs to sock something, and sock it hard, while your need is to outwit another living thing. To each his own, but to every man a way to discharge aggressions.)*

> *Something to think about. (If you can play the game without paying attention to it, chances are it's too easy to take your mind off your worries. If you could make your mind go completely blank at regular intervals, perhaps you wouldn't need a diversionary sport. But if Yoga is not your dish, choose a sport that engages your mental faculties even as it lulls them.)*

Ah, but this is dreaming. No one ever fell in love with a genetic table in view, and no one ever fell into a sport because it was good for him. That's as it should be, and in order that it should be easy for you to fall into a new sport, just for fun, the following pages parade the choices before you. Read —a kind of sport in itself. Picture yourself as a participant. See what strikes your fancy. Somewhere, on one of these pages to come, your eye will light; you'll stir in your chair; you'll start wondering if you really could learn to ski, or shoot, or ride, or whatever, at this late date. The answer is yes—you can. Try it, and see.

10. THE WARM-UP

To get you into the proper frame of mind, Henry McLemore here gives you his witty advice on "How to Be a Successful Duffer":

Do you hold your nose when you dive off the springboard?
Do you take six shots and five minutes to get out of a sand trap?
Do you get more blisters than aces when playing tennis?
In brief, are you a duffer at sports?
The chances are that you are a duffer, because of the millions of Ameri-

cans who play at sports each year only the scantiest fraction are champions or anything like it. The overwhelming majority are double-dipped, hand-carved duffers—men and women to the awkward manner born.

I am a member of this tremendous duffer family, whose brothers and sisters you find everywhere—untangling their snarled fishing lines from trees, playing shots from rough so deep and forbidding that Frank Buck would think twice before invading it, getting bumped on their noggins by booms and spars, double-faulting and foot-faulting, and executing belly-whopping swan dives from the edges of pools. A true duffer always will be a duffer.

Lessons from professionals do him little good. He will carry that loop in his backswing, that flyswatter tennis service, to his grave. The library shelves of the nation are overrun with learned books on how to become a champion by improving your form. The real duffer has no form and couldn't improve it if he did.

As for becoming a champion you can't fool us. Champions are harder to make than trees. To begin with, they must have great natural ability and an early start. Your champion horseshoe pitcher probably started pitching pony shoes when he still wore three-cornered pants, and your golf champion undoubtedly could put backspin on his milk bottle. Most fly-casting experts learned the rudiments by casting into the goldfish bowl from their bassinets. Anyone who is old enough to read is too old to start becoming a champion.

During the years I have been a member of the duffer family—my only real shame has been in front of outsiders. We members of the family understand one another, but occasionally we have to compete with nonduffers, men and women who are not bound together by the common lack of ability to do things well, and it's embarrassing. They patronize us. They smile indulgently. They make it known to us that they wonder why we struggle on.

As one who has long been inefficient at many sports I have felt the need for a manual or primer which would explain to the duffer how he could appear to be much better at games than he really is. So, during the years in which I have been a sports writer, I have been careful to observe and listen to the explanations that champions make when they slip temporarily into the duffer class and top drives, flub easy lobs, land sideways on a jackknife dive, and ride the best horse in the race and finish last. For the champs make the same mistakes that you and I do—only not so often. That's why they are champions and you and I are dubs.

There's another difference, too. When we duffers flop, we say "Oh, hell." When champions flop, they are ready with a profound explanation that may involve criticism of wind, weather, the tides, equipment, spectator noises, playing conditions, the referee, or the piece of chocolate cake they ate the night before. They make these explanations in highly technical terms and in my scholarly way I have been writing them down, often not knowing what they mean.

The result is a long-needed manual and guidebook on how duffers may make themselves look good when actually they are terrible. As soon as the sports season opened this spring, I tried it out at a week-end party. My theories worked beautifully. Not one of my fellow guests realized I was a duffer. When I packed up on Monday I had almost convinced myself that I was good.

Arriving late on a hot afternoon I was told by my host to get into a bathing suit and join everybody at the swimming pool. I would have preferred to have had him ask me to put on a pair of overalls and clean up the basement. My equipment for swimming consisted of a laborious side stroke and a fear of any water more than five feet deep. I reached the pool to find it alive with expert swimmers who were doing newfangled crawls and diving from platforms so high that it didn't seem right not to have firemen with nets below. My host introduced me around to the human sea lions who called for me to "come on in!"

I thought about that side stroke which Aunt Bessie had taught me when I was eight years old. She thought I was very graceful but something told me that these strangers would not see eye to eye with Aunt Bessie. Then I remembered the study I had made on how to look good at sports although a duffer. Standing there on the edge of the pool I thought back on my swimming data and decided to put it to a test.

"Remember the old dog paddle?" I shouted. "Watch me do it!"

Every eye was upon me as I jumped in with a huge splash and started dog-paddling to the other side of the pool.

My progress was greeted with roars of genuine laughter. Encouraged (and out of wind) I said:

"Remember this one?"

Then I went into Aunt Bessie's side stroke and again everybody laughed. Carried away by my success I suddenly found myself slowly sinking in the middle of the pool. I managed to cry:

"Come on, fellows! Pretend to save me!"

Then I went down for the second time. Fortunately, the expert swimmers were so intrigued by this that they joined in the sport and made what they thought was a mock rescue. They howled with laughter when I allowed them to pull me out of the pool and apply first aid.

Later, when I had revived, I thought I had better go off the diving board to impress them further with my athletic prowess. I was the center of attention as I stepped out on the board that was quivering almost as much as I. But again my duffers' manual came to my aid. I had picked up much technical knowledge concerning the sport. I knew about "carriage," I realized the importance of the "approach to the board." I had seen champions.

I made the classic approach, tiptoe and arch and all, then, just when they expected me to go into a beautiful swan dive, I laughed and said:

"Now for the old frog jump!"

Grabbing my nose, I jumped. My feet spread wide, and my free arm cut circles in the air. It was the only dive I knew. I will always remember it because my stomach is still sore.

My success was unbelievable. The men and women, who had been sailing off the board in lovely and intricate dives a few moments before, began trying my frog dive. They turned to me for advice and I actually found myself an instructor, showing them how to do it.

The next day I played tennis. During the ride to the courts I was positively cocky. I sized up my doubles partner and my opponents and decided they were much better than duffers and far out of my class. So I knew that I must waste no time in laying a foundation that would make them believe at the end of the match that I was really a fine tennis player, no matter what happened.

I recalled that all the good tennis players I knew never called a racquet a racquet. They always called it a "bat."

"Darn it," I said, picking up my racquet and shaking it, "I packed in a hurry yesterday and brought along the wrong bat."

My companions looked at me with new interest in their eyes. I had scored and I pressed my advantage.

"The weight in this bat," I said, "is too much in the head. I like a bat with balance nearer the throat. Nothing bothers you so much on half volleys as an unbalanced bat."

My companions handed me their racquets and asked my opinion on the balance. I held them over my head at arm's length and swung them delicately.

"Fine bats," I finally said judiciously. "I wish mine had as neat a balance."

Too, too soon we arrived at the courts. My companions began taking off their sweaters but I walked directly to the court and pressed my thumbs against the surface. Then, shaking my head in despair, I called a conference at the net.

"Terribly soft court, isn't it?" I said. "Not much bounce today. Pins us down almost entirely to chopping, doesn't it?"

The only reason I had decided the court was soft was that a feeble chop— a lamb chop, so to speak—was my lone tennis stroke. Well, I chopped and chopped and chopped. My partner and I lost the first set, 1-6, but my reputation did not suffer. Throughout the set I was careful to yell "Well hit!" or "Too good!" every time I missed a simple shot. These cries of flattery blinded my opponents to my own shortcomings. They believed they were playing super tennis and that I was merely the unfortunate victim of their blazing speed and control.

When it came my time to serve, however, I was strictly on my own. For a moment I was at a loss for an explanation of the weak, pitty-pat, girl undergraduate, service of mine. Then I remembered Henri Cochet, the little Frenchman who once dominated all the courts of the world, not with his speed, but with uncanny placement of shots.

"Placement of service is the thing, eh, partner?" I cried, and then put a powder puff across the net, ducking to escape the terrific smash that came back at my head.

"Peach! Peach!" I screamed, and then frowned at my racquet.

"I'm going to have to string my own bats after this," I said. "This gut is loose as spaghetti."

Well, we lost three sets in a row, 1-6, 3-6, and 0-6.

Under the shower I said to my partner:

"Odd, isn't it, how some players can't get their games together in doubles? Tilden and Helen Wills Moody used to have the same trouble we had today. Individually they were unbeatable; together they never could click. It was the same with us today."

"Never thought of that," my partner answered, "but it certainly sounds logical. Hope we can team up again some time."

The next day we were scheduled to play golf, and just before going to bed I looked out the window to see if there were any hope of a saving rain for me. All of the stars were out, and winking evilly at me. I stayed awake most of the night preparing a professional alibi for every mistake I could possibly make. First, my hook, which is chronic. I knew that of the 105 or so strokes I would need to get around at least 90 would be hooked. My two-foot putts are fairly straight. I remembered Bobby Jones once saying that a hooked ball got tremendous roll because of top-spin or something. I knew I could explain my inability to hit a decent brassie shot with the same reason that Tommy Armour once used in my hearing.

"The lies are too close for a brassie shot," he said.

I have often wondered what he meant.

I began my personal work on my opponent while we still were in the locker room dressing for the match.

"How long is the course?" I asked quite casually.

"Sixty-seven hundred yards," he answered.

"From front or back tees?" I quickly asked, remembering that I had once heard Lawson Little make the same inquiry.

"I don't know," my opponent replied.

"But it makes a great deal of difference," I said, and on the way out to the first tee I told him all about the yardage at St. Andrews, the Royal St. George at Sandwich, and Carnoustie, all of which I hope to play someday.

He seemed impressed, but I was taking no chances. I plucked a handful of grass from the first tee, tossed it into the air, and studied it with a frown on my face as it drifted down.

"Hmmmmmmm, cross wind. And a nasty one, too," I said. "A man would be a fool not to play a hook here."

He licked his finger and held it up as a test for the wind.

"You're right," he said, "but I can't control my hooks."

I leaped at him like a tiger. For ten minutes I severely cross-examined him on his game. I questioned him minutely on the following points: Did he use the overlapping or interlocking grip? Was he an open- or a closed-stance player? Did he have a tendency to shut the face of his club? Did he cock his wrists at the top of his backswing? Did he believe that the left hand was everything? How was his pivot?

For ten minutes he knocked the tops-off dandelions with a swing that I would have sold my soul to Mephistopheles to have been able to equal. Between narrowed eyes I watched him. I circled him. I adjusted his arms. Ordered him to keep his head down. Finally, I delivered my verdict:

"Old man, try a wee bit more right hand on top of the shaft."

I said that I would be glad to demonstrate what I meant by hooking every shot.

He argued against this, saying it would spoil my score, but I merely smiled and said:

"No trouble at all. We'll just call all bets off. What's another round of golf to me?"

I never have seen a more appreciative man. He won the first, second, and third holes with pars. On the fourth hole, which is a decided dog-leg to the right, I hooked into woods on the left of the fairway, hooked out of them, and then hooked back in again. I finally hooked onto the green in eight, and hooked three short putts for an eleven.

"Get the idea?" I asked him.

"Yeah," he answered, "that right hand is what does it, all right."

At the fifteenth green (I was ten down and sliding fast) he hit one of his few bad shots of the day. I walked slowly and solemnly across the fairway, put my arm around his shoulder in a comradely fashion, and said:

"Tck! Tck! Mustn't let your right shoulder collapse like that, old man."

THE WARM-UP   **157**

"Thanks," he said. "I'll watch it from now on."

I returned, addressed my ball smartly, and hooked sharply into the rough on the left of the green. If my opponent's shoulder had collapsed, both of mine fell clear to my waist. But I covered up quickly by turning to my caddy and barking:

"You overclubbed me again, boy!"

Approaching the eighteenth green I was twelve down and I knew that my only hope was to talk fast. My drive was fairly good with a slight hook on the end of it but I dug a six-inch divot behind my approach shot.

"Must be fresh sod on this fairway," I said, speaking loud enough to be sure my opponent heard me.

My ball rolled into a trap on the right of the green. I took out a niblick, tested it, frowned and put it back in the bag.

"Boy, my dynamiter," I said, and my caddy handed it to me with the air of one who has suffered too much already. I was on the green in four more shots and knew that I had to make my final face-saving speech of the day. I had it ready because I had heard pros put the blast on courses on which they had unfortunate scores. For good measure, I threw in some things I had remembered from an interview with Donald Ross, the great golf architect.

"The trap is furrowed," I said, "and the pin on this green is unfairly placed. Mighty coarse-grained sand in your bunkers here. And how about these greens, they don't get enough shade, do they, and somebody planted the wrong bent on this one. Your fairways are baked but maybe you'll get some rain soon. Go ahead and putt, you're away."

That night I was away on the first train. They were planning water polo for the morrow.

ESQUIRE'S THE ART OF KEEPING FIT

11. THE BIG TEN SPORTS FOR MEN

And now, let's take a look at the most popular sports for men. We begin with that exhilarating but frustrating, healthful but exasperating, apparently simple but devilishly deceiving game called golf.

GOLF

Somebody once defined golf as "the difficulty of attempting to put a small ball into a wee hole, with instruments ill adapted to the purpose." The confirmed golfer will hear his game so defined at least once a season, usually by one of the million-odd Americans who have given up golf for one reason or other. He can only smile. He knows what golf is:

... It's the soul-cleansing satisfaction of that *cra-a-ack* when a driver's head meets a golf ball in a perfect mating.

... It's the pure ecstasy of sinking a putt from off the green.

... It's the relaxation of pleasantly tired muscles and a pleasantly tired mind when the round is over.

... It's the coursing of ice-cold beer down a parched throat, a needle shower sloughing caked sweat off a hot, moist body, the precious treasure of a 79 card after weeks of playing in the nineties.

... It's a zestful, not too strenuous pastime, salutary both mentally and physically.

Perhaps you've heard the other side of the story—that golf is, for example, not relaxing but aggravating, that the average player's inability to master the game technically makes him tense, irritable, downright unhappy. It happens, but when it does the fault lies with the player, not with the game.

Says Lawson Little on this point: "The average businessman golfer rushes madly out to the club, thinking about letters he didn't answer, problems he didn't attend to, traffic accidents he narrowly missed, and places he must be right after he finishes the round. Then, too, he eats a big lunch, argues about who gets or gives strokes, doesn't warm up by hitting twenty or thirty balls, and is mystified and discouraged because he starts out 7, 8, 6. The same tense, worried routine before a round would add ten strokes to my own game. The businessman can cut strokes off his score *by playing at golf, instead of worrying at it.*"

Walter Hagen's attitude, expressed on the golf course when he was on his way to winning his first of four British Opens, would be the ideal approach for a new golfer to take to the game. Hagen's beautifully placed drive on one of the trickiest fairways at Sandwich took an utterly reasonless bound into the deep gorse—a shot, maybe two shots ... *gone!*

Somebody in the huge gallery was moved to offer sympathy: "Gee, Walter, that's tough luck!"

Chin up, grinning away, Walter Hagen replied: "Well ... *that's where it is!*"

Sportswriter O. B. Keeler has written, "I think golf's otherwise inexplicable appeal to the average individual lies in its curious similarity to that other game we limpidly call *Life*. A game of breaks. Good breaks from bad shots. Bad breaks from good shots. And he who can take the breaks and keep his shirt on and his chin up ... is the winner in the long run."

If you are having a little trouble with your own chin, these days—if, that is, you are fully aware of the virtues of golf as a sport but are beginning to wonder why it isn't more *fun* for you—Ben Hogan has some advice, next up.

And if that isn't enough to get you back on the beam, play around Tommy Armour's "Brain-Straining 18," page 166. One of golf's great advantages is that it can be played almost anywhere in the world—even in the armchair.

And even in the cold, cold winter, there are indoor putting practice and exercises for conditioning golf muscles. As a matter of fact, these might well be worth a try by the potential golfer. We know that they prepared at least one man for breaking eighty in his first season of play.

There is almost no end to the fascinations of golf—for golfers. Maybe this is the game for you, too. Try it and see!

WHEN GOLF IS NO FUN

Ben Hogan knows more than you might think about those times when a golfer's game goes sour. To wit:

When I got the man's letter I thought here is something a couple of books couldn't answer.

And he wanted me to solve his problem with an offhand reply on a sheet of paper!

What the fellow wrote was this:

I used to play a fairly good game of golf, getting several rounds a year in the seventies and going over 85 only two or three times a year. Now my game is always around 100—a few strokes under or over. I have taken some lessons, and I practice about one evening a week on the average at a stop-and-sock place. But my game is getting no better. I certainly don't enjoy my golfing as much as I did. Is there anything I can do to get back on my game, or must I realize I am forty-six years old and past the age when my golf can be improved? If I am going to be playing worse and worse all the time, then I am about ready to give up on the game entirely. It's no fun any more.

I feel sorry for that fellow. I have taken the same sort of punishment he's been giving himself. Before I really found my game I might be hot one round and cold the next for no reason I could figure out. After rounds when I wasn't scoring well I would practice for hours trying to get to hitting the ball, and finally go home disgusted.

When I found out from players like Nelson, Cooper, Armour and Smith what I was doing wrong and got ideas for correction, then I began to get some good out of practice. Now I will practice for an hour or two right after I've come in from playing a round well under par. My inquiring friend won't

do that. He probably goes in, takes his shower and has a few drinks to console himself for his score. That part, at any rate, should be fun.

What I've learned is that when a fellow is hitting the golf ball well he should try to keep in that groove until it becomes a habit. If he's developed bad details in his swing and tries to get rid of them without knowing how his swing looks or without being aware of the feel he should have at different stages of the swing, then his practice only deepens his bad swing.

The chances are that the fellow who wrote me never had what could actually be called a golf swing. When he was younger, when his eyes were keener, his co-ordination better and his muscles more flexible, it was natural that he would be able to hack at the ball fairly well without thinking about it at all. Adjustment for error was subconscious and fairly efficient.

Then along came the day when he tried to substitute his brains for his muscles. He heard some fellow say that he should keep his right elbow close to his body on the backswing, and he got so attached to that hunch that he ended up taking a lady-like jerky hack at the ball. Or the chances are about nine to one that his playing companions all kept telling him that he was taking his eye off the ball. Whereupon the victim stiffened himself so much that he almost broke his neck when he swung. Then, as he still had a miserable swing and got bad results, he gave up in profanity and dismay.

He thought he was the only one in the world who had become so stinking at golf he should give up the game. The sad part of it is that one of his type often does quit golf when some other discouragement is added to his scores. If his business slumps then golf loses a player. From what I've seen of golfers I'd say that about nine out of ten of those who gave up the game quit because there was no fun in their scores.

These people who get troubled about their scores to the extent that they quit the game make an expensive mistake. It's plain that if they get so disturbed about their scores that they worry themselves into giving up, their general morale needs attention.

The best thing golf can do for these fellows who get low-spirited when they bump into a tough problem is not to give them scores of 73, 74, and 75, but to get them to walking the four miles of an eighteen-hole round merely for the exercise and the congenial company. The first thing I'd honestly advise a fellow who is disgusted with his golf to do is to change the company he's playing in. If he changes to playing with fellows who enjoy themselves without worrying themselves and others about bad shots and high scores, he'll begin to relax at his game. He will get a better score because he won't be trying so desperately that he tightens up stiffer than a steel rail.

A man who is discouraged with his game gets disgusted with a bad shot and goes to his next shot either scared or in a mad mood. If he's scared he has an unreasoning hunch that brute force will hammer the next shot home. If he's sore he wants to take out this grouch on the ball. So he doesn't stop to think about the first two things: whether his grip gives him a chance to swing the club-head squarely into the ball, and whether the location of the ball with respect to placement of his feet will allow the club to do its work right.

Even if the fellow did stop to think, he probably wouldn't know what to do because he's so set in his own wrong way that the right way probably would feel awkward to him. That's why you hear men say so many times that the lesson they just took threw them off their game. It sure enough did. That is what the pro was paid for. The game the pupil had was lousy; he should have been thrown off it long ago. No effort at correction can be 100 per cent successful immediately.

It would amaze the fellow who is discouraged with his golf to realize what patience and heart have been required for many of the greatest pros to discover and overcome mysterious flaws that were giving them trouble.

Denny Shute was sick of his golf in 1928. He made a change in his grip that took him about a year to master. His first big victory was in the Los Angeles Open in 1930. From that he went on to win a British Open, two P.G.A. Championships, lose a U.S. National Open title in a play-off, and keep good enough to finish second in the 1941 U.S. Open.

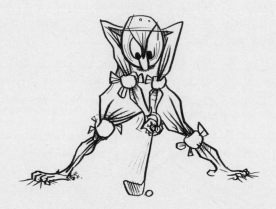

Ralph Guldahl went into a bad slump after finishing a stroke out of a tie for the 1933 National Open Championship. It took him three years of practising and studying before he came back to win two U.S. Opens and three Western Opens.

Hagen, Sarazen, Horton Smith, Lawson Little and other great stars have had their slumps. But they've also had the hearts that make champions. They've found out what they needed to get scoring again and they worked on it until they got it.

I wouldn't expect anyone like the man who wrote me the letter I quoted to apply himself to correcting his game with the same intensity, and as long, as the playing pros work on theirs. He'd be crazy if he did. He's primarily in the game for fun and unless he is willing to enjoy himself at supervised practice for some months, he'd better get used to the sort of golf fun that isn't dependent on the score card.

This past golfing season my correspondent has probably had plenty of business problems. He made dates to take a lesson, or to play. He rushes out to the club, throws in a quick lunch, makes a telephone call he forgot to make at the office, and hurries out to the tee tired already and with his nerves dancing.

I might tell the man that if I'd go out to a golf course the way he does I'd feel lucky if I ever was able to break 90. He's a nervous basket case before he gets to the golf course—and he blames his score for making him that way! It's not the man's golf game, it's his entire physical and mental condition that has upset him about his golf. I'll bet if he'd analyze himself frankly he'd find that he was easily and severely upset about other things undoubtedly more important than his golf score.

Adding it all up, I'd say that if the fellow is scoring around 100, he isn't doing bad. Considering what he's up against in factors that handicap the development of the physical and mental phases of his game the man is lucky to hit a shot well now and then.

If this man is really on the level about wanting to improve his golf, he can do what I've done for several years; take a putter and use it from fifteen minutes to a couple of hours almost every night putting at a glass laid on a carpet.

If he'll see where the ball is, with respect to his feet and eyes, when he gets uniformly good results, and how his grip is, and how the path of the putter blade is when he's regularly stroking putts into the glass, then he'll begin to get fun out of really studying his golf.

If he doesn't want to do that, what he wants is a miracle worked to improve his golf. Should there be any miracle that can be worked on a golf game I want it for myself.

When you get right down to it I guess that it actually isn't a few details about golf that have been bothering the man who wrote me. Maybe it's something he ate, the cold war, taxes or something else far away from a golf course. Golf is a very convenient thing for him to blame as the source of his unhappiness. He should be happy he has golf handy for that alibi and relief.

THE BRAIN-STRAINING 18

Here's a *new* game—progressive golf—and you can play it right where you're sitting. Your partner? *Tommy Armour.*

It's impossible for me to recall how many golf holes I've played, but in all the years of golf there are eighteen holes that are vivid in my mind as holes of unforgettable interest. Every time I've played them they remind me to be alert and thinking. They each have infinite variety, according to where the shots go. Invariably, I discovered, when I played them in thoughtfulness they rewarded me with delight; but when I treated them carelessly, they rebuked me with scores that punished not the mistakes of my muscles but the mistakes of my mind.

Here are the eighteen golf holes that, for me, would constitute the most majestic golf course that could be devised. It would test the golfer's mentality as well as his capacity to hit shots with the skill of a virtuoso:

HOLE	PAR	YARDAGE
Oakmont No. 15	4	475
Merion No. 2	5	555
Carnoustie No. 17	4	485
Pebble Beach No. 17	3	218
Yale No. 9	3	225
Pinehurst No. 11 (No. 2 Course)	4	433
Cypress Point No. 16	3	222
Pebble Beach No. 18	5	540
Oakmont No. 18	4	473
Oakmont No. 16	3	234
Sandwich No. 13	4	450
West Palm Beach No. 10	4	475
Riviera No. 18	4	455
St. Andrews (Old) No. 17	4	467
Pine Valley No. 5	3	226
Boca Raton No. 15 (North)	4	444
Carnoustie No. 18	4	450
Pine Valley No. 13	4	446

1. Oakmont's 15th is on club's score card as a par-four hole, although it's 475 yards long. That's 30 yards longer than the distance the United States Golf Association sets as top length for a par-four hole under normal conditions. A tee shot has to be long and pin-pointed to the left to give you a chance for the shot you have to play to the green. The green is the longest one on the course, but narrow. If you play too much to the right, there's a trap to the right of the green that costs a stroke even to the trickiest wizards of the wedge. When you mark down a five or a six on that hole, you damn yourself for not having had sense enough to see how you should have played the hole.

2. The second hole on Merion's championship East Course is 555 yards and not the toughest par on that course, according to the scoring of the 1934 and 1950 National Opens. But it accounted for costly sixes where par fives would have been the reward of headwork. There's rough and out of bounds to the right, and a wandering creek and trap hazards to the left. Merion is one of the few American courses that still has the exacting test of a genuine rough, instead of a shaggy fairway-imitating rough. The long hitter who has been able to stray all over most courses and scramble out in par must pause and think on his tee shot and second shot on this hole.

3. Carnoustie's 485-yard 17th and 450-yard 18th are contests with the wind, the water of the Barry Burn, and the undulating terrain. The holes are parallel, with the 17th played from east to west and the 18th (see 17, below), vice versa. The wind at Carnoustie is either an east wind from the sea, or a west wind. It rarely comes from the north or south. At the 17th, the wind twists along the left of the fairway, then crosses it. The drive must favor the right side. The green is in a hollow. Its narrow entrance is strongly protected by bunkers. With the wind against you, a second shot may splash into the burn. When you get to the green, you find it small and contoured in a testing way. Par four.

4. The 17th at Pebble Beach calls for the most accurate 218 yards a mortal can drive a golf ball and for more brains than most of us golfers have. If you get too far to the left, you're liable to be in Carmel Bay or on the rocky shore. A bit short when banging at the pin and you'll be in soft sand with a narrow green between you and more sand or, again, the bay. Too long and too far to the right and you're in trouble. The green is divided by a ridge across its narrow center. Unless you can *think* yourself an absolutely perfect shot of 218 yards off the tee, with a gusty wind against you, you'll have to do a lot of brainwork to catch your par here. Par three.

5. The 9th at Yale University's course is 225 yards from the championship tee, about 170 yards of it across a lake. The green is on two plateaus sepa-

rated by a gully which is part of the putting surface. There's a deep trap bordering the left of the green. The hole was designed and built by Charles Blair MacDonald, Seth Raynor and William Perkins, along the lines of a famed hole at Biarritz. This one is more testing than the original. Par three.

6. A deceptively easy-looking hole is the 11th on the No. 2 course at Pinehurst. It's a par-four hole of 433 yards with a trap at the left that is a tee-shot menace to be outwitted. You've got to be long to get past it. If you've got a slight hook to your drive, the ground slopes gently to this trap and steers your drive in. The tee shot has to be to the left to put you in a position to make a sharp shot to the green because there's a pine tree at the right bordering the fairway, just where the fairway begins to narrow down into the green. It's amazing how many approaches are just barely into the rough at the right—and are blocked by that tree. There is a hollow in front of the green which is liable to throw a running shot far off line. There's a clever guarding of traps around that green. The green is rolling, low in front, high at the back left where the cup is. This is a hole that gives your brains exercise over the full route from tee to cup.

7. The 222-yard 16th at Cypress Point is chosen by almost all widely experienced players as one of the world's greatest par-three holes. It's certainly the most picturesque of all of them. With the wind in your teeth, you may be short and sunk in the surging Pacific with a shot you thought would ordinarily be good for 250 yards. There are plenty of times when the most powerful and confident players aren't ashamed to acknowledge that discretion is the better part of valor—they bat their tee shots hopefully toward the narrow entrance at the left of the green, hoping the drives will roll on. Too far to the left and your par dies in a watery grave.

8. The 540-yard 18th at Pebble Beach is a dog-leg with the Pacific in the elbow and two trees at the right that are annoying, disturbing, or downright troublesome if you make too much of a mistake in keeping away from the danger at the left. There's a trap tightly guarding the right side of the green. Either you loft your approach onto the green over the hazard or ease your shot in front from left to right. You must hit your drive and second and third shots *with your skull* if you want a par or a chance of a birdie. Par five.

9. The 18th at Oakmont is a gigantic par four of 473 yards. If you go almost any place but down the middle, you've got to hope for a magnificent second to negotiate a mound in front of the green, or play safe and trust to heaven for a precise approach and one putt on a sloping, speedy green. You have to outthink this hole; you can't outslug it.

10. Oakmont's 234-yard 16th calls for a lusty and high shot that will have to hold to a green that slopes away from its center to surrounding traps, or for a shot that will fade and roll in through a narrow entrance to the left

of the green. Your decision on the shot that you'll play will have to be followed by masterly marksmanship. Par three.

11. A left-angling dog-leg, tough bunkering and a terrifying rough at the left make the 450-yard 13th at Royal St. George's Sandwich a hole that tests the thinking capacity of the player. The tee shot is made over a ridge that runs diagonally across the fairway. A bunker extends about two-fifths of the way across the entrance to the green. Guarding the green at the left is a deadly bunker. This is another of the great holes that deceive you. When the wind is right, the hole will eat out of your hand, but when the wind is against you—as it frequently is—this 13th will bite you. Par four.

12. The West Palm Beach Country Club's 475-yard dog-leg 10th presents problems that determine the golfing brains of the ordinary golfer and the star. To gamble dangerously with this hole requires a drive carrying from 195 to 220 yards, flirting with sandy rough at the right all the way. A big tee shot makes the second considerably easier but still exacting because of the rather close trapping of the green. From wherever you play your second shot to the green, the shot demands perfect execution. Par four.

13. Riviera's 455-yard par-four 18th has a blind tee shot from a tee on the low side of a dwarf canyon up onto a fairway that slopes to the right. It may give you an uphill or downhill lie for your long second. There's a stretched-out grove encroaching on fairway at right. The second shot ought to drift into the green from the left, or you'll be in trouble. The green is fairly large, but tricky and trapped close for a rather long second. On the bank back of this green and on the clubhouse lawn, tournament spectators by the thousands have watched the disasters of the fellows who failed to think their shots and to accompany their thinking with magnificent execution.

14. Being a born Scot, for me to even suggest a disparaging thought about the famous Road Hole at St. Andrews would be sacrilege. I and all my progeny would probably be permanently exiled from my native heath. Personally, I despise the hole—probably because I have never been able to play it well. St. Andrews 17th defies the modern concept of what constitutes a fine hole, but it has withstood the test of time. The tee is placed beside a railroad track. In front of you are the Forgan Sheds. The spelling of Forgan has always held great significance in connection with the playing of this hole. If the wind is against you—and I can assure you there is always a wind of some kind at St. Andrews— you play *to the left* of the Forgan Sheds. If the wind is on the left, you play over the "F" in Forgan, which calls for a carry of about 200 yards. If the wind is behind you, you go after the "R" in Forgan, which calls for a carry of about 230 yards. Now, presuming you have made any of these carries, then comes the major problem. The green is long, narrow, and approximately at right angles to where you are aiming. At the

left side of the green, there is a small, but deep, bunker. Slightly to the right of this is a dip which leads all mis-hit or too-close shots into the bunker. The green is narrow and very long. If you go over the green, you land on the famous, or the infamous, road. From there you have practically no opportunity to recover. Golf destinies have been carved on that slight pathway. But the penalty of getting over the green is far too severe for anyone to ever call this a really great hole. Par four.

15. Pine Valley 5th is a par-three hole, 226 yards long, with a carry of approximately 180 yards over water, bushes and bunkers, into a long narrow green straightaway from the tee. The penalties incurred for being short to the left or to the right are far too extreme. These prevent it from being a "great" hole, although it is a very difficult one.

16. Consider next the 15th at Boca Raton, North Course. A par four, this is *"it."* Slightly left to right, the main distinction of the hole is that it calls for two perfectly hit balls. The drive must be long and well placed. The second shot calls for anything from a three-iron to a brassie, depending on the wind. The green is beautifully bunkered. Perhaps the second shot is too difficult. I've played it for twenty-two consecutive years, and must say that it calls for the most exacting second shot of any hole that I have ever played. As I said before, this is it.

17. The 18th at Carnoustie is a par-four hole, about 450 yards long, with out-of-bounds on the left and a beautiful burn (or a dirty ditch) on the right. The carry from the Tiger tee, that is, the back tee, is 220 yards. A slice or a hook gets you into really desperate trouble. If, by some freak of circumstances, you hit a perfectly placed drive, you are then faced with problems even greater than before. Another burn faces you. It runs diagonally from left to right across the fairway and calls for a carry of 180 to 210 yards. With the slightest slice you are in the burn and with the slightest hook you are out-of-bounds. If you hit a really magnificent second shot, it is possible to make the green. Put the ball on that green in two and you can be sure that you've accomplished a real feat.

18. Pine Valley 13th is truly a great hole. Par four, the hole is right to left and even if the drive is hit in the correct place it still calls for a fine second shot. If the drive is not correctly placed, it calls for a very fine placement of the second shot which will then make it a pitch-and-putt for the four. The slightest deviation after the misplaced or mis-hit drive calls for a very severe penalty which might result in an 8, 9, or even more. The same situation exists after a perfectly placed drive—if the second shot fails to be good. It is always possible to meet with disaster.

You will notice that nine of the par-four holes I've selected are longer than the customary top par-four yardage of 445, but it isn't the length that makes these great holes. A hole that's merely long can be played in par by a golfer with a strong back and a weak mind. It's the length of the thinking from the tee to the cup that distinguishes these holes as well as all the others of this brain-straining eighteen.

THE RACKET SPORTS

Tapering off from tennis, because the doctor says it's too strenuous for a "man of your age"?

Consider squash rackets, page 173, but get your M.D.'s vote before you try it. It gives tennis very little edge in the department of hard exercise.

Consider badminton (below), a game that can be played indoors or out, as slow or as fast as you make it.

And then—don't laugh—there's table tennis, page 177. You may be surprised to learn that ping-pong, played well, can leave you breathless.

If you ever enjoyed swinging a baseball bat, try one of the racket games. That sensation of really *wacking* a ball is hard to beat!

BADMINTON

It may seem odd to see a healthy guy swatting a bunch of feathers, but it's no game for pantywaists.

Probably the way for the uninitiated to get the clearest mental picture of badminton is to visualize lawn tennis, which badminton most nearly approximates in structural setup and play, the two games employing in common a court, a net and rackets.

The court itself is forty-four feet long. For the two-handed, or single game, the court is seventeen feet wide; for the four-handed, or doubles game, an eighteen-inch alley is added to each sideline, making the court twenty feet wide. The top of the net, which is stretched across the middle of the court, is five feet, one inch high at the sidelines, and exactly five feet high in the center. Good, bad and indifferent badminton has been, and is, played beneath comparatively low ceilings, but to insure the opportunity of producing the proper variety of shots the game offers, fairly high clearance space is desirable. In most organized competition a minimum height of twenty feet is required, twenty-five to thirty-five feet is preferable and unlimited height ideal.

The light-framed rackets used in badminton are strung with a very narrow-gauge gut and weigh between four and five ounces. But here the tennis parallel ends for, in place of the ball traditionally used in racket games, there is substituted the delicate and contentious shuttlecock, or "bird." Usually weighing between seventy-five and eighty grains, it is composed of a cork base with a kid jacket in which are inserted sixteen guiding goose-feathers. The average lifetime of this fairly precious object is not much longer than the duration of one game.

The object of the game, then, is to hit the shuttle back and forth cross the net, keeping it within the boundaries of the court and not allowing it to touch the floor. A game consists of fifteen points during which *only the server scores,* and the serve is surrendered with the loss of a point. A match consists of the best of three games. If, and when, a score of 13-all, or "deuce," is reached, the side scoring the thirteenth point first has the privilege of allowing the game to run out at 15 points, or the alternative of "setting" the score at 5, thus extending the game to 18 points. If, and when, a score of 14-all, also "deuce," is reached, the side scoring the fourteenth point first has the privilege of letting the game run out at 15 points, or the alternative of "setting" the score at 3, thus extending the game to 17 points.

Like tennis, golf and similar games, never smacking of the lustiness of those sports involving physical contact, badminton was destined at various periods during its evolution to be classified as "sissy." Maybe it was, once upon a time, but today's typical picture is that of two trim young men in light shirts, shorts, sneakers and the pink of condition, but breathless, running each other ragged about the court, chasing the bird from baseline to net, net to baseline, retrieving, clearing, feinting, dropping, smashing, and dripping perspiration like a hard running horse.

It can be played less strenuously. In fact a beauty of badminton is that dubs can have fun at it. Unlike tennis, you need not be perfectly matched. The game is a neat sort of athletic dance—a give-and-take of racquetwork and footwork, that the lackadaisical can enjoy and the most ardent eat up with exhibitionistic prowess.

It is a game of grace and accuracy. Only the very heavy shuttlecock, rubber-weighted for windy days, flies fast enough to elude the eye. The light shuttlecock, used by indoor gentlemen all the time, and by outdoor men on calm days, can always be followed in flight. It can be smacked right at you; or it can be lifted into a graceful defensive curve, like the path of a mortar, to descend in a deceptive drop. The game is one of surprise, of change of pace, of all the ruses of any court-and-net game except that the shuttlecock does not respond to "english." The man with the racquet can not misshape the shuttlecock as he does a tennis ball, to make it dance lemon-shaped to the bewilderment of the amateur—but rather he depends upon the versatility of muscular control. That is, he sends a swift one, a high one, a low one, a cross-court one and constantly exercises the guile of restraint.

Accuracy and hitting the bird squarely are prime factors in badminton, but the real art of the game lies in the player's ability to anticipate and deceive his opponent and to alter the pace of the shuttle, which can be hit surprisingly hard, or again, merely touched. When a good player hits a really hard smash the shuttle leaves the racket at a speed of sixty or more miles an hour. But the hardest hitters can barely hit the shuttle from one baseline clear across the other. That may give you some notion of the tremendous change that may occur in the bird's flight during a rally on the forty-four-by-twenty-foot court. However dainty the flight of the shuttlecock may appear, remember that the shuttle does not bounce, and that the ability and stamina required to reach it before it hits the floor and to keep it in flight makes badminton a really tough game.

The outdoor version is usually more casual than the indoor. The court, quickly laid out with a ready-made tape on the lawn next to the country house, blends with the landscape. The game blends well with such accessories of country life as beer, ale, cocktails and highballs. It is not so strenuous that a drink will impair your skill. A game does not last long, and the returning breadwinner has time for a turn at it before dinner.

The game can be as fast as you like it, or as slow. Try it sometime!

SQUASH RACKETS

Squash rackets is a whirling, exhausting, bitter game that can be played for fun but that more often is played in the spirit of root hog or die. Two contestants with no fear of heart failure isolate themselves in a windowless, high-ceilinged room and then proceed to go mad. The play is forcing and, in a way, dirty, for it is calculated to make the opposition run, leap, twist, and at last come close to collapse. The tempo rises as the game progresses. The rackets speak with a sharper tone, and the ball as it hits the front wall snaps like the breaking of timber. The strategy of attack and defense becomes intricate and must be executed with split-second precision. Power, speed, endurance, and craftiness must be available in large measure, and they must be synchronized so that on point after point the wearing destructiveness of the pace can be maintained. Between points the players may lean against the walls for support, their faces empty of color and sweat dribbling onto the floor; but when the ball is served again, so fanatical is the bugginess that the game breeds, they are after it tirelessly, relentlessly—all they know or feel is that they must meet the competition and, if possible, overpower it.

Squash rackets flourishes because it is a fighting game. It is the pat answer for the man who dislikes the airy gracefulness of badminton, the galloping boredom of volley ball, the twitching of ping-pong, and the inconsequentialities of such indoor activities as deck tennis, box ball, and tiddlywinks. In squash rackets you can get hold of the meat. You can use your physical and mental capacities right up to the limit. You never have the frustrated feeling of not being able to let yourself go. When the ball rebounds off the front wall and you move into position for the shot, you have an awareness of freedom that no other game can give. You can make a soft shot, loop the ball high into the air, send the ball through any crazy angles that you choose— or you can lay into it as if you wanted to knock the walls down. Laying one away, smacking the ball so hard that it becomes a squirting black streak —that is the kind of catastrophic, complete satisfaction that is somewhere on the other side of Paradise. And the competition is no remote, cobwebby thing: it is right beside you, alive, tangible, fighting. You don't need a telescope to see that you are concerned with a battle.

Technically pictured, squash rackets is indoor tennis with the two contestants playing on the same side of the net, the ball being returned by rebound off the front wall of the four-walled court. The net is a metal "telltale" which rings with a deafening clamor when struck by a low ball. It is nearly flush with the front wall, and its top edge is parallel to and not quite knee-high above the floor. The racket resembles a round-headed fly swatter in shape, and would lead anyone who had never seen the game to believe that it was a sissies' pastime. The ball is hollow and is made of black rubber; it is about the size of a golf ball and weighs thirty grams; in theory at least it makes a squashy sound when dropped. The standard American court is about the size of an upper-middle-class living room, the length being thirty-two feet and the width eighteen feet six inches, but the height must be at least sixteen feet. Painted lines define the court boundaries, which for practical purposes are limitless since even a beginner rarely double-faults, and it is a crazy wild man indeed who cannot play his shots above the telltale and below the sixteen-foot mark on the front wall. Entrance to the court is made through a small door in the back wall, fitted so that the joints are even. Illumination comes from overhead or from high on the court walls.

This court layout means that the players face the front wall as in handball, swinging rackets around each other's ears and keeping out of each other's way. Since the ball is light and smooth-surfaced, it is probable that the hard-hit squash ball travels faster than the 125 miles an hour ascribed to some tennis services. The swing of the racket is an even whiplash from the wrist which has the effect of an explosive; the weight of the shoulder is behind it, and the body moves forward slightly to give the shot full authority. The ball is served as in tennis. Then play continues until a racket is broken, someone falls into a faint, or the ball hits the floor twice on the same shot. The right of service, which carries some advantage with it, goes to the winner of the preceding point. The first player to win fifteen points wins the game, unless it goes to deuce, and a match consists of the best three games out of five.

Squash rackets is an importation from England, and is descended from the ferocious game of rackets, which is believed to have originated in a seventeenth-century debtor's prison. Rackets has to a large extent been superseded: it is too expensive for anyone but a debtor or a well-heeled capitalist, and, besides, since it is the "fastest game on foot," it demands near-perfect conditioning. The rackets court is almost twice as long as the squash rackets court and is surfaced with a special imported material applied by English workmen. Four officials are needed to conduct a formal match, one of them being occupied mostly with handing out new equipment. Bats may be broken at the rate of two hundred dollars' worth an afternoon; the ball has to be replaced about every ninety seconds.

Originally intended as a training game for rackets, squash rackets has become the game to play. It is strenuous but does not keep a contestant doing the hundred-yard dash for an hour on end. It is less dangerous than rackets, for not all rackets players go through life keeping both their eyes. Officials are not needed in informal play, and only one is required in matches between clubs. The racket, though it is never guaranteed and will break easily enough if slapped against a wall, can be made to last a full season.

What constitutes a good squash rackets player has not been determined.

A little skinny guy can take a fall out of an ex-football player, or vice versa. Power counts, but it is not everything. Speed counts, but you can often find a stocky chunk of a man playing such a canny game that he does not have to be fast. A rangy man with a long reach seems to have an advantage, but let a cold-blooded mite go into the court with him and the outcome is not predictable. All other things being equal, it is plain fortitude that wins, the willingness to keep going when your heart is pushing into your throat and to step up the competition when you would rather lie down and die.

Coaches teach a varied, brainy game with emphasis on skillful stroking, but young players, unless they are of the stuff that makes champions or near-champions, almost inevitably turn on the power and burn up energy by the tank car. The ball may sail high, hitting side wall, front wall, and back wall before it hits the floor—there may be terrific collisions between players—but this recklessness to a young man is fun. It is an absolute release of vitality and gustiness, and is especially esteemed after a day of paper or book work.

As an average player grows older, he has to forego climbing up the walls and turning hand springs. His game becomes calculated and tricky. He hits long when he seems to be hitting short, short when he seems to be hitting long. He mixes soft shots with hard shots, and plays for position. He goes for the kill only when he is reasonably sure of getting it. And if he is a proficient older player he can throttle a young man's game so effectively that he might as well be playing with a baseball bat.

Age does not wither nor custom stale. After forty a man can take his squash rackets or leave it alone, but usually he takes it. Before a match he may have to oil his joints and apply special supporters, but the pleasure he gets from subduing young upstarts is worth the trouble. There are plenty of players of over fifty who can win from young men of no inconsiderable ability. Harry Boakes, one of the grandest of grand old men, was playing a creditable game at eighty-two years.

One great advantage of squash rackets over many other sports is that the beginner can have as much fun as the expert. He is not forever chasing balls and being reminded of his mistakes. While he is learning he may not win half a dozen points in half a dozen games, but he does not have the worry that he is making a fool of himself. Another advantage is convenience. If you have a match scheduled for five in the afternoon, you can be sure, barring violent acts of God, that five is the time you will play. Wet weather or darkness makes no difference. You don't have to assemble a team. You don't have to drive miles into the country, hire a caddy, and spend the afternoon taking your exercise. You merely make sure that you have an opponent, go to the court, and stage the battle. Within an hour you will have had all the exercise that a nonprofessional needs.

Squash rackets will never be popular in the sense that it will draw big gates and make the headlines. The construction of the courts makes large crowds of spectators impossible. A court with a seating capacity of three hundred is exceptional, and the usual capacity is about fifty. There has been some talk of building glass courts at least for the championship matches, but, by and large, most players feel that the game belongs to them and that commercializing it would only take the sport out of it and breed a new race of tramps. For their own playing they are satisfied to go off by themselves and have it out without benefit of officials or spectators. That they love the game is indisputable. In the fall of the year when the smoky haze settles over the horizons, they regret the finish of outdoor sports but have the satisfaction of knowing that for the next six or seven months they can engage in an indoor sport for which they do not have to apologize to anybody.

TABLE TENNIS: MORE EXERCISE THAN YOU THINK!

People who are familiar with the real *sport* of ping-pong, as distinguished from the basement-playroom version that most people play, are apt to see red when a scoffer says, "Ah, there's nothing to that kids' game."

As a matter of fact, table tennis *is* good recreation for the youngsters, but it is also a stern test of the ability and resourcefulness of an adult. It takes years to master all the strokes and learn the various intricacies of spin shots. Cannon-ball serves? No, but a first-class player can put so much stuff on the ball that the average novice would be doing well if he got a third of them back on the table. The element of spin on the ball is part and parcel of the modern game and is one of its fascinations. Exercise? We could show you a big man who indulges three or four times a week and who, in the past four months, has lopped off twenty-one pounds! Devotees would like nothing better than to watch some of ping-pong's scoffers, who have never taken a crack at the game, huff and puff and groan and altogether wilt after an hour's workout. Excitement? Cock an ear, sometime, to the incessant roar of the cheering crowds at a table tennis tournament!

Not so many years ago tennis and golf were called "minor sports." Golf was "an old man's game" and tennis, with its white trousers and "love game" business, was frequently associated with pretty boys and pink tea. But they were games that had the real stuff and time proved it. Table tennis, too, has finally won the praise and respect of the leading figures in athletic circles everywhere. As Arch Ward wrote in the Chicago *Tribune*, "I don't believe the general public realizes the physical exertion and scientific play table tennis demands. I didn't until I saw it. I consider it a fine, vigorous form of exercise."

Coleman Clark of Chicago, once holder of a shot-put title, said, "Table tennis as played today is just as strenuous, just as fatiguing as any of the so-called 'he-man' sports. It's fine entertainment, but you can also get a real workout from it. In my opinion, it requires just as much stamina as wrestling, boxing or football."

Here is the original vest-pocket game which can overnight convert a home into an athletic club with the outlay of only a small sum for equipment. Behold the only active sport in captivity that is adaptable to home, office (are we putting ideas into your head?), barbershop, night club, prison cell or what have you. In contrast to leisurely golf, for example, where, taking everything into account, a full half-day is taken up for eighteen holes, table tennis is an efficient lunch-counter proposition. No time wasted—just peel off the coat and go to it. (Tournament players are always uniformed.) Like medicine it can be taken in measured doses. If you are itching for a vigorous workout you can get one in an hour, or if you just want enough to relax, a couple of games will do the trick. Always easy to find a partner, too, even if you have to fall back on the wife. As anyone can catch on to the hang of the game in no time it's a royal family diversion. Incidentally table tennis is being played more and more in the open and on porches.

Suppose you'd like to have a ping-pong set up at your house. How large a room do you need to play in? The table is nine by five feet, and thirty inches high. There should be a minimum of two and one-half feet at the sides and four feet at either end, but for expert play there should be eight to twelve feet at either end, and more room on the sides. (For tournaments the association specifies a minimum runback of fifteen feet.) An ample playing area will enable you to perform the classical strokes of the game far more easily. As a white background makes it hard to follow the ball, walls should be treated with some solid color other than white. Three one-hundred-watt lamps with shades, strung in a line down the center of the table, are infinitely better than one lone, bare sixty-watter.

In buying equipment, be sure to buy the best. In the long run you will find it cheaper and you simply can't do justice to the game if you use inferior merchandise. Insist on the official, five-ply veneer, three-quarter-inch, painted table, and procure the large, pebbled-rubber rackets which are infinitely superior to the sandpaper kind. There is a great deal of difference in balls, nets and brackets, too. Here again it will not pay to skimp.

And now a few hints on how to play the game, and a brief clarification of the most controversial rules.

As there is no doubt that the "tennis" grip is vastly superior to the old-fashioned "penholder" method, adopt the former.

The serve puts the ball into play. Be sure that you use the "bounce ball" service, wherein the ball is struck behind the table so that it first touches your court, and passing over the net, touches the receiver's half of the table. Disregard the minor courts made by the white line running down the center of the table as these are used for doubles play only. Direct "over the net" serving, without the ball first having touched your side of the table, is illegal.

Also, the number of "let" serves which you are permitted is unlimited. Finger-spin and knuckle-ball serves, once allowed, are now barred. Place your serves and keep them low so that your opponent cannot smash them for sure points.

A game is 21 points and a match either best of three, or best of five games. After every five points service changes. At 20 all service alternates after each point and the player who first scores two successive points wins the game. Only one service, mind you, not two as in tennis.

In playing first learn to keep the ball on the table. No slugging yet. First accuracy and control. Return each ball on the rising bounce, directly after it touches the table—half-volley it—on its first bounce.

Volleying, or striking it on the fly, is not permitted. Just keep pushing it back and forth. If the ball comes to your right side use your forehand. If it is directed at your left side or straight at you, your backhand will come into play. Keep the other fellow guessing by aiming the ball "where he ain't."

Now learn to chop, or cut the ball. This is a defensive shot which you should use when your adversary drives the ball so hard that you are forced back several feet behind the table. (Warning—if you haven't got at least five feet of clear space behind the table do not bother to learn to chop.) As the ball approaches you draw the racket back and to the side, shoulder high. Now swing forward and down with a sharp, short stroke, meeting the ball at the crest of its bounce with the top edge of the racket tilted back. This stroke will put excessive underspin on the ball and make it difficult for the other fellow to lift it back over the net.

Now learn the offensive stroke, a drive, for you will not be content to win always on your opponent's errors. You will want to get the thrill yourself of winning points outright with sizzling aces. This calls for the topspin drive, a stroke which permits you to hit the ball hard and still remain on the table because the overspin (acting like a topped drive in golf) causes the ball to dive downward after it passes the net and not fly out beyond the table. Start the stroke low, about table high, and swing crisply forward and up.

The use of rubber rackets in executing properly effective topspin and underspin shots is of great importance. Rubber is what puts lots of stuff on the ball and is to the racket what chalk is to the billiard cue.

As the strokes of table tennis must be made much faster than those for playing tennis, your shots must be shorter and less sweeping. Hit from the elbow more than from the shoulder and let the wrist help out. Bear in mind that the chop is the easiest way to return a hard-driven ball, if you have five or more feet of clear space behind the table. Here is the clue on how you can win in cramped quarters. Keep the ball in play by pushing, now and then placing the ball. Eventually your adversary will present you with a ball you can drive. This will be difficult for him to push back, and he can't chop it back for lack of room! So he pays the bets.

If you wish to progress rapidly and go far, by all means engage the services of a competent instructor. Mixing it with different players will likewise be beneficial; hence, you should welcome the opportunity to compete in league and tournament play. If an exhibition match or a tournament is announced in your community don't miss it, as a great deal can be learned by observation.

Much of the game's present popularity can be attributed to the hard-smacking lads who have made table tennis almost as exciting to watch as it is to play. When a couple of these wizards face each other across the table and start walloping the little white pill, you see an exhibition of speed and scientific play as fast and thrilling as any other indoor game in the world. Bang-bang-bang-bang—it sounds like machine-gun fire as the ball shoots back and forth. Sometimes the celluloid sphere travels just a little faster than your eye can follow. But still these boys keep socking away. These are the players who put the fireworks in the game. Like to join them?

SKI? WHO, ME?

Can you learn to ski when you are no longer young? Robert M. Coates did, and here's his advice to the man who might like to follow in his tracks . . .

The question is, can a man who has reached, say, his early thirties, and has never been on skis before, learn to ski? A further question, of course, might be, why should he?

Any man who has reached that age and has seen friends of his pay out big money for ski boots, ski pants and a jacket, skis, woolen shirts, socks, sweaters and other paraphernalia, who has seen these same friends, laden down with all this equipment, starting out for a skiing week end and has made note of the severity of their schedules, who has seen them return, weary-eyed from lack of sleep, slightly bruised, a little hung-over—well, there is every reason, on the face of it, why such a man might think himself well out of the whole damned business and devote himself instead to some less demanding sport, like badminton.

On the other hand, skiing—but I'm not going into the usual panegyric about skiing at this moment: the crisp, virginal snow, the swift downhill run, the jovial camaraderie of the ski lodge afterward, and so on. Skiing happens to be far and away my favorite sport, but it may never be yours, and if it isn't, no amount of impassioned description of that sort can make it so. Moreover, those aren't the reasons I like it either, or at least they aren't the main ones.

The snow, certainly, has something to do with it. I'm convinced that no one who doesn't love snow, just snow, for its own sake, as a garland for fence posts and shrubbery, as a cleaner, more symmetrical foliage for tree branches than any summer has to offer, as a brightener of the barren landscape and a tincturer of the wintry air—as, indeed, something to love almost physically, to fall into, to feel against the face, to see against the sky—such a man can never love skiing. He might better spend his winters shivering in Florida.

The downhill run, granted that you've chosen a terrain for it that's within your capabilities, has its satisfactions too; indeed, they're the principal reasons for skiing. But these come when you've achieved a certain degree of expertness. They're the end result, and not the beginning, and to list them among the *attractions* of skiing, among the things that lead you to take up the sport in the first place, implies a logical fallacy; it's like saying that you decide to learn to play tennis because you enjoy trading shots with Gonzales or Mulloy or Talbert.

When I try to decide really why I like skiing, I find myself thinking persistently of dancing, and so I may as well put the word down and try to reason it out. There are certainly definite relations and I would set down, as one more rule-of-thumb bit of advice for the putative beginner, that if you aren't a fairly good dancer, with enough feeling for the dance so that you find it hard to sit still when good music is playing—then, again, skiing probably isn't for you.

For skiing, though it may seem odd to say so, is really very much like dancing—if you'll overlook the fact that it's done alone, on a slanting surface that is a good deal more slippery than any dance floor, and at speeds which, although they seem a good deal greater than they actually are, can still range up to forty or more miles per hour. (Racing skiers, with special equipment, have been clocked at upward of seventy.) Otherwise, the same co-ordination and sense of balance are required as in dancing, as well as very much the same kind of rhythmic feeling, and it's notable that I've never yet met a very good skier who wasn't also a naturally good dancer, and—given the training—vice versa.

I love skiing, finally, because in a peculiar way it's a remarkably foolproof sport. By this I don't mean that it lacks danger, but that its pleasures are direct and self-contained, and so depend less than most others on outside circumstances. You don't have to have partners to go skiing, as you do for tennis or bridge.

You can ski alone; in fact, that's what you always do, once you start down a slope, no matter how much company you may have at either top or bottom. You can ski anywhere, in your own back yard if you have any snow and a slight slope there, or cross-country or on a mountain. And as its pleasures are self-contained, so are its accomplishments. When you make your first good Christie or tempo turn, or when, later, you come down a difficult trail just exactly as you want to come down it, checking speed when you need to check, running straight when you dare to, going into your turns just right and coming out of them all set for the next one, hitting bad spots and never letting them throw you and taking full advantage of the good ones—when you turn in a good performance at skiing (good, I mean, for yourself, and the hell with the experts), well, you *know* it, with a kind of whole-bodied internal satisfaction that's half muscular and half mental, and has nothing to do with whether anyone is watching you.

So, then, there you are, thirty-five years old, we'll say, and you've decided you'd like to learn skiing. There's no question at all but that you can, and I could give you a sizable list of famous people who have actually done so, like Lowell Thomas and Harvey Gibson, the banker, and Claudette Colbert and John Atherton, the artist, to support my contention. I could also cite my own experience, for I learned at about that age, and though I'll never be an expert skier in consequence, I've at least reached the point where I can ski pretty much anywhere, without too much danger to life and limb.

I learned by the book—by which I mean that, since I happened to live in the country at the time, I simply bought a ski manual and went out on a hill and tried to put the instructions the book contained into practice. I shouldn't recommend that method. Ski instructors look wonderful on the slopes, but they just can't write, and when they try to describe the simplest maneuver they get so involved that it's practically impossible to unravel them.

You'll need lessons, right out there on the slope where you can watch what the man does and try to imitate him, and then hear his criticism afterward: and you'll hear plenty for ski instructors are not noted for their reticence.

It's no fooling about needing good equipment, incidentally. When I started, I approached the sport with a kind of inverted pride, which made me feel that until I was a good enough skier to use them, good boots and skis were beyond me, and it would be sheer ostentation for me even to think of buying them. As a result, I did my first year or two of skiing in a pair of old hunting boots, pine skis, and leather bindings—and I suppose set myself back at least a year in point of progress.

That was nine or ten years ago, when skiing was much less well organized than it is now, but you still find a good many people going about the business of learning to ski in much the same fashion—buying cheap things to start with, on a kind of vague notion that they're likely to ruin it anyway, while learning, and they'll buy some really *good* stuff later, when they know how to use it.

That's foolish, as foolish as it would be to start playing tennis with a $2.98 racket, or learn bowling with a lopsided bowling ball. In fact, it's more foolish, for skiing, for a man to be proficient at it, requires thinking and acting at higher speeds than tennis, and an exactitude greater than bowling, and while an expert might ski fairly well, if he had to, with bad equipment, the beginner would be licked at the start.

In the matter of dress, you can wear anything from a pair of old levis to the nattiest custom-made ensemble without appreciable difference in your performance on the hill. But your boots and your skis and your bindings are the three things that, combined, really make or break your skiing, and these should be first-rate. Get good, solid-soled, steel-shanked boots, with a strap to hold them firmly to the ankle. Get good hickory skis, not too long, and with steel edges.

The steel edges will make them cost more, but steel edges will give your skis a bite in the snow on turns and a feeling of confidence generally that is invaluable. While an expert might get along without them, a beginner will be handicapped all the time.

As for length, the standard rule is this: that the skis should be as long as the man who wears them can reach with his upstretched hand. But that, I think, is a leftover from the days of mountain skiing, when long skis were necessary to keep a man from sinking too deeply into the soft, unpacked snow customarily encountered. On the kind of smooth, well-packed slopes you are likely to encounter, I've a feeling that you'll manage better with a slightly shorter article. I'd say, get them about a foot longer than your height, if you're of average weight, and an inch or two longer if you're heavier; you may ski a bit slower because of it, but you'll find them a lot more controllable, and at your age, you're not out to break records—or are you?

There are a few final words of advice that are usually given to the beginner. There's the question of terminology, in which such words as slalom, schuss, kanonen, flush, gate, vorlage and geländesprung are inspected, dissected and defined. There's the question of waxes—the greasy substance you put on the bottom of the skis to make them go faster—and much can be said about when to use Klister and when to use paraffin, and when to combine them both. I propose to skip both questions, on the theory that you'll pick up that knowledge soon enough by yourself.

What I want to do is to get you skiing, and the best way to do that is to bring up one other maneuver, so far left unmentioned—the fall. Don't overlook the fall. You are taking up skiing just to have fun with it, and the importance of the fall in that respect shouldn't be underestimated.

First of all, it's the great equalizer. Experts fall as well as beginners, and the sooner you learn that fact, and learn too that they get just as much snow down their necks and arise just as shamefacedly, the more cheerful you'll feel about the whole business.

The fall, too, in an odd way, takes fear away. Skiing really isn't dangerous, despite the awesome names that have been given to some of the trails (Nosedive, Thunderbolt, Shincracker and Rattlesnake are a few of the famous ones) and the general aura of frightfulness with which the sport has been surrounded. You will probably come down the Nosedive at Stowe or the Shincracker at North Conway yourself someday, and live to tell about it.

But there are times when you need to stop, and stop fast, and if a turn won't do it for you, a fall will. Fall cheerfully, carelessly, and unself-consciously, fall freely and with abandon; fall lustily. Once you've mastered the fall, so you can fall with aplomb and get up with confidence, you'll practically have mastered skiing.

WHY HIBERNATE?

Skiing is just as strenuous or as leisurely a sport as you care to make it. If you want to, you can pack the day's trip with hair-raising thrills and cover yourself with sweat and glory or you can travel across country more safely than you can travel across town; without turning a hair. If you go sensibly clad you can be warm and comfortable even in subzero weather.

The thick blanket of winter snow raises the lower contours and irons out the rough places in the topography of the countryside so that you can go places and see things that you could never reach on foot, on horseback or by car. The impassable gully or swamp of summertime becomes merely a dip in the winter skitrail and fences and walls are no longer barriers or restrictions.

You hit only the high spots. The skier travels through the winter woods as silently as a flitting ghost.

There is no crackling of twigs or rustling of leaves to frighten off those hardy birds and beasts that, like himself, have the necessary guts to brave the rigors of the northern winter. Every bend in the trail opens up a new vista to the lover of the picturesque. Every turn, dip and rise in his path offers the skier a new problem to solve and a new sensation in its successful solution.

If you are hell-bent on thrills you can always find them in hilly country. Ski-running or sliding down a steep hill on skis is without a doubt one of the most exciting experiences a human being can undergo. It is a well-known fact that the sensation of speed increases the closer you are to the surface over which you are moving. An aviator at high altitude has little or no sensation of speed. The man on the boatdeck of a fast liner envies the surf rider and the passenger on the streamlined express train doesn't get half the kick out of a hundred miles an hour that the motorcyclist does. The skier, almost in actual contact with the snow, beats them all.

So much for the pleasure and excitement. How about exercise?

As soon as a skier puts on his skis and pushes off with his poles he becomes, to all intents and purposes, a quadruped. Going along the level the arms supply about half the propelling force. Up a moderate slope they do most of the work except under very favorable snow conditions when "backslip" is at its minimum. Up steeper slopes where it is necessary to "herringbone" the legs come again into their own although the arms still have plenty to do. Even in ski-running the arms are exerted very strenuously in maintaining the balance.

Crossing bumps and pitch holes on a fast descent where the skier alternately crouches low and straightens up again, the joints of the body get a limbering up that few other exercises will provide. But skiing isn't all a matter of tearing madly downhill. Every slide has its corresponding climb and until he masters the art of tireless climbing the skier gets plenty of exercise going up steep slopes.

Is skiing good for reducing? That depends entirely on you. By the time you have snatched an early breakfast, caught an early bus or train and climbed a few steep hills you will undoubtedly have taken off several pounds. But after you have swooped down a few good long hills with the crisp winter air blowing the cobwebs out of your brain and the foul city air out of your lungs you are likely to finish the day with such an appetite that you eat yourself all out of shape again. But after your general health has improved and common sense has triumphed over nervous greed you will at least have substituted hard muscle for flabby fat.

Age or previous experience have little or nothing to do with your ability to enjoy this sport. Active expert skiers range all the way from seven to seventy, and many of the older ones didn't go into the game till after they were forty or more.

Take skiing where you enjoy it most—on woodland paths, downhill, or off the jump. But taken any way, it lifts the heart and the spirit as high as the peaks around you.

So in the winter, in the one season when open-air exercise and sunshine are most needed, don't hibernate—ski! Don't be one of those people who confine their winter excursions into the great outdoors to brief dashes across sidewalks from overheated buildings to overheated cars. Get out in the snow—and ski!

BEFORE YOU GO SKIING

Practice these easy exercises while you brush your teeth, shave, talk on the phone, or drink a cocktail.

The place to start learning to ski is on the bedroom, bathroom or office floor, with a turn perhaps on the stairway. The place for those who ski to avoid wasting time getting broken in, or broken bones, is the same.

Clarence Streit, who devised these preseason ski exercises, wrote:

"My idea of the ideal ski exercise is that it should be clearly and effectively designed (a) to help directly one's skiing and (b) to be done while phoning, dictating, drinking a cocktail, enduring a bore, shaving, brushing the teeth, rubbing in the stuff alleged to defeat baldness, or something else. And I've got just such an exercise in my small collection.

"It's as simple as standing on one leg. In fact, that's it—just standing on one leg.

"My exercise No. 1 is The Stork: Stand on one leg (holding the other just off the floor) as long as you can, then shift over to the other. After two or three minutes of the Stork you will find the muscles and tendons around your ankle and knee beginning to get plenty of quiet exercise keeping you balanced on that leg."

Here are the other at-home ways to train your ski muscles:

Exercise No. 2 is the Cossack—the Stork made much more strenuous; it's not for babies. Stand on right foot and slowly squat on the right heel and then rise again, never letting the left leg touch the floor until standing again. In other words, lower and raise the whole weight of the body with one leg. Then repeat with the other. This builds powerful knees, ankles, and leg muscles while developing balance and habituating one to shifting the body's weight. It may prove too hard at first, but with practice and the help of the other exercises it will come.

When you can do it fairly easily, do the Cossack dance. That is, when squatting on the right heel, tap the floor with the extended left heel, bring it back under you and shift your weight to it while extending the right and tapping the floor with the extended right heel, then bringing it back and shifting your weight to it while extending the left, and so on. To develop the side muscles of the knee, sometimes extend the free foot sideways instead of front, tapping the floor on the right side with the right heel, and on the left with the left.

Downhill

3. Stand with both feet parallel, close together (to make balance harder and therefore improve it, toe of one foot at instep of other, heels on floor (low heels), arms down sides loose, body straight and loose. Keeping the trunk straight bend the knees as far as possible without raising the heels, straighten up, and repeat till tired or bored. To relieve monotony swing the knees to right or left when bending.

If you brush your teeth or shave or telephone while doing this, so much the better; it not only saves time but develops co-ordination. Practice shifting the weight with this by putting the weight sometimes as you bend mostly on right or left foot.

A variation is to stand straight and without bending try to strike the shoulder with the knee. But don't shave while doing this one!

Stem

4. Stand straight, pigeon-toed, and push the feet simultaneously a foot or two sideways while keeping the weight evenly distributed and heels and toes on the floor. Keep the knees as close together as possible while doing this. Bring the feet back to first position by the opposite pull and repeat, not ad nauseam. Vary this by shifting weight from one leg to the other when separated, and by keeping one foot straight and pushing out the other— a half stem. One can do an amusing dance with this exercise or combine it with brushing the hair.

Christie

5. The Whirl: Stand as in No. 3 with legs bent, but with trunk parallel to shins. Jump straight up and whirl in the air, attempting to go around as far as possible and light standing, balanced. Repeat, whirling in opposite direction. If you find you do better in one direction, whirl more in the other. If you can whirl round either way and light almost in your tracks

in good balance and can do this four or five times each way without tiring, you are in fair condition, and you will be able to whirl even more than once round. The Whirl develops and trains the up-swing and side-swing muscles of the knees and by exaggeration accustoms one to the basic Christie movements while at the same time developing the ankles, springiness, balance, and leg power. To develop side-swing do not jump up more than a few inches, for the higher you jump the less you whirl. To develop up-swing jump higher and whirl less.

6. The Christie: Stand as at the start of the Whirl, weight on advanced foot, straighten knees smartly and just as this movement lifts your weight slightly from the floor, whirl or skid round ninety degrees or more in the direction of the advanced foot, keeping both feet parallel and touching the floor. Repeat, starting with the opposite foot forward and turning in its direction. Try it with weight well forward and also toward heels.

To become more accustomed to very upsetting conditions in which the Christie must be done on skis—namely, a slope where one foot is higher than the other—practice this exercise on a stairway. Stand on two steps toward the edges with the foot on the lower step advanced, whirl 180 degrees on the lower foot, the upper foot landing on the step below the pivot foot. Repeat in opposite direction. One can go downstairs this way—if the family or neighbors permit.

BOATING

As Glen Perry put it in *Esquire,* "Yachting has a great effect on those who follow it. It demands knowledge, which can be acquired by practically anyone who wants to acquire it. It teaches self-reliance; it frequently demands nerve and cool, calculating courage; it makes necessary instant and correct decisions. It's good for a man's morale to get into a jam at sea and fight through it. It makes him wonder whether the boss is so tough after all. When you go to sea, you're on your own. There aren't any traffic cops to help you, and it's up to you whether you get home or not."

But that angle of it isn't what takes people into boating. It's the sheer joy of it, the sense of being independent and free to go where you choose, as you choose, under pleasant circumstances. It's . . . well, it's just that there's something about a boat that gets you.

BOAT? WHAT BOAT?

Thirty years ago the term "yachting" conveyed a Currier & Ives picture of white-flanneled, blue-jacketed gentlemen grouped picturesquely against an eye-filling background of dashing waves and white-winged yachts of liner-like proportions. It was then principally an activity for the wealthy few, and the public diffidently looked upon it as a sport as exclusive as polo or racquets.

Today all is changed, and with good reason. Yachting today is a sport for the masses, made possible by thousands of miles of ideal waterways, by the surprisingly moderate cost of boats and by the proportionately low cost of operation and upkeep. On our three seaboards, on our thousands of lakes and rivers, we find that bank presidents and butchers, family scions and the local milkman are all enthusiastically "messing about in boats." This is due in large part to the fact that it can be enjoyed, and actively participated in, by all members of the family. No less attractive is its endless variety including the sport of racing, the pleasure of cruising—of inshore and deep-sea fishing —to say nothing of the endless fun of operating one's "home afloat." Best of all, there is the knowledge that once aboard, you are king of all you survey; your ship is a self-contained entity, while stretching out before you is an endless and ever-changing horizon beckoning you on to new delights and surprises. Be your "yacht" a real deep-sea craft or a converted cockleshell, she's the darling of your eye—and you wouldn't trade her for all the cup defenders ever built!

Now that we have sold you on yachting as a major sport, let's presume that you are one of the many neophytes who have cast longing glances at every boat that you have seen, and that you are now ready—come what may —to take the plunge and to become a yachtsman yourself.

Before buying a boat, the first factor to be considered is—how much *can* you spend? Secondly—where are you going to use this boat? On a river, lake, or are you on the seaboard where your range of activity is practically unlimited? Thirdly—for what purpose do you wish to use it? For cruising, for day trips, or do you want to race? Fourthly—do you want a sail or power boat (or a sailboat which is equipped with an engine, which is commonly known as an "auxiliary")?

As to the first question: before parting with so much as a penny there are these simple truths which you must consider:

1. The financial axiom in boat buying is that "upkeep" is a more essential factor than "purchase price." You may have your eye on a sixty-foot cutter which is to all outward appearances a bargain, but have you thought to consider that her annual maintenance may easily exceed your initial investment?
2. Never so much as consider buying a secondhand boat without having it inspected by a reputable yacht broker or naval architect.

Know what you are buying, and if you don't, make a boon companion of someone who does!

3. Whereas it is often advisable for the tyro to begin with a second-hand boat, it is equally true that in the long run you will usually save money by buying a new one. Moreover, the financial depreciation of a yacht is far less than that of an automobile. A ten-year-old vessel, if she has been kept in good condition, can be resold for as much as fifty to sixty per cent of her original purchase price.

4. Don't make the common mistake of getting a boat too large for you to handle, especially if you are a beginner. If you do, she will be a millstone around your neck. Be content to start in a small way, and then let experience be your yardstick.

Question two is of equal importance. A sailboat is rarely practical on a river—that is, unless the river is large and the boat is small. River banks obstruct air currents, and the actual river current is often too much to contend with. However, this question is so tied up with all manner of local conditions that it can only be answered by a local authority. (The yachting fraternity literally breeds "local authorities," so you won't have any trouble on that score.) Go to the local boatyard, marine supply dealer or yacht club and weigh their advice carefully.

The answer to the third question also varies. A recent survey indicated that no less than 85 per cent of the yachtsmen contemplating new boats wanted them for cruising, and but 5 per cent of the balance were interested in mere day sailing (excluding those interested in day racing). You'll have much more fun if you cruise, even if your voyages cover only a few miles. If you want to race, make sure you have someone to race against! Inquire about and find out what are the most popular classes in your particular locality.

The pros and cons of the motorboat vs. the sailboat are endless. It is a question of local conditions and personal preference. There is nothing quite so exhilarating as sailing, and nothing as maddening as sailing under unfavorable conditions. The modern power boat is a miracle of compact efficiency. Equally, stock auxiliaries are superbly built, and today boast of luxuries unheard of a few years ago. Moreover, the prices of stock boats are about one-half those of similar craft custom built. A good point to remember is that the maintenance cost of a power boat is considerably less than that of an auxiliary of the same size. (The operating cost of a power boat increases in proportion to the size and speed of her engine and whether or not she is single or twin screw.)

The various types of sailing vessels are many, and to the landlubber the legion of classifications will seem almost incomprehensible. There are schooners and yawls, sloops and ketches, catboats (now rapidly disappearing) and cutters, and each one of these names signifies a different "rig" (the arrangement of the masts and sails). Their hulls differ according to the whim of the individual designer, and you will therefore find vessels both long and narrow, short and broad, deep draft or "skimming dishes"—or just plain nondescript and "tubby." But there are reasons for all these physical variations.

Motorboats are equally individual in both external and internal characteristics, and the individual variations of their hull form and cabin plan are endless. The advantages—or disadvantages—of all these differentiations enable you to pick and choose according to your individual likes and requirements.

Now let us assume that you have just purchased a bright and shiny boat, and while you are a devil on skis and championship material on the tennis court, there is no gainsaying that (where boats are concerned) you don't know the bow from the stern, or the port tack from a starboard channel buoy. You will find there are a hundred hands ready and willing to introduce you into the so-called mysteries of being an accomplished yachtsman. Your yachting friends will, for some reason known only to themselves, spend hours patiently showing you the preliminary "ins and outs." On the other hand, every boating center has a score of young boys who have apparently spent their waking hours in anything that will float and who will, for a mere pittance, act as your coach on your first experimental voyages. Many yacht clubs and yachting associations hire instructors for the express purpose of coming to your aid.

Inquiry will reveal yachting associations which give classes (gratis or for a small fee) in small-boat handling, piloting, seamanship, elementary piloting and navigation.

Government charts and publications of navigable waters provide endless cruising destinations. A number of the larger gas companies each year distribute thousands of cruising charts and guides. These same companies, through co-operation with their gas dealers at various ports, will hold or forward your mail, dispatch your laundry, order your groceries—and even provide you with a fresh-water shower. And it's all absolutely free! Moreover, if you are a member of an established yacht club, you are in turn a welcome visitor to other clubs along the way.

Unless you live on the water's edge, probably the local yacht club or municipal yacht basin will be your "marine garage." The dues of such organizations vary from a few dollars a month to a veritable king's ransom. But you can always find the club which fits both your requirements and your pocket-book.

There are a score of books and articles which deal with yachting and instruction, and their study will set you well ahead in your career as a shell-back. But observation and experience are the greatest teachers of all, and sharp eyes and a remembrance of your first mistakes will rapidly change you from an ignorant landlubber to a competent mariner. And don't be afraid to ask questions!

Little can be said for the man who complains, "My wife doesn't like the water." Nine times out of ten the fault is his own, for many men do not realize there is no fun in merely being a passenger. The oft-heard statement that "women have no place on a boat" is sheer rubbish. Let the little woman have her trick at the wheel, do her share of the work aboard ship, and she will take to it like a duck to water. For that matter, some of the finest racing sailors in the country are women (as a good many men regretfully admit).

The idea that a small boat is not safe for children is equally silly. The younger generation is a lot safer on the water than within striking distance of the average motorist. Teach them to swim, give them confidence in the ship and in themselves, and you will never have a moment's fear—except when you fall overboard yourself!

It all boils down to the simple fact that yachting knows neither sex nor age, and it really is the finest family sport ever invented.

If you live in the Middle West or on the North Atlantic seaboard, your boat must be hauled out of the water during the winter months to escape the rigors of wind, ice and snow. Boatyards range from waterfront junk heaps to models of efficient operation. They should be selected after much careful observation and comparison.

The growth of yachting areas in the United States is but another evidence of the rapidly increasing popularity of the sport. On every hand government, state and municipal agencies are rapidly increasing all manner of yachting facilities. Throughout the nation rivers and lakes have been dredged, channels and harbors improved. Buoys, beacons and lighthouses are now almost as numerous as road signs.

There you have it: a streamlined picture of the popular pastime of "messing about in boats." Few are those who, once they have been introduced to its countless attractions, have escaped its contagious fascination. For fun, for health, for a satisfying antidote for the miseries of the world, there is nothing quite like it.

What can you get from a motorboat cruise that you cannot get from a trip by land or air? Not speed, of course. But you can get a freer mobility, and more of certain kinds of comfort such as privacy and cleanliness and quiet; and sometimes economy; and you can get a new and different view of places and people—people met by water somehow are different from those met by land, and some say, easier and more likable. And above all, you can get freedom: freedom of living—to sleep, eat and dress as you choose—and freedom of movement—to stay forever or pick up and go whenever you want, unfettered by timetables or traffic lights or creeping processions of Sunday drivers.

You can get all these things, that is, unless you give them up for distance covered. You can get all this in a few miles of running provided you take a day to do it, and you cannot get more in eighty miles a day, and you'll get less if you make it 160.

You can shoot right down the middle of Chesapeake Bay, running day and night, and turn around at Norfolk and shoot back, and you will not have had as much out of it as if you had set forth to explore every little inlet, with a maximum daily run of six hours, and had never got beyond West River. There are exceptions, of course, dictated by local conditions, but in general the way to get the most comfort and pleasure and whatever else it is that makes for the fascination of cruising is to start reasonably early in the morning, head for a safe, comfortable anchorage that you can reach by early afternoon—stop sooner if you come to a likely spot—spend the rest of the day sleeping, eating, fishing, loafing and exploring the possibilities of the place afloat, aswim and ashore, and never to leave it for another until you have reasonably exhausted its possibilities. There is always a next time for the next place.

The pleasure to be had from a cruise depends, obviously, on the nature of the cruising ground, to a large extent. Items such as interest, scenery, climate, the prevalence of fogs, the complexities of tide and current, are highly important, of course, but in general the best waters for the kind of cruise we are talking about are those with many bays and inlets and few large cities— it is no fun to pitch at anchor in an open roadway, or pick your way through driftwood, tugs and ferryboats past the New York waterfront—waters such as Puget Sound, the upper Mississippi, Chesapeake Bay, the upper Hudson to the lakes and certain portions of Long Island Sound, the Great Lakes, the St. Lawrence and the Maine Coast. If your home port is in a region that suffers from lack of natural harbors, such as parts of the Great Lakes and

Pacific Coast, head for the nearest waters with islands or bays, reach them with the best speed consistent with comfort and safety, and do your easy cruising when you get there. Inland and coastal, there is plenty of cruising ground in all possible variety, and the limitations of your choice are solely those of inclination and the amount of time you have to spend.

Even if you cannot spare many days at a stretch you can often get in a good deal of cruising in fairly remote waters by adopting the week-end commuting method. A Philadelphian of our acquaintance managed to cover almost all of Chesapeake Bay by this scheme, leaving his boat wherever Sunday evening overtook him, going home by rail or motor, and returning to the boat on the following Friday. He spent a summer at this and then, being a real easy-cruiser, spent his three weeks' holiday in the fall loafing around two or three places that had struck his fancy as he passed them.

Your typical easy-cruiser is not such a hit-or-miss fellow as his goings and comings might indicate. His movements may seem a bit eccentric, but the chances are he has planned most of them well in advance. When he decides on an expedition to new waters he is likely to learn all about the region from books and any other sources he can find, and especially from brother cruisers who have been there, and then he notes on the chart, tentatively, his ports of call—places of interest ashore, pleasant anchorages, and a base depot or two for getting supplies and overhauling. Then he traces his general route, arranging, where it is possible, to come back by a course different from that on which he went out—going out along one shore of Long Island Sound, for example, and coming back along the other. Where no circular route is possible he may step off distances on his chart and plan his cruise—still tentatively—by the skip-stop method, stopping at the odd-numbered points on the way out and the even-numbered on the way back.

He makes no rigid schedule, though—that would be a most frightful violation of the spirit of the easy cruise—and he will probably be disappointed if even his sketchy program isn't thrown out of kilter by pleasant surprises and new whims. He will stick to it as long as it serves, but will ask his way, too, as he goes, and before the voyage is over he may have discarded it altogether. And most important of all, while he may bone up in this way on an extensive tour, he is prepared to feel content if he accomplishes only a small part of it—to spend as much time as he likes on the early stages, if they prove enjoyable, and let the rest of the cruise go hang.

He plans short days' runs, of course. He intends, in general, to cast anchor long before dusk, but otherwise to end his run at such times as local conditions indicate. He makes a note to reach Block Island, for example, when the tide that day is right for fishing, to make Chestertown with time enough to see the Colonial brick houses and still have a swim before dinner. He hopes his cruising ground will prove so interesting that he will spend a lot of time ashore just nosing around. He learns what he can, in advance, of local weather conditions—such as that on most parts of Chesapeake Bay there is a brief squall every afternoon in the summer—and he caters to them: he isn't playing Hardy Norseman, you know. He intends to do most of his running by day, but he gives himself leave, in advance, to heave up the hook whenever the moon shows full and free.

The most nearly ideal waters in the world might as well be Niagara Falls, so far as the easy cruise is concerned, in the wrong kind of boat, and it is one of the larger mysteries of all time, to the experienced easy-cruiser, how many wrong kinds of boat there can be—for him. One will have too much open cockpit for his climate, another too little for fishing, the engine will be hard to get at in a third, still another handles badly, and so on *ad infinitum*—and besides all this, there are a hundred delicate questions of construction and power. A landlubber shopping for his first boat is all too easily pleased, but the longer he sails the more choosy he becomes.

Then what is the right kind of boat for your easy-cruiser? The best he can get, of course—the best for his particular needs and for the waters where he is to cruise. But he cannot tell what that best is until he has crept up on it, so to speak. He could get demonstration rides on the various stock models and learn a good deal, of course, or if he can draw on some fund of skill with hulls and motors he may find some used custom job that is exactly the thing. But if, though he is an out-and-out beginner, he has it in him to become an expert, he is quite likely to join a yacht club before he selects a boat. (It would be interesting to know, incidentally, how many members of yacht clubs never do own a boat!) There is nothing easier to get than rides on fellow members' boats and by the time your beginner has sailed in a dozen varieties of craft he should come pretty close to knowing what he wants for himself.

He will probably have revised downward his notions as to size, for example. Unless he's going in for the de luxe sort of thing—seventy-five-footers, stewards, all that—he will have found out that one paid hand in a smaller boat spoils the fun, and that a forty-footer is about as big a boat as he can take care of comfortably, single-handed. He will have come to appreciate the importance of the most worrisome thing in motorboating, the fire hazard, and he will have made up his mind whether a Diesel engine, with its almost complete lack of that hazard, is worth to him the comparatively high initial cost.

He will have got over the "roughing it" idea, too. It sounded grand, at first, but as he went along he found that he wanted all the comfort he could get, and he began to be critical of such details as bunks, galleys and interior architecture. He learned what kind of stove and what kind of cooking fuel served him best, whether he liked his bridge deck forward or amidships, and he gained decided ideas as to whether he wanted several small cabins or fewer larger ones. The chances are that here, too, he revised his first notions downward. His first mental pictures of cruising probably took in a large, jolly company of family and friends; that part of the picture grew dim with time. Crowding, he saw, was the curse of cruising—the great mistake as to space comfort and temper comfort. It is amazing how much six people can get in each other's way, after a couple of days, on even a thirty-eight-footer, and how the oldest acquaintances reveal hitherto unnoticed mannerisms of the most intolerable sort. So your easy-cruiser rarely thinks of taking more than three other people—and them hand-picked—in a boat that sleeps six, if he is to be out for more than a week end.

He has learned all this, he has got his boat, and he's off. When, after a night or two, he has slept himself out, he's up with the dawn, surprising himself, perhaps, but finding the nights better for sleeping than for bridge, making a good breakfast, if he is to be running at midday, so that a cold lunch will do then, stopping ashore for frequent meals but keeping a full larder aboard so that he can be independent of the land. He's off on a three-hundred-mile course and if it comes up to expectations he'll not cover a third of it.

MEETING NATURE HALFWAY (OR MORE)

Hiking

Going for a walk may not sound like much sport, nor exercise, either, but it *can* be. It can be exciting, invigorating, refreshing, everything the doctor ordered and the city-jaded spirit hoped. Hike in a group, as a member of one of the nation's countless walking clubs, or hike on your own. But rediscover your legs and you'll discover a sport that is a hobby and vice versa. Walking has everything—except speed.

You may be surprised to know that there are now no less than nine hundred miles of mapped trails in Glacier National Park alone—or that you can hike from Maine to Georgia along the backbone of the Appalachians under the guidance of the famous "AT" blaze mark—or that New York State officially publishes a free, thirty-two-page pamphlet on *Catskill Trails,* or *Lake Placid Trails* or *Trails to Marcy*—or that established hiking routes, such as the 250-mile Long Trail through the wild Vermont hills, are so adequately spotted with lodges or shacks that you are sure every night of having at least a bunk mattressed with fragrant pine boughs under you and a solid roof over you if you're on a lengthy trip.

How fast will you walk these trails? Many people feel that a regular pace of four miles an hour on the level is a good thing to shoot at. The truth is, you've got to be in good condition and accustomed to walking in order to maintain that pace for much more than a single hour. Three m.p.h., is more comfortable and rational for general use, and even that will be too fast if you are a nature lover who likes to stop and look at things.

How far in a day? You can figure that for extended trips, hill and dale, twenty to twenty-five miles a day with a twelve-pound pack is good enough and not unpleasant when you're in condition. But the beginner who does twenty-five miles once a week will be doing plenty. In hilly country with a mixed crowd, fifteen miles with packs will prove a good day's work.

Hills, however, knock all calculations askew, and the flat-country walker who brings his past performance records into the mountains—even our sissy Eastern mountains—is doomed to disappointment. One mile an hour there is frequently good time when the trails climb, and if the grade is steep and rough, you'll be mighty proud to do a thousand to fifteen hundred feet every sixty minutes.

This, of course, means trail hiking, not open rock work which is slow and punishing. And even on the trail, comparative times mean little unless you know the terrain.

The best advice anybody can give the novice is, take it easy. Only the suckers start off the season with a ten-mile jaunt—and they don't do any more jaunting for some days thereafter. Walking seems easy because we all do a little of it every day. But when you begin knocking off mile after mile, that's a horse of another color—and you seldom see the real color until tomorrow.

This is doubly true where people who have spent the past fifty weeks in an office chair suddenly start to compress a month of climbing into a two-week vacation. Steep trails are mighty tough on the hearts of the inexperienced, and no one knows how much damage has been done to untrained hikers who were ashamed to admit exhaustion until they were ready to drop.

Some of the other mistakes beginners make concern clothing—especially footwear. The pros and cons of this topic would fill a book, and when you consider the range from the featherweight Indian moccasin to a pair of seven-pound alpine boots, each with its proper function, you can understand why. This, however, doesn't simplify matters any when you get into a sporting goods store and a salesman babbles glibly about "molded-sole hunting boots," "Maine guide shoes," "woods boots," "mountain climber's shoes," and what not.

Whichever you decide on, keep two things in mind. First of all, never go on a hike with new shoes that aren't thoroughly broken in by considerable wear around the house, on short walks, etc. Second, buy walking shoes of a larger size than street shoes and have them fitted over the kind of socks you'll wear. Hiking socks should be woolen and thick: they will influence the size shoe you need.

A hiking shoe should be snug in the heel; easy across the ball of the foot; and very roomy in the toes, especially if you walk in hilly country where the downhill drill kills the babies with short shoes. But you can't gauge these three factors in silk socks—as so many greenhorns try to do.

The bag? Yes, by all means carry a bag—a backpack, not a valise!—if you start on any hike that promises to be longer than five blocks. Don't fall for one of those single-strap side bags because they look light: they hold next to nothing and they drive you nuts in three miles. If you don't need much capacity, you can do with a small rucksack or knapsack; but in any case get the type which has two broad shoulder straps and carries on the back with the load weight suspended from the *center of the top.*

In packs, of course, you'll find as much variety as there is in footwear, each with its loyal adherents. The Adirondack guide swears by the pack basket, while the northern Canadian prefers the tumpline or head-strap pack: the Nessmuk pack is quite different from the Swiss rucksack, and so it goes. When all is said and done, a Boy Scout haversack suffices for most of us unless there are prospects of doing a great deal of hiking with fair loads. In which case nothing, in my opinion, compares with the expensive Norwegian or "Bergans Meis" packs with their perfect balance through a one-point top hanging and their even distribution of weight by means of a light, tubular steel frame and back bow which rests just above the hips. Apart from spreading the weight, this frame also keeps the pack away from your back by the width of a hand, allowing needed ventilation to cool you. And a bellyband which fastens in front also keeps the load from swinging around under your chin every time you bend over.

The principal trouble with many ordinary packs on the market (aside from the fact that they aren't hung so they can ride on your back instead of rolling all over) is the fact that the straps are so narrow or tight that they cut into the shoulders. Other things being equal, take the broadest web strap you can get.

Whatever kind of bag you pick, however, you will cram too much duffel into it at first and then gradually taper off to a sensible load as time goes on. It is perfectly possible today to pack a single tent, sleeping bag, cooking utensils, toilet articles and necessary extra apparel in less than twenty pounds, so when you start collecting stuff for an afternoon's jaunt, bear that in mind! Twelve pounds is enough for anybody to carry who isn't in the Army.

The mention of back packs, incidentally, brings up the point that the poncho is a much more satisfactory bad-weather garment than the raincoat. Among other things, you can wear it on top of a pack if that should be necessary.

As for the contents of a pack, it is silly for one man to try to tell another what to put in, yet a few sundry items merit mention because most novices overlook them. Most beginners, for instance, can well afford to carry a small can of "baby talc," especially if they're wearing new clothing or shoes which may cause trouble. A sheet or strip of chiropodist's moleskin may also prove a lifesaver when shoes *begin to rub*. But don't ever put anything like that on top of a blister. The best blister treatment is to puncture it with a clean needle, cover it with saturated gauze, and fasten that to the healthy skin with adhesive. A little bicarbonate of soda in water makes a good antiseptic solution for the gauze—and when a party of any size goes on the trail, one of them should carry a small, ten-cent box of bicarb. Not only is it the best tooth powder made, but it also serves as a mouth wash, indigestion remedy, burn poultice, antiseptic wash for cuts, scratches, insect bites, or what have you?

Other items commonly forgotten are: extra matches in a waterproof container; a change of socks; a flashlight; some toilet paper, even for a half-day hike, an extra pair of eyeglasses if you normally wear them, because they're broken mighty easily in the woods.

Naturally, we're talking about one-day tramps, now; not overnight trips or long tours. When you get into the realm of the latter, there's nothing like the good old Colorado system of pack trains which leaves all your unencumbered energies for panting!

Under the general heading, "Miscellaneous," sundry recommendations come to mind, to wit:

When climbing it is good policy to rest two minutes in every twenty. On level ground many hikers stop five minutes every hour.

In the woods never step on any obstruction you can step over. And don't walk so close together that the fellow in front slaps your face with every tree branch. It's your business to stay back, not his business to hold each twig for you.

In a party keep an eye on the weakest because tired novices are often too proud to acknowledge fatigue. When a hiker starts "tripping over shadows," he's tired no matter what he says.

In mountain hiking it pays to dress for both July and January—wool does it.

It is customary to figure on a one degree drop in temperature for every three hundred feet of elevation and, besides that, you've got unbroken wind on the summit. Indeed, it should be a rule for beginners never to go above the timber line unless they're with somebody who's had experience. Every once in a while, you know, some hiker dies on Mount Washington in the confusion of an August snowstorm, so it pays not to be too rash.

The most efficient way to walk is pigeon-toed. On level walks a free arm movement helps your speed. Likewise, locking the knee firmly as the rear foot comes off the ground gives so much spring that it is difficult to walk slowly in this fashion.

This, of course, applies to walking rather than hiking over rough ground, but if you're one of the millions who seldom do much else but the former, try this system of locking the knee (with a smooth action, not wooden-legged) and see how much more efficient it is. You'll be stiff at first on the day following a mile of it, but that very fact indicates that you're getting something out of walking that you never got before.

When you begin to get tired, whistle march tunes. It's an amazing help.

And remember, finally, that the second or third mile are the toughest—and that after the fifth, there's nothing to it!

As for where to walk and when, you can get plenty of information from your local newspaper, from Chambers of Commerce, from State Conservation Departments nearly everywhere. Some of these publish maps especially for hikers, but if you aren't familiar with the Federal geological survey maps, don't fail to write to Washington for them. These maps come on sheets about sixteen by twenty inches representing about 215 square miles in area. The usual scale is about one mile to the inch and these topographic maps shown every detail which is of importance to hikers: marsh land, springs, sand, falls or rapids, cliffs, depressions, etc. By means of brown contour lines—each line indicating an elevation of twenty feet unless otherwise indicated—the hiker can tell exactly what kind of terrain is ahead of him; how far he is from habitation or water; how high the trail climbs and how steep the grade is at any point.

A state is divided into quadrangles (there are 294 separate maps for New York State, for instance), so the thing to do is to write the U.S. Geological

Survey, Washington, D. C., for the index map covering your particular state and, from that guide, order the specific quadrangles you may need.

Do this, in fact, whether you plan to do much walking or not. For the odds are ten to one that when you begin poring over this fascinating diagram, so different from the motoring maps we've grown accustomed to, the lure of those contour lines will get into your blood.

The first symptom is the good old itching foot followed by a long vacant stare out of the window which carries your eye far beyond that drab house across the street and into the distant rolling hills where flinty pavements become moss-padded paths—and the turmoil of a pell-mell civilization subsides into the whispering of the trees—and the sweet, fresh breeze from God's heaven blows the cobwebs from your brain and the unpaid bills from your conscience!

You may even decide to try the Pacific Crest Trailway—a mixture of heaven and hell, a tonic for the spirit, a threat of death and a challenge that only the bravest can fully answer. It is a wilderness pathway from Canada to Mexico, 2,156 miles of the toughest terrain and most magnificent scenery in America. It leads across flowered alpine meadows, winds through dim and dusky forests, and curls along the lips of crags and precipices up into a frosty other world where Nature throws the book at you. It presents every imaginable hiking thrill from long, gentle slopes to rough and rocky wilderness. But the average explorer can travel the whole trail without undue danger or hardship if he chooses not to attempt the difficult peaks. Many men are devoting all their summer vacations to the project of hiking the whole distance from Canada to Mexico, piece by piece, picking up the trail each year at the approximate spot they left off the year before.

The novice usually endures considerable discomfort before he learns the secret of hiking—how to lean forward so the weight of his pack is high on his shoulders and not pulling at his arms, how to open his bed only when he is ready for it and thereby keep out snakes and animals, and how to rest standing up to avoid the stiff muscles he gets when he lies down for even a few minutes. The temptation to stretch out for a while to regain strength is tremendous, but experienced hikers have found that in high altitudes and on rough terrain reclining tightens the muscles so that more climbing right away is painful if not impossible. He also learns how to gauge his ascents to be off the peaks by noon and thereby avoid serious storms, and how to pitch camp at the foot of hard climbs so that he can make it fresh in the morning.

At the same time he is learning these things, he is learning others perhaps more important. He is discovering legs and lungs and an appreciative peace of mind that he may have all but lost in the daily routine of his life in town.

In the freer, inspiring air of the mountains, he realizes they are still the most impressive things on earth. And in the awesome majesty of the mountains just before sunrise, when all is silent and cold and the huge forms loom through the ghostly dimness, he may have a spiritual awakening that no church could give him.

GOING UP?

No one but a goof climbs mountains, you say? Maybe so. But after you've leaned back on your ice-ax and swooped in a flashing glissade down some tilting snow field; or after you've wriggled up a narrow chimney by bracing your knees on one side and your back on the other with nothing but empty space hanging down beneath your tail; then you begin to feel that there's something to it after all. The solid meat of unrivaled exercise forms one basic ingredient. Word-beggaring scenery furnishes another. Throw in the spice of adventure and you have the makings of a sporting dish fit for any king.

In spite of all this, mountain climbing in America is surprisingly neglected.

There is no reason why it should be, for we have right in our own back yard a goodly number of pinnacles which compare favorably to the much-advertised Alps. The most fertile field, naturally, is in the Rockies: more specifically, in Glacier National Park; in Wyoming's incredibly rugged Wind River Range and Grand Tetons; in Colorado's Elk Mountains, convulsed Needles, and magnificent San Juans. Too, there are the back regions of the California Sierras, notably the Palisade section, and the sweeping glaciers of Mount Ranier and Mount Hood.

Here we sit, then, next door to several hundred square miles of mountain country jammed to the eyebrows with good climbs. The matter of location settled, the only thing remaining is to pick out a summit and go up it. And here is where the implements of the mountain climber's calling come in mighty handy.

We'll assume you've already obtained a staunch pair of comfortable shoes (not knee boots, which cramp leg action) and that their extra thickness of sole bristles with Swiss mountaineering hobs and edging nails. At first sight they look as though packing them around would wear out a circus strong man, but before you're safely back in camp you'll be plenty thankful for all this solid leather and hardware which rests between you and the ground. The splintered acres of sharp, flinty rock that girdle every peak will tear ordinary shoes and ordinary hobs to mincemeat. Except for occasional tough going on a smooth cliff, tennis or other rubber-soled shoes are worse than useless. They'll shred into nothing before you are well started. All such abuse to your pedal extremities is to be studiously avoided. A mountaineer's feet are, at all times, his main asset.

Of mechanical aids, the most valuable is the rope. It serves a variety of purposes, all designed to help the climber keep from breaking his neck. And—as you value the skin on your shoulder and in your crotch—get a soft one! A hard twist rope will cause more agony than ever did Penitentes' hair shirt.

It is generally advisable to rope up as soon as the going becomes difficult. When tying yourself in, use a butterfly or bowline knot—never a slip knot. Only one person moves on the rope at a time. The others, before or behind him, keep the rope taut but not too tight to allow ample freedom of motion. Here is where the process known as belaying comes into play. The duty of the stationary members, obviously, is to check any incipient fall. Equally apparent is the necessity of a solid standing place and a firm hold on the rope. You get this sometimes by looping it over a convenient rock; or, rocks failing, over your shoulders or knees—any way so that your arms won't have to take the whole shock of a falling body; for, unless you have the physique of a Londos you'll never in the world be able to hold a hurtling 175 pounds of man with your unbraced hands.

Naturally, if your grip isn't good and your balance isn't solid, you'll be jerked from your perch, and in turn you'll jerk the next fellow from his. Whereupon the rope suddenly switches from a life belt to a suicide pact. Falls are rare, but they do happen sometimes. Inasmuch as you can never be certain when your comrade may slip, it is wise to play safe at all times and be sure that you take up a belaying position you *know* is substantial.

Relying on the rope while climbing is Cardinal Sin Number One in the mountaineer's book of ethics. You must go ahead as if it weren't there, never putting so much as a fraction of an ounce of your weight upon it. Its purpose is that of a safety device and nothing more.

Yet it is a marvelous thing what this hempen strand does for one. You know the dangers of a fatal slip are reduced to a minimum.

The psychological effect is immediate. Confidence leaps back full-fledged. With a rope around your middle you can climb places you wouldn't even dream of tackling without one and still not so much as lay a finger on it for support.

It is in descending that the rope serves its most useful function. As every boy knows, it is quite possible to get up a place then not be able to get back down unaided. You use the rope for this. It is convenient. It is speedy. And it packs with it a thrill no roller coaster in the country can equal.

It is called rappeling. You find the middle of the rope, loop this over a projecting rock (or *piton*), and drop the two ends over the cliff's edge. You straddle the rope, facing inward, pull it diagonally across your back, over your shoulder, across your chest and out behind.

Now for the fun. Fall backward into space. You won't go far—just far enough to catch your breath in a wad in your throat. Your hand on the rope which plays out behind and beneath you acts as a brake; the friction of the rope between your legs and across your shoulders keeps you from gathering too much speed. (Catch on why you want a soft rope?) You brace your legs against the cliff to keep from spinning around like a top. The nearer you come to a right angle position with its face, the better luck you'll have.

Then just drop . . . down . . . down . . . as fast as you care to let yourself go. In a few minutes you'll be at the bottom of a precipice it took you hours to climb. And, unless you foolishly let go of the rope with both hands you'll be there sound of wind and limb and eager to try it again.

Next to the rope the ice-ax is the most stable part of the mountaineer's equipment. A handy little thing it is, too. It's a staff about hip-high with a steel point on the bottom. The business part consists of a double head, one end of which is a long, stout point; the other presents a broad cutting surface, adz-shaped. It is indispensable for chopping steps in steep glaciers or in the ice tongues which lick up the couloirs.

The ice-ax also serves as an aid to glissading, as sheer and swooping a form of excitement as can be found—skiing possibly excepted. This is sliding on your feet down a snow field. You use the ax as brake and rudder by dragging it in the snow, very necessary where the course is littered with crevasses and boulders. On long, unbroken slopes it is possible to get in some tremendous runs.

And that's about all there is to ordinary climbing.

Practice is the keynote of mountain craft. A gradual progression from difficulty to difficulty gives you the *feel* of the thing, just as continual work with a horse gives you that delicate sense of balance so necessary for rough riding.

The beautiful part of it is that you don't need a towering peak to become a proficient scrambler.

The New England climbers have the right idea. Deprived of lofty mountains, they utilize the next best things. On Sunday mornings they throng to stone quarries, to seaside cliffs, to river bluffs—to anything just so it is rocky and perpendicular. They carefully select the worst-looking spot they can find and then go up, using the full regalia of the mountaineer on the way. As a result they learn to the fine point of exactness all those details of cliff scaling so dear to the heart of a technical climber.

This is *not* mountain climbing, however. In the first place any peak, no matter how softly rounded, presents problems all its very own, problems no Palisade on the Hudson can begin to touch. Foremost of these is the factor of altitude, a thing which will wreak havoc with sea-level lungs, and which, if you try too violent exercise without first becoming acclimated, will make your sweat taste of every cigarette and cocktail you've inhaled for six weeks previous. That leg which was so steady at four hundred feet will palpitate in the most extraordinary manner at fourteen thousand.

Despite the fact that the possibility of tragedy abounds on every summit, still mountaineering is not dangerous except as the climber himself makes it so. The majority of deaths arise not from the sport *per se* but from the nature of those who attempt it. Mountaineering's sometimes thin margin of safety allows of neither carelessness nor inexperience.

If, however, you stick to elements within your control, you'll find all the adventure, exercise, and scenery you want. If your sense of balance is something beside a part of your ear and if you *always* give the mountain credit for being a worthy opponent, then there'll be no disasters to send your relatives into a dither of horror. In the meantime common sense will soon enough teach you to test holds for solidity and whether or not it is safe to step onto any particular spot. This much done, technical skill follows as a matter of course.

And if you don't have common sense it won't make any difference how technically correct your climbing is. As a matter of fact you'll probably end up being run over by a streetcar. So you might as well go fall off a mountain and have some fun while you're doing it.

CAMPING IN THE OPEN

All primitive people are at home outdoors, and occasionally a civilized man is able to master the art, too. He cuts his camping equipment down to essentials, and thus accomplishes what going outdoors is supposed to accomplish: he really gets back to the simple, to the primitive, really leads a life unburdened by the care and worry and constant friction of *things*.

A few things are necessary—something to sleep on or under, an extra pair of socks, a knife, a cup, a light hatchet, a waterproof match safe. A light batteryless flashlight comes in mighty handy on a dark trail. A miniature first-aid kit is a comfort.

But there is more than mere comfort in this business of going as light as possible, out into the woods. There is something wonderful about it; something which you really must experience to understand. Maybe no one else can give you an inkling of what it is. The nearest idea is to describe it as a feeling of release, of utter freedom which comes when you at last stand rid of the shackles of civilization, of the constraining influence of things, and get close, really close, to Nature.

"Meeting Nature Halfway" we called this chapter. Robert Ruark went halfway around the world to meet her, and for him the trip was necessary, but let's hope you can find her closer to home. Look, listen, *feel,* and maybe she'll tell you something like this. Mr. Ruark:

It was about 5:15 p.m., 108 miles northeast of Oran, I remember, when the starboard gunners shouted, "Torpedo off the bow!" The helmsman tried to swing her so the thing would run parallel to us, but the old bucket was bottom-heavy with about nine thousand tons of high explosive and she was sluggish as a sleepy sloth. Whatever it was took a long time coming, but not long enough to dodge it. As I recall, I didn't pray, even though I had seen that afternoon, and on other days, what happens to a ship that gets smacked with a crawful of high ex. I felt a vague regret over the fact that getting blown up at the age of twenty-seven left a lot of pleasant things undone, and that was about all. Whatever it was hit us with a dreadful crash. The deck plates popped and spouted flame. The ship took a list, and was knocked heavily off her course. The feeling then was impatience that she didn't blow and get it over with. But no last-minute consignments of soul, no death-brink stammers of apology for what had been a short but gaudy life amongst the shattered Commandments. She didn't blow. And I uttered no prayer of thankfulness. I just figured that if there wasn't enough sincerity in me to pray ahead of it, there wasn't much point in praying behind it. The Lord and I did little business together in those days. It was more or less as if we had been introduced by the wrong folks.

If we can flash forward about nine years, now, I will tell you about a wordless prayer I said. I said it through my pores, sitting in a grove of trees in Tanganyika, East Africa, hard by a crocodile-infested river called the Little Ruaha. There wasn't anybody around at the time but the Lord and me and some wild animals. I didn't make any sort of formal speech out of it. Just told Him thank You very kindly for not blowing up the ship that day in the Mediterranean, and for letting me live till this day. It was a little late coming, this thank-you note, but I never meant anything more vehemently. And so far as formal religion goes I am a very irreligious fellow, who smokes, swears, drinks whisky, ogles girls and at that very moment was paradoxically interested in killing things.

I was very grateful to be alive, at that moment, for I was alone in the nearest thing to the Garden of Eden I ever expect to see. We had stumbled, while on safari, onto a piece of land which had largely been untrammeled by human feet, and uncontaminated by human presence. The exact location remains a secret. The place was too good for man to louse up. Its keynote was perfect peace.

We were out after kudu—greater kudu—one of the more elusive and possibly the most beautiful of all African game. He is as big as a horse, and as dainty as his tiny cousin, the dik-dik. He has enormous backswept upcurling horns that completely spiral twice, ending four or five feet from his skull in shining ivory tips. His coat is delicate gray, barred in white, and there is a chevron on his nose, and his heavy neck wears a long dark mane. Also he is ordinarily twice as wild as any other animal, save possibly the bongo. A man is lucky to see one kudu in many months of hunting.

Here the kudu were comparatively as tame as the little Thomson gazelle. I suppose we saw sixty or more in two weeks, and might have shot twenty if we counted the immature bulls. The cows were as tame as domestic cattle, nearly. I shot one kudu bull, because I wanted the trophy badly. The rest of the time we just looked around.

We marveled. Here was country as the first man saw it. We were camped on the river's edge, beneath a vast grove of acacias. It was like living in a natural cathedral, to look upward in the cool, created by the flat tops of the giant trees, with the sun dappling here and there to remove the dank darkness of moist forests. It reminded you of sun rays streaming in through the stained glass of a church window. The straw beneath the trees had been trampled flat by all the generations of elephants since the first elephant. The silence was unshattered by traffic sounds, by the squawk of radios, by the presence of people. All the noises were animal noises: The elephants bugled and crashed in the bush across the little river. The hippos grunted and the lions roared. The ordinarily elusive leopards came to within fifty yards of the camp, and coughed from curiosity. The hyenas came to call and lounged around the tents like dogs. Even the baboons, usually shy, trotted through the camp as if they'd paid taxes on it.

The eland is a timid antelope, a giant creature who'll weigh up to two thousand pounds, and who almost never stops moving. He is as spooky as a banshee, and unless you chase him on the plains in a car, a couple thousand yards away is as close as you're apt to get. Here the eland came in herds, walking inquiringly toward you. The same applied to the big Cape Buffalo, who ordinarily snatch one whiff of man-scent and shove off. The buffalo walked up to us here, their noses stretched and their eyes placid and unafraid. We watched one herd of a hundred or so for half an hour, and finally shooed them into the bush.

The impala, lovely, golden antelope with delicate, lyrelike horns, are usually pretty cheeky little cusses, but here they were downright presumptuous. As we drove along the trails in the jeep, we would have to stop the car and drive them off the path. They leaped high above the earth for sheer fun, not from fear, and one little joker actually jumped completely over the car—just to see if he could, I suppose.

Even the crocodiles seemed unafraid. They slept quietly on the banks, and didn't bother to slide into the water at our approach. The guinea fowl, usually scary birds, were as tame as domesticated chicken. We must have seen at least three thousand one morning, and they neither flew nor ran to the nearest exit. They walked with dignity.

This place had been seen only by one other safari, and was not despoiled by natives. The locals lived eighteen hard miles away, and they were not a tribe of hunters. They grew crops and grazed cattle, and robbed wild beehives for honey, and generally did not even tote the customary spear, which is as much a part of native equipment as the umbrella is to the Londoner. One grizzled grandsire, eighteen miles away on the Big Ruaha, told us solemnly that he had lived there all his life and had never seen a kudu. We saw fourteen that day.

You felt that here was a capsuling of creation, unsoiled, unspoiled, untouched by greed or selfishness or cruelty or suspicion. The white hunter, Harry Selby, whose life has been spent among animals, out of doors, gasped continually at the confidence and trust displayed by the profusions of game. We didn't want to shoot; we didn't even want to talk loud. Here you could see tangible peace, here you could see the hand of God as He possibly intended things to be. We left the place largely as we found it. We felt unworthy of the clean, soft blue sky, of the animals and birds and trees.

It was not until we found this camp that I became aware of what had happened to me in Africa. It had been happening daily, but my perceptions had been so blunted by civilized living that I had somewhere lost an appreciation of simplicity, had dulled my sensitivity by a glut of sensation and the rush of modern existence. All of a sudden I was seeing skies and noticing mountains and appreciating animals and cataloguing the flowers that dot the yellowed, grassy plains of Africa. I was tabulating bird calls and marveling over the sheer drop of the Rift and feeling *good*. I was conscious of the taste of food and the sharp impact of whisky on a tired man, and the warmth of water in the canvas bathtub, and the wonder of dreamless sleep. I was getting up before dawn and loving it. I was desperately anxious to win the approval of the blacks who made up my safari—me who never gave much of a damn about presidents and kings. I was feeling *kind*, and acutely alive, and very conscious of sun and moon, sky and breeze and hot and cold.

This has to be a paradox, because my primary business in Africa was killing. I was there to shoot. And I shot. I shot lions and a leopard and buffalo and all the edible antelopes and all the good trophies I could rustle up. But I never shot needlessly and I never killed anything for the sake of seeing it die. We killed for good trophies, and we killed to feed sixteen hungry people. Killing does not seem wrong in Africa, because the entire scheme of living is based on death. The death of one thing complements the life of another thing. The African economy is erected on violence, and so there is no guilt to shooting a zebra that the lions will have tomorrow, or a lion that will eventually be a hyena's breakfast when he is too old to defend himself against an ignoble enemy.

This is a hell of a way to write, for a professional cynic, but you see I'm not really cynical any more. What has wrapped us all in a protective armor, an insulation against honest stimulation, has been an artificiality of living that contrived civilization has thrust upon us to the detriment of decency.

Things are very simple in the African veldt. You is or you ain't. You are a courageous man or you are a coward, and it takes a very short time to decide, and for everyone you know to detect it. You can learn more about people in three days on safari than you might run down in a lifetime of polite association under "civilized" circumstances. That is why very few foreign visitors are speaking to each other when they finish a long trip into the bush.

There is no room for selfishness. A safari is as intricate as a watch. It is pared down to the essentials of good living—which is to say food, transportation, cleanness, self-protection and relaxation, or fun. It has a heavy quotient of hard work, in which everyone has a share. It is like a ship, on a long cruise, in that respect. There is a thing for every man to do, and if he fouls out on his duty the failure affects everybody, to everybody's hurt. A sloppy gunbearer, who lags behind, can get you killed. Indecision on your part or the part of any vital member of your party can get you killed. Cowardice can get you killed. Lack of caution can get you killed. You shake your shoes each morning on the off chance a scorpion has nested in your boot. . . .

When you live among phonies long enough, when your life is a vast and complicated cocktail party of communication, pose, frustration, confusion, pressure, refinement and threat of indistinct doom, you can forget that the human body is a very simple organism with very simple demands. It does not take much to amuse a monkey, but we have seemingly overendowed ourselves with playthings, with extraneous fripperies we call necessities, with gimmicks, gadgets, gizmos and distractions that completely obscure the basic truth that a night's sleep, a day's work, a full belly and a healthy elimination is about all a human organism needs for satisfactory existence. The refinements come later, of themselves.

I find today, to my dismay, that while I live in New York in an approximate palace—freshly decorated, at God knows what cost in blood, sweat and money—I was happier in a tent. It kept the rain off me, needed no lease, was easily movable and did not require air-conditioning. The bed was a cot, and tired as I was nightly it could have been upholstered in spikes without disturbing my rest.

Now I'm back on my old routine of toying with a chop, and spending eight thousand dollars for a dinner I don't want, but I don't like it. I recall a fellow by the same name who used to pick up a whole guinea fowl and devour it with great enthusiasm, and who never cared too much whether the tommy chops had been cooked sufficiently or not. Cold spaghetti tastes great out of a can. Beer is never better than when warmed by the sun, due to no refrigeration. I read a lot of mishmash about diet—in the words of my friend Selby, the hunter: *Gimme meat, and skip the extras.* In Tanganyika

I ate like a starved cannibal, and lost weight. There I was eating to live—not to sell books, not to be entrancing, not to be stylish. I was eating because I was hungry, and was burning up enough of what I ate to keep me thin enough to climb a mountain or crawl through a swamp.

You realize that a man who earns a living with two fingers on a typewriter has always accepted the A & P, the local supermarket, the utilities company, the waterworks, the central heating and the highway department as part of his life. All of a sudden, save for a few conveniences, I was right back with the early man.

If we wanted light we either built a fire or turned on a very primitive lamp. Fire we always needed, if only to fend the hyenas off tomorrow's dinner, and always in the starkly chill nights to keep from freezing. So we had to pitch camp where dry wood was. And close to where water was. And where dry wood was, and water was, and food was, you had to travel. In the absence of a highway department you have to take a *panga* and cut your own roads through dense growth, or build your own bridge, or pave the bottom of a stream with rocks you have painstakingly gathered.

I had accepted light, heat, water, roads and food. Especially food. You flicked a switch, screamed at a janitor, started the car and let her ramble, or picked up the phone and called the grocer. The most intimate contact with food I ever had was when I ate it and when I paid the bill. Now I was for the first time in the bacon-bringing business, which is to say that sixteen people ate or didn't eat according to what I could do with the business aperture of a rifle. Not that my wife, the hunter, or I would starve, of course. But there were thirteen hungry black mouths, used to consuming ten to twelve pounds of meat a day—*eaoh*—wondering what goodies *Bwana* was going to fetch home that day to plug the aching void. By goodies they meant *nyama*—meat. Zebra meat, eland meat, buffalo meat, any kind of meat. I was the Chicago stockyards, the slaughter pens, the corner delicatessen, in their simple and direct minds. This was a new thing. I hunted for it, and I found it, and I shot it, and we butchered it, and then we ate it. What we didn't eat was made into *biltong*, dried meat or jerky. The hyenas, the jackals, the vultures and the marabou storks cleaned up the odds and ends.

There is a neatness to Africa that needs no sanitation corps, no street-cleaning department, no wash-down trucks. What the hyenas and jackals don't get the buzzards get. What they don't get the marabou storks get. What else is left around the ants get. There is no garbage—no waste.

Maybe that's one of the things that hit me hard. No waste. Back home I seem surrounded by waste—waste of money, waste of time, waste of life, waste of leisure, mostly waste of effort. Away out yonder, under the cleanly laundered skies, there seems to be a scheme that works better than what we have devised here. There is a dignity we have not achieved by acquiring vice-presidencies and a fifty-thousand-dollar bonus and planned economies and the purposeful directorship of the world.

The happiest man I ever knew is named Katunga. He is an old Wakamba, whose filed front teeth have dropped out. His possessions are four wives, a passel of old children, young children and grandchildren. And *pride*. Katunga is known as *Bwana* Katunga to white and black alike, because Katunga is the best skinner of animals in the whole world. He achieved his title because he once approached Philip Percival, the now retired dean of all white hunters, and spake thusly:

"*Bwana,* I see that all white men are called *Bwana. Bwana* means Lord, or Master. Now I, Katunga, am an atheist, because my father was good enough for me. But to be called *Bwana* means that a man is master of something, and I am master of my knife. I am the best skinner in the world. Why cannot I too be called *Bwana* Katunga?"

"*Jumbo, Bwana* Katunga," Mr. Percival said, and *Bwana* Katunga he has remained. He sings as he skins. He is a happy man, with a sense of humor, and he has never seen Dagmar or Milton Berle, and he disdains a gun as an unworthy weapon compared to a knife. Nor does he pay a tax or fret his soul about extinction. Death holds no horror for him.

One day just before I left East Africa I heard Katunga speaking more or less to himself, as he flensed a Grant gazelle I had shot. He was surrounded by his usual clique of admirers, for Africans are great listeners.

"I am an old man," Katunga said, "I am not so very long for safaris. Someday soon I will die. But when I die—when I, who am now called *Bwana* Katunga, die—I will have left my mark. The safaris will pass my *boma*. They will see my houses, and my maize fields. They will see my wives and my children and my grandchildren. They will see what Katunga has left behind him, and they will say: '*King-i* Katunga lived there!'"

And true enough, *Bwana* Katunga will have become King, since he realizes his worth and anticipates it before time awards it to him. Not many captains of our industry can say as much.

The best man I ever met, white, black, or varicolored, is named Kidogo. Kidogo is a Nandi boy, about twenty-eight years old, who was my gun-bearer. He is rich according to his standards. He has wives and children and herds of cattle and grainfields. He has been to English-talking school and it has neither made him a scornful African nor a wishful Englishman. He will work harder, give more of himself to the problem at hand, sleep less, complain less, be more humble, more tolerant, and more efficient than any "civilized" person I know. With it he retains a sense of humor, too, and a vast pride in himself as a man. He hunts as a gunbearer for the best hunter in the business only because he loves the hunt and he loves the hunter and he loves the business of being with *Mungu,* which is God, no matter how you spell it or conceive of it. I feared the scorn of Kidogo more than ever I feared the wrath of God or man, and it pleased me that finally he approved sufficiently to make jokes with me. A joke from Kidogo was accolade enough to make my year. It told me I was a fairly decent fellow, worthy of association with a superlatively brave man, a tolerant man, a *good* man. Apart from the joking compliment, he showed no surprise when his bossman casually assumed that I would join them in a happy little adventure called "pulling the wounded buffalo out of the bush." Kidogo tracked the blood spoor for me, with his life on the line ahead of me. He seemed confident that his life was in good hands, since he had no gun. Adam, the other tracker, showed the same sort of confidence in Selby, and to be accorded a similar consideration as Selby was the deepest bow to my ego I ever experienced. Because Selby is the all-time pro at standing off charging buffalo at four feet.

I still thrill, from time to time, about the dedication to danger that was given me by three relative strangers. "Clients" are generally told to wait in the jeep until the dirty business of finishing off a wounded, dangerous animal is complete. If they are "good," or nonabrasive clients, they might be asked if they care to join in the dubious fun of extracting a sick, sore, and angry animal from his bastion in the thorn. We hit a buffalo hard. Twice he went to his knees, but nevertheless recovered and took off with the herd.

"Let's smoke a cigarette and give him time to stiffen," Selby said. We smoked the cigarette, Selby, Adam and I. Kidogo doesn't smoke.

"Well," Selby said, directly to me, crushing out his smoke, "let's go and collect the old boy." No ultimatum to wait in safety. No request as to whether I wished to play. It was assumed by Harry Selby, who is half buffalo and half elephant, and two lean blacks who live by danger, that I was naturally going to tag along. No Pulitzer Prize, no Congressional Medal of Honor, would ever give me the thrill I got that day out of casual acceptance as an equal.

You see there is a thing about the buffalo. He is a very naughty creature, as Selby might understate it. He is so bloody awful, horridly, vindictively naughty, after he has been hurt that he is almost impossible to kill. He will soak up bullets that would stop elephants cold, and still keep coming. He can run faster than you can. He can turn faster than you can. He will hide if possible and take you from the rear, and he can hide in bush that wouldn't cover a cat. He weighs in the neighborhood of 2,500 pounds. He will hook you with his razor horns—he charges with his head straight out and his eyes open—and then he will go and pick you up from where he has thrown you and he will throw you again. When you cannot move he will jump up and down on you with feet as big as flatirons and as sharp as axes. He will butt you and kneel on you and if you climb a tree he will stretch that big snout up and lick the flesh off your feet with a tongue like a rasp. When he is wounded and you are up against him there is only one logical development. You die, or he dies, because he will not run away. He just comes, and comes, and the brain shot sometimes won't stop him. Most wounded buffalo are killed within a hand's reach. The starkest fear I have ever known was given me by buffalo, until the fear became a fascination, and the fascination an addiction, until I was almost able to observe myself as another creature, and became bemused by my own reactions. I finally courted buffalo as a hair shirt to my own conscience, and almost would have been interested objectively to see how many possible ways there are to be killed by one.

In this trip to Africa, and in my association with Selby, Kidogo, Adam, and a few lions, leopards, buffalo and other vindictive insects, I had the opportunity to find out about courage, which is something I never acquired from the late war. I know now that I am a complete coward, which is something I never would admit before. I am the kid with the dry mouth and the revolving stomach, the sweaty palms and the brilliant visions of disaster.

But cowardice has its points, too. There are all gradations of fear, and the greatest gradation is the fear of being known to be afraid. I felt it one day after a lengthy stalk through awful grass after a wounded buffalo. When I finally looked at him, and he looked at me, and there wasn't any tree to climb and no place to hide, I was the local expert on fear. At less than fifty yards a buffalo looks into your soul.

I unlimbered my Westley-Richards double-barreled .470, and let him have it where it hurt. Then I went off and was sick. And then for the next several weeks, I had to force myself to inspect his relatives at close quarters. I was frightened of embarrassing Harry and Kidogo and Adam by my own cowardice, so my cowardice conquered the minor cowardice, which only involved dying, and so we went and sought the buffalo. Ditto lion, leopard, rhino. Likewise snakes. A small cobra is very large to a man who fears caterpillars.

I learned, on this expedition, about such things as grass, and its relation to rain, and its relation to game, and game's relation to people, and people's relation to staying alive. There is a simple ABC here: When it rains too much, the grass grows too high. Also trucks get stuck, but the main point is that when the grass grows too high you can't get there from here. You stay where you are, and all the frantic cables from home can't reach you.

Also when the grass is too high the game is in the hills, and you can't get to the hills, and furthermore the carnivore which live off the game are out of sight, too, because there ain't no carnivore where there ain't no game. The lions and leopards and cheetah can't operate in the high grass because the Tommies and Grant and zebra and wildebeeste know that the carnivore can't operate in the high grass. And it is an amazing thing that all the hoofed animals drop their young when it is raining so hard that nothing predatory can move much, which gives the young a short chance to stay alive. Me, I always thought pregnant animals went to hospitals when their time came on.

I learned something of females on this trip, too. Such as how the male lion seldom kills. What he does is stand upwind and let his scent drift down. Once in a while he roars. While he is creating a commotion the old lady sneaks along against the wind and grabs what she is sneaking after and then she breaks its neck. And brings home to father the spoils of her effort. We have reversed this technique in this country.

The emphasis on sex is very simple in Africa, having little to do with the citified voodoo with which we have endowed it. Sex is not really a symbol, nor is it hidden, psychiatry-ridden or obscure. There are two sexes—*doumi*, the bulls, and *manamouki*, the cows. They work and they breed and they die. There is no such thing as a sterile man, because the woman shops around amongst the village until she breeds. Breeding is thought to be highly important, since it begets *Mtotos*, and children of both sexes are highly regarded as both nice to have around the hut and valuable in an economic sense. Neither sex of animal nor human group seems overworried about morality as we know it, or the implications of sexual jealousy as we know it. They got sex, and are content, and do not need a Kinsey lecture to impress its importance on each other. They also have sun and rain and seasons, and if they take the sheep and goats into the huts at night it is to keep the sheep and goats from harm while simultaneously keeping warm. It makes as much sense as tethering a poodle to a restaurant radiator.

What I have been driving at all along is an explanation of why I want to go back to Africa, again and again and again, and why I think Kidogo the gunbearer is most important to life. It is because I discovered in Africa my own true importance, which is largely nothing. Except as a very tiny wedge in the never-ending cycle that God or *Mungu* or somebody has figured out. The Swahili say: *"Shauri Mungu"* meaning "God's business," when they can't figure out an explanation for why it rains or they lost the way to camp or there aren't any lions where there should be lions.

In Africa you learn finally that death is as necessary to life as the other way around. You learn from watching the ants rebuild a shattered hill that nothing is so terribly important as to make any single aspect of it important beyond the concept of your participation in it. You are impressed with the tininess of your own role in a grand scheme that has been going on since before anybody wrote books about it, and from that starting point you know true humility for the first time.

I believe today I am an humble man, because I have seen a hyena eat a lion carcass, and I have seen the buzzards eat the hyena that ate the lion, and I saw the ants eat one buzzard that ate the hyena that ate the lion. It appeared to me that *Mungu* had this one figured out, because if kings fall before knaves, and they both contribute to the richness of tomorrow's fertile soil, then who am I to make a big thing out of *me?*

It was not so much that I was a stranger to the vastnesses of Tanganyika, which are not dark but joyous. It was not that I was lost in a jungle so much as if I had finally come home, home to a place of serenity, with a million pets to play with, without complication, with full appreciation of the momentary luxury of being alive, without pettiness, and finally, with a full knowledge of what a small ant I was in the hill of life.

I belonged there all the time, I figured, and that's why I say I had to go to Africa to meet God.

SWIMMING FOR FUN

Swimming is the all-around healthiest exercise there is. It makes you waggle practically every muscle you own without violently pulling any single one. It mends your posture, and it's good for your gizzard and other organs. It takes off fat where you're bunchy, and it puts on flesh where you're scrawny. It makes you husky but not muscle-bound, lean but not skinny. Water and sunshine fix you up outside and in, softening, toughening and clearing up your skin, and of course plastering on the old coat of tan; soothing those frazzled nerves and filling you full of Vitamin D. True, but a dull reason for going to the beach.

For a change and a rest? That's your story, and you almost believe it.

Really, you're going for the purpose of having a good time, and you might better face the fact.

A lot of people go off to have a good time around the water . . . and don't have it. If you take the trouble to look at them you can see with half an eye what's holding them back.

Superstitions. Inhibitions, and that sort of thing.

Take the case of Mr. B, a typical Athletic Compulsion subject. You'll have to watch him closely to notice anything odd in his behavior; it's only when he takes his daily swim that his quirk is evident. Here he goes now. That's him over there on the beach. He takes a deep breath. His jaw sets. He's off!

Down the beach and headlong into the water. A flat racing dive. He's up, now; he's swimming. Zam, zam, zam, his flailing arms pummel the water. His churning feet leave a wake of spreading foam. Zam, zam, zam; he's halfway to the float. On he goes, unfaltering. He's almost there. Zam, zam, zam; he reaches the float, snatches himself out of the water, sinks down on his stomach, lies there. Now it's his heart that's going zam, zam, zam; and his lungs are going wheeze. Return to your bridge game for half an hour, then take another look at the float. Aha! B is on his feet again. Again the chest expansion, the facial expression of purpose. The racing dive, and here he comes, zam, zam, zam, zam. When he gets ashore now, and throws himself down panting on his blanket, we can forget him. He's through for the day. Poor Mr. B.

Poor Mr. B. There's nothing that man would rather do than swim; yet once a day is all he can take. Naturally, at the hideous pace he sets himself. Why doesn't he take it easy? Athletic Compulsion.

B is a reader of magazines, a goer to moving pictures, a liver, in other words, of an average life. He reads articles on swimming, he notices advertisements of bathing wear, he sees swimmers in newsreels and sports shorts, and in meets and exhibitions now and then. Wherever he notices people swimming, it seems to him, they're swimming fast. It's crept into his subconscious; he's built up, quite without realizing it, the belief—the superstition—that somehow it isn't sporting to swim unless you swim like the dickens all the time. He can't go slow. Athletic Compulsion.

Mr. McL's condition is more obvious than Mr. B's. You can spot Mr. McL any time except when he's in bed, and often then. He's a victim of the Ironman Delusion. Watch him as he arrives from the city, at five-twenty-five the afternoon of the first day of his vacation. By five-forty-seven he has dumped his bags in his cottage, hung up his dinner jacket to unwrinkle for an evening of dancing, got into his shorts and bathrobe, and trotted halfway to the cove. By five-fifty-three he has arrived, still trotting, at the cove, doffed his robe, and trotted on into the water. His is no sprinting style, but rather the long and powerful stroke of the marathoner. Darkness, fortunately or unfortunately, forces him to leave the water after only eleven round trips to the float. He trots back to the cottage, takes a shower, puts on his dinner jacket, and steps out.

Ah, Mr. McL—how fortunate you thought to prepare your tux for this evening! You don't know it, but this is your last evening of dancing *this* vacation.

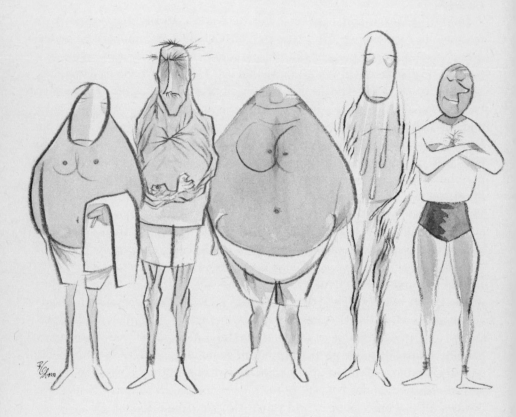

Nine o'clock tomorrow morning will find you on the beach, stripped to the sun, starting your first water marathon (there'll be another around noon, two more only slightly shorter during the afternoon). Ten-thirty will see you taking a brisk run on the beach. Between swims in the afternoon you'll have an hour of volley ball, an hour in a rowboat, and a couple of twenty minute stretches of calisthenics. You'll go home and fall asleep in the bathtub, and move from there to bed about twelve-thirty.

The next day you'll feel not unbearably crisp and crinkly on your back and shoulders, though you'll be quite red; yes, really *quite* red. You won't discover the blisters until after your three o'clock mile; you won't get out of the sun, of course, until the sun goes down. But you won't feel hungry, somehow, for dinner; "too tired," you'll tell yourself. You won't sleep worth a hoot. And, what with the fever, the weakness and the pain, you won't get out of bed in the morning. But don't worry; it's only a matter of time before someone will discover you and call in a doctor, who will doubtless be gifted enough to cure those burns so you can get out of bed by the end of your vacation.

Don't feel too sorry for Mr. McL; if sunburn hadn't got him, some other result of his idiocy would have. He was doomed from the moment he forgot that it's possible to enjoy vacations just taking it easy—from the moment he became a prey of the Ironman Delusion.

No ironman is Mr. W; no athlete either, and he knows it. Mr. W is a Danger Deviser. Mr. W's mind has two parts, a department of storage and filing where he keeps all the accidents and mishaps he has ever heard of, together with original ones he has invented, and a department of inspiration and creation where he is able to fashion at a moment's notice from four to seven accidents to fit any given situation. Mr. W. sits in the shade of a large umbrella throughout the day, wearing a visor and smoked glasses and quivering periodically with apprehension. Why he ever bothered to take off his clothes and come down near the water is a problem you must solve for yourself if you want it solved.

Now then:

Who are you?

Mr. B, Mr. McL, or Mr. W? Well, you're all of them to some extent; everybody is. Each of them, as you've seen, has been unable to cut loose and have a thoroughly good time. And you're all three!

Look yourself straight in the eye, and say to yourself in a rich baritone, "I realize fully that I am Mr. B, Mr. McL, and Mr. W." By doing that you've cleared half your hurdles.

More specifically, about your Athletic Compulsion: You don't want to look like a dub in the water; everybody is a good swimmer nowadays, and you're not going to lag behind. So you swim harder than there's any need to. (An Athletic Compulsion may be present in any pastime, as a matter of fact; but right now we're talking about water and swimming.)

Just how critical are you of other people when they swim? Critical . . . why, you seldom even notice other swimmers. And other swimmers seldom even notice you. So skip the self-consciousness; forget it; slow down and have a good time. Take it easy.

Your Ironman Delusion is a little less simple. The McL in you is no show-off; as his initials might indicate, he's Scotch, and thrifty. He's come down here to have a good time, and he's going to make certain he's having one every moment. Fine; perfectly natural; but he doesn't think very clearly, and he certainly lacks imagination. He can't seem to remember that he's no athlete, that he's not even in especially good shape for a nonathlete. And on the other hand he can't invent ways of amusing himself which aren't unnecessarily strenuous.

An old codger who used to spend two weeks every summer at a little beach in California had the right idea. He may have been a McL to begin with, but years had cured him of his Ironman Delusion without robbing him of his love of long swims. He got himself a plank about four feet long, eighteen inches wide, and two or three inches thick. He rounded off the corners and nailed some old rubber hose all around the edge for a buffer. He used to be out for hours cruising around the bay on that thing, swimming and pushing it, lying on it and paddling and kicking, often just lying on it and drifting. He got his time's worth out of every moment of his two weeks, and he didn't kill himself off either. He dawdled around rising and falling on the waves and watching the little people on the beach and dodging the seagulls and giving his ears a rest from chatter.

How is the water where you swim? Clear? If it's not absolutely murky, you ought to be able to find more interesting things under the water than on top of it. It's rather difficult to observe things beneath the water, though. You can't see down from the surface very well, because ripples distort your vision. And if you dive or swim underwater you still can't see clearly; the lenses of the human eye are set to receive light coming through air, and when your eyes are in contact with the denser medium of water your vision, though it's undistorted, is blurred.

To look down from the surface, you need to smooth the ripples somehow. The best tool is what's variously called a waterscope, an aquascope, or a waterglass; simply a bucket with a glass bottom. Cut the bottom out of a pail or a large tin can, seal on—with putty, liquid solder, even candle wax or adhesive tape—a piece of flat glass. Set the waterscope on the water, press it down so the glass end is clear in, and look into the open end. You can see just as if there weren't any water. If that's too much bother, simply stick a three-foot length of four- to six-inch pipe endwise into the water and look through it. There's no positive smoothing of the surface, like that accomplished by the waterscope, but the pipe acts as a windbreak and does away with most of the ripples.

For seeing clearly while you yourself are underwater, the most satisfactory thing is a pair of water goggles; you can buy them at most sporting goods stores around the water. Adjust them so they fit good and tight. And have a few drops of water inside each lens when you put them on; then you'll have something to rinse the glass with if it fogs up.

You can get an unblurred look underwater, not badly ripple-distorted, just by trapping bubbles of air against your eyes. Put a hand on each side of your face, like a horse's blinder, with the thumb toward your ear and the base joint of the forefinger against the outer end of your eye socket. So long as your face is pointed straight down you can hold air in front of your eyes; if it leaks out, bubble some more in from your mouth.

Long swims with a plank to rest on, easygoing underwater explorations —those are just two of the possible ways of getting a kick out of the water without giving all you've got all the time. Is there a surf? Try riding it on a board; or without a board, just floating on your face or your back. Is there a beach? Lie down on it and relax. Delusion or no delusion, you are no ironman, and you better realize it before you spoil your vacation altogether. Take it easy.

Take it easy in the sun, too. Naturally you'd like to get tan as soon as you can. All right, do it—but don't try to get tan *sooner* than you can. On your first day, give yourself an hour in the early morning sun. Then stay in the shade till late afternoon. See how you look; if you look O.K., take another hour. Give yourself an hour and a half next morning, if you aren't too burned. And so on. If you use a little judgment and have plenty of pigment in your skin you can tan yourself nicely in a week. Cook yourself thoroughly the first day and you'll not only have a miserable time but lose your opportunity for a tan besides.

Beware of misty days, by the way. Infrared rays will come right through water vapor and burn you, but ultraviolet rays are stopped, so your burn never does turn into a tan.

Now for the Danger Deviser, the Mr. W in you. A lot of your fears are exaggerated; a lot more of them are totally unfounded.

Lurking behind all the other fears is that of drowning, a grotesque and shapeless sort of fear—and in itself a very foolish one. Nobody ever just drowned; invariably something happens first, to lead to the drowning. If you don't believe that, go on in the water and try to drown yourself. Just try. So cross drowning, as such, off your list.

You've heard a lot about undertows. They exist, all right; but you've got the wrong idea of what they are. You think, or at least most people do, that an undertow is a downward swirl which seizes you in its icy grasp, pulls you to the very bottom, and sits on your chest, sneering. Fiddle. An undertow is no more than a current, underwater, which moves in the direction opposite to the current on the surface. Where water is coming in, in waves on the surface, it's usually going out again, beneath. If you stand up in the surf, perhaps the undertow will sweep your feet out from under you. But if you can swim—and all this is on the assumption that you can—what do you care? Suppose it's a very devil of a current, close to the surface and too strong to swim against? Drift along the beach fifty or a hundred yards and you'll find you can come in all right.

Another thing you're constantly expecting to be grabbed by is weeds. Weeds don't grab people; they're not meat eaters. If the weeds are underwater, lie close to the surface and you won't even know they're there. If they're spread out on the surface, you can see them and swim around them. As a matter of fact, you can, if you're willing to take your time and go slow, swim right through any clump of weeds in the Western Hemisphere. Or Eastern.

If somebody throws you right in the middle of a marine thicket, lie level on the water, take small, conservative strokes, and you'll have no trouble swimming out.

You're afraid of cramps, and certainly people do get them in the water now and then. There is one cramp which is dangerous, cramp of the stomach or diaphragm; cases of stomach cramp are very rare. A cramp anywhere else can be broken by forcibly stretching out the affected muscle. Cramp in your foot? Pull your toes up toward you with your hand, and straighten your knee; it will hurt a little, but it will break the cramp. Cramp in the calf of your leg? Cramp in the back of your thigh? Same treatment. Cramp in the front of your thigh? Get hold of your foot and pull it up till the sole is against your buttock; then hold it there and swing your knee down and back under you. Cramp in the shoulder muscles back of your neck? Force your head forward till your chin is on your chest, and roll it from side to side.

You can break cramps in the water, or you can swim ashore and then break them. But whichever you do stay out of the water for a little while, and give the muscle a rubdown to help circulation.

Learn to float in some position, on your back or with your feet hanging below you, so that you can keep your nose and mouth above water without moving a muscle.

If you can do that, Mr. W, the chances against your drowning are a million to one.

Don't swim within two hours after eating.

Digestion usually takes that long, and though nobody knows what causes stomach cramps, swimming while you're digesting food seems to have something to do with it.

Don't swim when you're feeling off form, or when you're very tired or very hot. Or When You're Plastered.

You aren't normal under those circumstances. Your judgment is bad, as well as your physical condition and endurance.

Don't swim absolutely alone; always try to keep within sight and hollering distance of somebody or other.

And all of you—B, McL, and W—for safety, for health, for enjoyment: take it easy.

BODY-SURFING

Not since Guy Gilpatrick introduced the fascinating game of swimming underwater with a hooked fork to catch octopus has any sport as exciting and exhilarating as body-surfing been invented. Within the past few years this novel pastime, sometimes known as "wave-riding," has taken California by storm, and is now spreading rapidly to the Atlantic seaboard and even to the vacation spots around the Great Lakes.

Body-surfing, as the term implies, consists of turning your body into an animated surf board, and using it to ride the waves, a sport that combines the thrills of tobogganing with the breath-taking plunge of the Big Dip on a roller coaster.

The action goes something like this:

You wade out to where the first line of breakers is curling shoreward.

You take a deep breath, shoot to the top of the wave, and launch yourself with one fast stroke.

Then, if your timing has been correct, you find yourself poised at the crest of the breaker, looking down into a fearsome chasm, sometimes from ten to fifteen feet deep.

With a thrill comparable to a high ski jump, you find yourself dropping dizzily down the precipitous wall of water.

And, as you reach the bottom of the slide, you are hurtled shoreward like a torpedo, pushed ahead of a swirling spray of feathery spume.

That is real body-surfing, without doubt one of the most spectacular, and pleasurable, water sports ever developed.

There has, of course, always been known and practiced—in the East as well as the West—a simple type of wave riding that consists of lying flat in the water with legs and arms outstretched. If you follow this method you jump into the wave after it has broken, and attempt to ride what is known as the "bore," that is, the broken surf. A good swimmer can ride a considerable distance in this manner, with his head down and his body completely submerged.

But with the highly developed method used by the expert body-surfer it is possible to ride huge waves, sometimes fifteen feet high, catching them before they have broken. And you ride them, head and shoulders out of the water, the entire distance from the breakers to the shore, often fifty yards or more. The bigger the wave, the better the sport.

In riding a wave you are, in effect, sliding down a steep slope, and you continue sliding until the pressure of water back of you carries you onto the beach. If you are unusually expert you can ride in a zigzag fashion along the side of the wave as you progress shoreward. Or you may turn flips as you slide down the incline, or do a barrelroll and continue to ride on your back, or use another rider for a surfboard. There are infinite variations.

To get the full effect of the wave's pressure the water must bear against some part of the body. And the easiest way of obtaining this pressure is by bending the knee and forcing the body down. But the most important factor seems to be the hunching of the shoulders.

Flattening the chest and hollowing the shoulders causes a pocket to form under the body that acts, in effect, exactly like a sea sled. This inverted V shape allows the forward part of the body to rise up out of the water. Thus the swimmer can breathe comfortably, and even carry on a shouted conversation during the entire length of the ride.

Just what to do with the hands is a subject of heated discussion among the body-surfers, but all agree that they must be kept back. Experience has demonstrated that the "behind the back" position, as advocated by Duke Kahanamoku, is essentially correct. A radical modification of this position has, however, been recently developed by modern surfers which, it is claimed, tends to prolong the ride. This latest development consists of placing both hands between the legs, thereby accentuating the hump and the hollow under the chest. An experienced lifeguard who has tried every style maintains that this position is by far the most effective.

Both balance and steering are controlled by raising or depressing the shoulders. This part of the art is not difficult to acquire, and can be learned perfectly after a few attempts. If the beginner will remember that his body is being synchronized with the speed of the wave he will quickly acquire the proper technique. The general consensus of opinion among the experts is that any swimmer, no matter how poor he may be, can become a good body-surfer if he will follow the rules and practice faithfully for a few months—or a few years.

BOWLING

If you like a sport that will test your mettle without breaking your back, try bowling. If you've never bowled before, stop in some alley and watch the old hands perform: they pick up a ball by its finger holes, balance it a moment, swing it behind them in an arm-length arc, and walk smartly up to the foul line with a final genuflection as the ball swings forward. How sweetly it hugs the boards as it hums down the sixty-foot stretch—how soul-satisfying the crash of "timber" as the missile shoots into the "1-3 pocket" and thirty pounds of polished lumber are swept helter-skelter into the pit!

Team mates yowl in unrestrained delight; rivals admonish their man in even louder voices to go and do likewise—and before you know it—you want to peel off your coat and bowl, yourself.

Do it!

Bowling is a game in which brawn is unimportant, so the field is wide open for any normal individual who can stand up. Anybody can aspire to be a good bowler regardless of age, physical perfection or athletic experience.

Those elusive yet simple elements—timing, rhythm and control—are the basis of skill on the alleys.

Millions of people have frequented the alleys for years for the simple reason that bowling is a swell game. It is good, lusty exercise; it is an ideal vehicle for complete mental relaxation; it is a friendly, neighborly game. Skill is involved, to be sure, but not the exacting skill of golf, the lack of which converts a sport into an embarrassing misery for the novice. For the truth is that bowling can be thoroughly enjoyed with less proficiency than almost any other game you can mention. And the best way to prove that is to watch some newly formed club of women, most of whom never had any athletic training before, having the time of their lives on the alleys despite the fact that three balls out of every four rolled land in the gutter long before they reach the pins!

Then, too, there is enough competition in bowling to make it exciting, yet that competition is not acute in the sense that it is directly physical or even greatly dependent upon physical strength. Two players of widely different muscular development and athletic education can bowl against each other with complete satisfaction. At the annual tournament the contestants' ages range from eighteen to sixty-five and in many sections of the country father-and-son tournaments are even more popular on the alleys than on the links. Husband and wife can bowl together with infinitely less risk of divorce than they are exposed to at golf!

Being all-inclusive, bowling is easily the most sociable of all games and therein lies its strength. The backbone of the sport in this country are the teams and leagues from offices, factories and mills which have bowled two or three evenings a week for years. Anybody from the boss to the office boy is eligible on equal grounds, and for that simple reason practically every leading concern in the country has fostered bowling as the ideal breeder of improved industrial relations.

When you first try bowling you may find that the sixteen-pound ball is too heavy for comfort. So use a lightweight ball: you'll find all weights in the rack. You will also discover that laying the ball down on the boards isn't quite so simple as it looked: usually you heave it and bounce it so awkwardly at first that it wobbles off into the gutter and accomplishes nothing. Unless you are amazingly inept, however, several of your first half-dozen balls will miraculously remain on the alley all the way down to the end. And once you've seen a couple of sturdy pins clonk against each other and then topple off out of sight, you've gotten the taste of blood that will never be completely satiated.

Even at the start, strikes will come frequently enough to strain your vest buttons, for this is a game peculiarly kind to the novice. As you improve your eye and develop that elusive trinity, timing, rhythm and control, you will find yourself steeped in a pastime which lures you on and on.

Like golf, too, bowling is not physically violent. You'll sleep like a top after three or four games, all right, but there's no danger of overdoing it for one very simple reason: your thumb will get sore from the friction of the finger grip before you can bowl too long for your own good! It is good exercise—principally because it gives the abdominal muscles a much needed workout—yet it carries its own curb to excess.

The smart thing to do, in the beginning, is to ask one of the attendants at the alleys to give you some tips—provided you don't personally know some kegler who will be delighted to do that for you. Neither of them will charge you anything (bowlers are like that!) and one or the other will be able to show you how to keep a larger percentage of your balls on the alley bed. They'll emphasize the necessity of the straight arm; the importance of a three- or four-step approach rather than the flat-footed stance; the advantage of keeping your feet wide apart; the necessity of bending at the hips; the reason for rolling the ball rather than throwing or bouncing it. As you progress they will demonstrate the difference between the "straight cross" and the "hook" delivery; the reason for seeking the "1-3 pocket" rather than aiming flush for the head pin; when to bowl from the left-hand side of the alley rather than the right; how to "shave" a pin when shooting the spare ball on a "railroad," and other things to improve your game.

Meantime, you'll be having a good time, some good exercise, and the rare and invigorating chance to make a big noise.

The average man or woman who bowls may not appreciate the psychological value of the game, but intelligent psychiatrists do and recommend it as a mental relaxation. The former Governor Adams, of Colorado, used to explain his frequent trips to the bowling alleys on the grounds that it was the only readily accessible game which tired his body and rested his mind in a short time. And if one attempted to get at the root of the recent popularity of bowling among the "upper crust," he would inevitably arrive at that conclusion as the explanation.

For entirely beyond the appeal of the game as a game, the critical analyst will see in it something which we, who live under increasing pressure, have been mutely crying for. In college we got it easily in gang formation by smashing up the town after the big game—and in adult life many still achieve it by attending conventions, getting marvelously tight and throwing the furniture out of the hotel windows.

In short, the savage in us still rebels at the damnable orderliness of conventional civilization. Individually, we are afraid to flaunt public opinion: in a sympathetic group we are delighted to blow things helter-skelter. Hence the popularity of bowling.

For the essence of bowling is that it permits the most strait-laced citizen to unbend long enough to blast into utter confusion a regimented array of ten neatly arranged objects.

Bowling is the civilized man's last chance to make a hell of a racket without apologizing to a soul!

VARIATION ON THE BOWLING THEME: CANDLEPINS

If you're already a bowler, and such a good one that the business of knocking down pins that are four and one half inches wide is becoming monotonous, consider New England's game, candlepins.

First-rate fat-pin rolling by top bowlers, New England thinks, is a constant procession of strikes, the same old story, requiring rhythm of movement by the bowler and accuracy, to be sure, but withal, monotonous as burlesque jokes. But in candlepins—ah! The strike is a rarity—four to ten in a ten-string match between champions—and the target pattern is forever changing.

The candlepin is fifteen and one half inches tall and bellies out only slightly from a two-inch base to a two and thirteen-sixteenth-inch center. It jumps more when it is hit than the bottlepin, and consequently, unless a split hit is nearly perfect, may spray out between other pins and into gutters and pits without touching them. The sweep, as of a broom, of bottlepins is missing, and the game becomes more of a dead-eye business.

The ball is small in comparison, too—not to exceed four and one half inches in diameter or two pounds ten ounces in weight—and presents the proposition of hitting a small target with a small ball instead of pitching a huge ball at a huge target.

With no finger holes in the ball, candlepin bowlers can adopt various styles. The most common is the slight curve ball that hooks into the one-two slot as it approaches the pins, yet a virtually straight ball is used by many speed bowlers.

Unlike bottlepins, an added help—and sometimes added hazard—is allowed in candlepins. If the pins, tipped over, do not roll from the plate where the other pins are standing, but stay on the alley or roll against these upright pins, a player may shoot at this toppled "deadwood" and attempt to clean up a spare or, if a third ball, extra pins. This deadwood is usually helpful but, on occasions, swings into positions where a two-inch end, facing the bowler, must be hit at a certain spot to be thrown against the pins still standing.

HORSES

Something about horseflesh. Your knowledge of horses may be limited to the pari-mutuel odds or you may be a julep-drinking breeder. It really doesn't matter. You don't have to know a walk from a gallop, or the withers from the crest—horseflesh in action holds an unbeatable thrill for everyone. Though horses are bigger than men, and often smarter, men have mastered them. That's a part of the thrill. Yet horses are a big chunk of nature, and that's another part of it. Whatever the reason and whether the sport is racing or hunting or breaking, you can be sure of one thing: If it's horses, it's exciting.

HORSEBACK RIDING

Good riders are born but they can also be made. The ones with long legs are the born ones. Anybody who's at all keen on it can learn, however. Six to ten lessons, under competent instruction, will suffice; after which regular practice counts for a lot, since brains learn quicker than muscles.

Anyone's enjoyment of horseback riding will be improved by some acquaintance with the principles underlying horsemanship.

Some riding enthusiasts have the cowboy complex and imagine, quite mistakenly, that they are exhibiting the highest type of equestrianism when they ride as fast as possible.

You will encounter others who assert they go riding for pleasure and exercise and would scorn any attempt at "fancy" riding.

Yet no one need apologize for equestrian style. It is as essential to perfection in riding as form and stance are in golf.

It is important to good riding that the rider bestow upon his horse some affection, consideration and understanding of his mount's character. He may well occasionally wonder what a horse thinks about.

It is only fair to say, in speaking about form, that there are different "schools" of riding, each with a partly different practice. To some extent you take your choice. In the Army and through the West, wherever the deep stock saddle is used, they ride "hard," sticking tight to the saddle without posting. In an English or flat saddle one posts, or rises at the trot. Once mastered, either style is equally comfortable and presentable. Both require balancing the body vertically, aided by "knee-grip" or firm hold by the muscles from the knee up the inner thigh. Similarly, there are several approved ways of holding the reins, each with a different reason; in the left hand only, or with the right hand over the left, or with the right snaffle rein withdrawn in the right hand or with two reins in each hand. All these are chiefly matter of opinion. The horse has his own ideas about them.

Everyone, including the horse, agrees that the two main requirements for good riding are light hands and secure seat. The trained rider sits up very straight with spine supple and with just enough rein length so his mount feels the touch of his hands all the time but not an ounce more. We control the horse by putting a curb and a snaffle bit in his mouth, because it is a tender part, yet unless we handle him skillfully we can soon undo this means of control. Continual pulling paralyzes the sensitive nerves and makes the horse "hard-mouthed," after which he no longer feels a signal to slow or stop and, if sufficiently annoyed to bolt, cannot readily be brought down. Kindness to animals and self-preservation both suggest light hands.

Stable manners are not incompatible with table manners as long as one does not get them mixed. There are certain things one can do that will show grooms and others present that one has the *savoir-faire* when it comes to horses. For example, suppose that the horse you are to ride has been saddled and bridled, ready for you to mount. You approach in a gentlemanly and dignified manner, the picture of composure whether you feel it or not. You do not raise your arms or voice or otherwise disconcert the horse. Instead, you come up to him at nonkicking end and hold out your hand in a friendly way, palm up. He will probably nibble at it, expecting to find a lump of sugar or a carrot, although he knows neither can comfortably be eaten with the bridle on. You rub the sides of his cheeks where the leather chafes; you do not pat or stroke his face—and you leave his ears alone. It is perfectly proper to talk to the horse, if you know what he likes to talk about. Otherwise, prepare to mount.

It is at this point that the novice will betray himself. One should remember always that one can easily get oneself mistaken for a proper horseman or horsewoman, if one will go through certain simple motions. Take pains to examine the curb chain under the horse's chin, passing the fingers over it (ostentatiously, of course), to make sure it is comfortable for him, then to feel if the girth is secure and next to inspect the stirrups for correct length. For this purpose you stand at the horse's left (called the near side, possibly because it is when one stands there), nonchalantly take the stirrup iron with the right hand and slide it down the full length of the stirrup leather. Taking a step back from the horse, you reach the tips of the fingers of your left hand to the buckle on the stirrup leather, where it is attached to the saddle, and with the right hand bring the stirrup iron up under your left armpit. The length of the stirrup from buckle to iron should be the length of your arm. Take up or let out a few holes to adjust it exactly. Not forgetting that you have two legs, you pass around in front of the horse and in the same way adjust the stirrup on the off side. Return from the "off" to the "near" side via the safer route.

Picking up the reins is the next move preparatory to swinging gracefully up into the saddle. To the beginner it may now seem as if the horse had somehow acquired a whole bunch of reins. If temporarily confused as to their proper order, pause a moment. Look critically at the horse's neck as though to convey your poor opinion of the groom's curry-combing. This will give you time to recall that there are two bits, to each side of which is fastened one end of a narrow strap or rein. The upper bit is the snaffle; the lower is the curb. The snaffle rein has a buckle exactly in the middle, while the curb rein is sewn together. You place the snaffle rein on the curb with the buckle over the sewn spot and pull the reins through your left hand with your right. You now, unless you have performed some sleight of hand, hold four lines issuing from your right fist. It is a simple matter to extend the fingers of the left hand like a fan and insert one after another between the four reins so that the little finger is between the first two; then a finger, then a rein, until you have run out of fingers. You will be pleased to discover that you have thus separated all the reins with fingers and arranged them snaffle-curb-curb-snaffle, which is exactly as it should be. The ends of the reins fold over the index finger and the thumb is clamped down, tightly and permanently, over all four. Hold your reins lightly, with your wrist bent outward, but keep that thumb there.

You are now at liberty to swing gracefully up into the saddle. It will help if you rest your left hand, which is holding the reins, on the horse's withers, just forward of the pommel. With the right hand take the stirrup iron, face the horse's flank or tail and raise your left foot very high, so you can place the ball of it on the stirrup iron which your right hand is holding ready. Next put your right hand on the rear end of the saddle. As you are now standing on one foot, the right one, it is the only one you can spring off. You aid the spring by pulling yourself up with both hands. As your weight is transferred to the left leg, you swing the right leg out over the horse, moving the right hand quickly from the rear to the front of the saddle, to get it out of the way of your right leg, and down you come to rest facing forward in the saddle, gracefully.

Looking as much like an equestrian statue as possible, you feel stealthily for your right stirrup and, having gained it, so place your feet that the ball of the foot is resting on the iron. The habit of riding thus with the stirrup iron under the ball of the foot should be cultivated, as it makes it easier to keep the heels down.

This is the time when you decide which is your favorite method of holding the reins. The rein length is adjusted so that you can just feel your horse's mouth when your hands are in your lap as if you were reading a book, which is perhaps what you wish you were doing. Your heels are pointed slightly out and well down and your legs below the knee are well away from the horse. Thumbs, as always, firmly on reins. Having succeeded in giving everybody present the impression that you are an experienced horseman, it only remains to be seen whether you can ride.

To signal your horse to go forward, you bring both heels in to touch his flanks. Don't tickle him, don't kick him—touch him. Whether you are wearing spurs or riding "naked," he will know what you mean. He should proceed at a walk. If for any reason whatsoever he trots or acts foolish, keep your hands down, chin in, elbows clamped at your sides, stiffen your straight spine, and lean back a little. This brings your weight, as much of it as is necessary, to bear on both bits and is the correct way to stop him. As soon as you have checked him, release the pressure promptly, but continue to feel his mouth as he walks, taking up and letting out slack on the reins by flexing your wrists, not by moving your elbows or forearms.

This is a good time to resolve that no matter what your horse does, you will not permit yourself to lean forward. You do this because you know that you cannot control your horse if riding in a forward position. You are also aware that nobody ever fell off a horse backward. Riders who are thrown go over the horse's head or shoulders, so that he who remembers to lean backward as much as is necessary to keep the body vertical, will retain his seat. This is what is meant by riding on balance.

Knee-grip is very useful as an aid to balance, as is a supple body, nowhere tense. If, in spite of good intentions, you find yourself getting pitched forward by the motion of the horse, you do not hold on by the front of the saddle, which simply pulls you farther forward, but grab the saddle behind you and pull yourself back to normalcy.

For the first ten minutes at least, you walk your horse. He may have been standing for hours in his stall or he may have been recently fed. While he is limbering up, you practice correct posture. Sitting up straight is all-important. The spine is ordinarily flexible and counterbalances the motion of the horse, yet it must instantly become rigid against any sudden movement requiring you to lean back.

One should regard the sky and the tops of trees, because this induces an easy freedom which adds much to one's appearance on horseback. Too many anxious people come in from a ride having seen nothing all the time but the horse's withers.

If you will notice other persons as they ride by, it will help you learn what to do and what to avoid. You keep to the right and pass anyone you overtake on his left. Although the thing may happen to you, it is not considered seemly to dash past others on the road, as it incites their horses to follow yours. An even worse social error is coming so close to another rider as to catch his stirrup; this is too easy a way to spill anyone to be regarded as showing any great finesse in homicide.

Guiding the saddle horse is not quite, perhaps, what you'd expect. A draft horse is steered to the right or left by pulling on the right or left rein. When riding, however, directions are given in a very different way. A touch of the reins, midway up one side of the neck is the signal. To swing around to the left, for example, as in turning around on the path, you move your right hand slightly to the left and raise it a trifle, until the reins touch the right side of your mount's neck, when he will turn obediently around to the left. Horses thus trained are said to be neck-broken or bridle-wise. The reins signal is usually augmented by a touch of the spur. To illustrate, if wheeling right, in addition to touching the left side of your horse's neck with the reins, you bring your right heel in just behind the girth.

The next step up after walking is trotting. You simply touch your horse with your heels. Then, as he trots, you either bounce helplessly or post; that is, bounce purposely. The latter is precisely 50 per cent less wearing, since you evade just half the bumps. As the right shoulder of your mount moves forward or his right hoof comes to the ground, whichever you find it easier to look at, you rise very slightly in the saddle, remaining in the air by gripping with the knees just long enough to miss one bounce, then descending and repeating the process of rising as the right shoulder goes forward. In learning to post it is very easy to get worked forward into an unbalanced and helpless position. This can be neatly avoided by thrusting the stomach forward as you rise or post, which helps to keep your shoulders back and your body vertical in consequence.

If you don't care two oats about your horse's mouth, you can pull yourself up to post by means of the reins. In fact, even with good intentions, you are likely to find yourself unconsciously jerking on the horse's mouth just a little, each time you rise, unless you watch closely. The proper thing to do is to let the motion of the horse under you start you up and to maintain yourself a little above the saddle by knee-grip. Your elbows should be holding twenty dollar bills against your sides, not flapping like wings, and your hands should be raised just a little higher than when walking and just as light on the horse's mouth.

You will see any number of "passengers" jerking the reins in the horse's mouth, wiggling the left elbow to help them rise, and banging their feet against their mount's flanks at every stride, the effect of which is usually to urge him on faster. When you see for yourself how awkward and ludicrous this makes them appear, you will probably become a lifelong convert to correct form. Keep the calf of the leg well away from your horse, with your heels down and toes in. In equestrian parlance, when you are rising each time his right hoof comes to the ground, you are "posting right." Take care to vary this during the course of your ride by sometimes posting on the left foot. Posting is an easy rhythmic motion and perfectly comfortable and graceful as long as you maintain a balanced vertical position.

The canter is a distinct gait, best described as a slow, measured gallop. You will find it the most comfortable sort of motion as it is the most natural gait in a horse. When cantering, the horse "leads" with either the right or the left forefoot. To put him into a canter from the trot, walk or standing position, turn his head a little to the left and at the same instant touch his right flank with your heel. He will lead off with the right forefoot, or if you reverse the reins and heel signals, with the left.

The motion of the rider in cantering is called "jockeying"; it is something no jockey ever does. The main thing to remember is that your seat never leaves the saddle. It will, of course, at first, but it shouldn't. By being extremely flexible at the base of the spine and leaning back again each time the jumpy motion of the horse tends to thrust you forward, you can keep a silver quarter on the saddle under you all the time you are cantering.

If you see some dub being bumped up out of the saddle as the horse canters, you can be sure he has forgotten to lean a little backward. The rider who appears to be a part of his horse always moves in counterbalance with him, coming forward to meet a backward thrust and leaning back to oppose the forward impulse, thus keeping his body vertical with respect to the earth—in other words, riding on balance. In this sport we insist upon balance as much as a bank.

The easiest thing to do on horseback is the fast gallop. You simply sit your horse. The faster he goes, the easier you find it to do so. "Chasers" are people who take advantage of this by simply running a horse fast all of the time. Usually they are the poorest riders. To a horseman a great thrill consists of giving a lively horse a burst of speed yet having him always collected —as the expression goes, "keeping him in your hand." The rider with sensitive touch is always in communication with his horse, none the less so because they are taking Blarney Stone Hill fully extended. To stop your horse or bring him down to the slow trot after a run is the real test of your handling. You should be able to have him up reasonably short, without pulling too hard or too long and without having him pull against you. A horse likes to be let out for a stretch and frequently gets quite excited about it. With hands down, elbows clamped to the sides, do not pull with your arms but just lean back so he feels your pressure signal on the bit. As soon as he responds by slowing his pace instantly relax. Then signal again. And again. This gives him the idea of coming down quietly to a walk.

Jumping is distinctly an advanced accomplishment but simple enough after a good seat is acquired. Just be sure you get a horse of the hunter or jumper type, as not every horse can or wants to jump. Then do little jumps frequently, at first, to get the "feel" of it. Canter up to the jump with loose reins, hands on the horse's neck, and stand in your stirrups. The great trick is not to get thrown forward.

The passing of time will suggest that you return to the stables. Bringing the horse in cool and dry is the mark of a gentleman rider. To do so you must walk your horse on the last stretch of the way home. This is a good time to slip your feet out of the stirrups and get down into the saddle, as it helps develop a seat and makes losing one or both stirrups occasionally a matter of little consequence.

On arriving at the stables, you dismount by simply reversing the procedure of mounting. That is, you place both hands on the front of the saddle, stand up and swing your right leg backward over the horse's quarters and come down on the ground with your right foot. Your left foot is then removed from the stirrup and you are once more on terra firma. Possibly you now have a new respect and affection for it.

Incidentally, it is manners to unfasten the girth, curb chain and neck strap yourself, before leaving. Also tip the groom if you ever expect to ride out of that stable again.

No rider is properly equipped who does not wear spurs, with or without rowels, yet no one is entitled to spurs who cannot keep his heels down and away from his horse. Don't be squeamish about spurs; they are not cruel. They are used principally to signal commands. Spurs are the badge of the graduate rider.

The temptation is irresistible, in an ex-cathedra dissertation of this kind, to indulge in a few well-modulated "Don'ts." Beginners are always told, "Don't lose your head, always keep cool." It is good advice, but scarcely practical. The reason behind it is sound, because it is undeniably true that the horse can tell when the rider is alarmed or uncertain. There is nothing very mystifying about this phenomenon; usually the nervous rider unconsciously clutches more tightly at the reins, which is fairly unmistakable telepathy to any horse. It would be less easy to explain how it is that any experienced horseman can feel what is going on in the mind of the mount under him.

Everybody knows he should not be afraid when riding, any more than when playing poker; admonitions to have courage are a little futile. It is much more to the point to say, "Don't be indifferent." You and your horse and the fifty yards of road ahead comprise a whole world, in which there is something new to be learned—every minute.

Don't miss a move your horse makes; for example, note if his ears are up and forward, indicating interest and contentment; or backward, indicating distrust or discomfort; or if they are constantly being flicked forward and backward, one after the other, indicating amusement and attentiveness. Study your horse and yourself all of the time. If you are escorting a lady, ride on the right (except when instructing or coaching) and observe how the two horses get on together, whether they are equally gaited, whether they act in unison, whether they can be kept together at the slow trot, what their individual peculiarities are. No couple has ever been known to run out of conversation who are keen riders; there are always the horses to talk about. Don't hesitate to talk to them and guide them by the sound of your voice. Don't forget, after they have done a good spanking trot or performed handily in a canter, to buffet them heartily on the neck; a horse is naturally modest but don't think he won't appreciate your praise and respond to it with affection. No one will ever really ride a horse who cannot love him.

FISHING

"When the sun is right; when the stream is good, and the wind small; when trout are coming well, fishing produces a kind of happiness which is sustained even during the moment you pause to examine it. The only other sport I know which has this quality is drinking. In both, an illusion is created, justified, and maintained over a period of time. While it lasts, you are a human being—in fact, one of the best!"—EDMUND WARE

"The thing that irresistibly attracts us fishermen is the primitive urge we inherit to go out and capture one of nature's wild things. We don't buy it or barter for it. We go directly to nature and take it through our own patience, skill or just plain good luck. There's satisfaction in this, such satisfaction as is not felt by simply carrying home a fine, fat fish from the store.

"This should be easy to understand. You go out, for instance, to a mountain stream. The white water boils down through the narrows and breaks over great rocks. Here it flattens out into a deep, smooth run, swinging in under some gnarled cedars to a dark, shaded pool. Now, you don't know what is down in that water. There is mystery and uncertainty. Time turns back five thousand years and it is a matter of life and death to take a fish out of that pool. Your ancestors didn't have a split bamboo rod and tapered leader but they were no more in earnest. When finally you lay a big rainbow in your creel, let no man try to tell you that here is just four pounds of dead fish. You know better!"—DAVID M. NEWELL

WHY MEN GO FISHING

To the question, "Why do you go fishing?" there appear to be three standard rejoinders, all of them emphatic.

First: "None of your business." (This is probably true.)

Second: "To catch fish." (This is probably false.)

The third rejoinder, "For the fun of it," is everything and nothing. *Why* is it fun to go fishing?

Edmund Ware explains it this way:

The first fish I caught was a bluegill. We also called them "kivvies" or "punkin seeds." I was seven years old, and the bluegill perhaps one. I have tried very hard to remember accurately what my sensations were—and not what, as a sportsman or fisherman, they ought to have been.

Here's what I think I remember: (1) An unexpected and highly exciting tug. (Surprise.) (2) As I derricked the bluegill onto the bank, there was a pleasing but easily conquered resistance. (Achievement without personal risk.) (3) The thought: this fish came up out of the water, but to look at the water you wouldn't know there was anything down there. (Mystery and fascination of a sphere alien and unknown to myself.) (4) The fish is fine to look at. Nice colors. He is alive. He is flopping. (Joy of bossing completely a life not my own, without getting socked for it.) (5) He might flop back into the water. But I want him up here on earth where I can touch him, and look at him. So now I will kill him. (Possession.) (6) There! I have killed him! Once he flopped, but now he's dead and just quivering. Alone, I have killed him. (Valor, and fine feeling of savagery in killing.) (7) Is he good to eat? (Hunger.)

Right after number six, the kill, I am bound to think I remember a waning of elation. That was a climax, and its moment must have been great stuff, for I wanted an immediate repetition—a second drink. I recaptured the sensation in some degree by exhibiting the bluegill to my father, and describing its catching. Thus, bragging became an important element in the fun of the whole episode.

In the catching of that bluegill are most—but not all—of the reasons why fishing is fun. The control beyond arm's reach of something alive and wild is fun. It gives you a sense of projecting your own power. This is very flattering, even when the object controlled is only a rubber ball on an elastic, or a ten-ounce trout on thirty feet of line. The fact that such a trout actually requires very little power to control adds nothing to the fun. Therefore, the fact is submerged. Any fact which adds nothing to the fun of fishing is similarly submerged. I am all for the process, too.

This far-reaching of power is fine stuff. It is why boys and their fathers throw stones. To connect with a stray cat from a distance of twenty yards is sheer perfection in delight. Think of the enormous lift the hunter gets when the mountain goat tumbles off the cliff six hundreds yards away a second after he squeezes the trigger! Just think of the astonishment of that goat. You caused it from a distance. It is necessary to *see* the results in order to get fun out of them. The hunter *sees* his game fall. The fisherman not only sees his salmon leap clear of the water, but he *feels* him.

I am pretty sure that the greatest sports have in them an element of danger. This disturbed me for a while, because the greatest sport in the world is, of course, fishing—and I could not honestly see any danger in it. I could see danger in a rough stream or lake, or in wading certain savage rivers, but that is a pure background danger and you can walk out of it any time it ceases to be fun. There is some danger that you will lose the fish, but it's insignificant. The real danger is that the fish will lose *you!* You can call this the fish's danger if you want to, but that's quibbling. In fact, when you've got a good fish on, you can feel his danger so keenly in your wrist that for excitement purposes it becomes your own.

Casting a fly does not require much dexterity, actually, but it gives the fisherman a *sensation* of great skill. The gorgeous, moving curves of the rod and line amaze him, and he feels himself a truly remarkable fellow for creating such beautiful motion with his wrist. As a matter of fact, if he co-ordinates average well, it should take him about twenty minutes to learn the dark mysteries of such creation. But the fun is there, and the soundlessness of the line unrolling on a long cast will fascinate me forever—I hope. So will the elaborate, cunning, and probably meaningless designs of certain flies which resemble no insect known.

One of the greatest joys of fishing comes when you are actually examining a fish you have just caught. This special joy is difficult to explain. It is a kind of furtive triumph akin to successful and justified eavesdropping. By reason of your own luck and maneuvering, you are now looking closely at a live, wild thing which has been beautifully trained to keep its distance in order to survive. You are the only human being ever to see these magnificent colors, this greatest of all streamlining, this now defenseless self. You are a kind of privileged miser. By reason of this close, possessive scrutiny, you feel curiously enriched, like a spy who has gleaned all manner of dirt. Hunting has this quality, too—except that the hunted, when you walk up to it after a good shot, lacks just one thing: life. When a thing lacks that, it has lost something in fun value, even while it may have gained in trophy value, or fun after the fact.

In most sports, the element of competition is requisite. I am inclined to believe that competition is superfluous to fishing, if not actually injurious to its fun. We have experimented with all manner of competition during fishing, and it's no go. At the trout club we have tagged trout, and the fellow catching the fish with the lucky number got the pool. As an innocuous form of gambling, it was fair. As fishing, it was the bunk. The fellows who were serious fishermen forgot all about the pool and just fished, and were faintly chagrined to take trout with little brass paper clips on their tails. The fellows who were interested in gambling forgot all about their fishing, and you could tell by the way they unhooked nonpaying fish that they were fishing for a number, not for fun.

At least one trip a year has a fellow along who suggests "a fin for the biggest, a fin for the most." This way fish, fishermen, and fishing all suffer. You have no time to examine your trout, to speculate on what lies beneath the water, or to note with any special pleasure your sensations of laziness and warmth and escape. A big trout, or a lot of trout, should be caught for your sake, or their own sake, and not for the sake of collecting a couple of fins. I do not say that gambling isn't fun. It's a very stirring form of fun. But it is not fishing, any more than a slot machine is a fly rod. As for competition, how can there be any when there is no antagonist?

The more interested you become in fishing, the more interested you will become in its high escape quality. If you have nothing—no wife, work, or woes—from which to escape, you will begin inventing obstacles after you have fished a few seasons. The angling husband frequently hopes that, as he leaves the house with his hallowed equipment, his wife will say: "Silly!" He wants her to say this so that he can say: "Well, by God! It isn't!" and depart with the impressiveness of a launching coal barge—into a background on which he holds his own sacred patents, all masculine.

The fisherman at work feels not only at peace with his background, but glorified by it. He takes unto himself its apparent wildness, and gives to it the honor of his awareness. Here, his savagery and his cruelty are fine attributes. They belong. At home, he might chastise his son for annoying the goldfish; but here, he will partake ravenously of his son's triumph in catching trout. I am certain that those who have not felt this difference in background are those who condemn fishing and hunting because these sports are cruel and predatory. Of course they are! That's one of the exhilarating things about them! Yet sporting editors, in answering the spoilsports, seldom if ever admit it. Instead, they roll off phrases about "the heritage of our forefathers." Some even go so far as to call this heritage "noble." It seems to me that what we inherited from our forefathers is first of all, life. Once in a while life may achieve nobility, but it practically always achieves cruelty. I am not even sure that that is too bad. All I know is that it is true. I have never read any arguments which justified hunting and fishing on humane grounds. Why should it be justified on those grounds? One of the reasons why fishing is fun is that its background justifies a fellow in a brief respite from being humane.

I am indebted to my father for introducing me to the sport of fishing. But I doubt if he ever witnessed the light of nobility shining from my eyes while I was catching white perch. What I see in my own son's countenance when he has a pickerel on are savage delight, greed, triumph, uproarious excitement, and, if he loses the fish, disappointment. From these expressions, and from his occasional outcries, I gather that he is having a hell of a good time. While it lasts, he is not humane. He is human. And he seems to have escaped from everything—home, boredom, adult control, the cognizance of mosquitoes, and his own obscurity.

Fishing is fun because it lets you indulge most of your human qualities without getting hung for it. If you can also catch its grace and see its beauty, there's an extra dividend. Sometimes there is stealth. Always there's surprise and curiosity. Except to other fishermen, there is no kindness—even when you return a trout to the water unharmed. You return him because you've had enough, or because the law requires it, or because he is too small for bragging or eating purposes, or so you can hope to catch him next year when he's bigger. No, you cannot be kind. You can be gentle in your methods, but the results are the same.

From all these ingredients, fishing derives its fun. When the sun is right; when the stream is good, and the wind small; when trout are coming well, fishing produces a kind of happiness which is sustained even during the moment you pause to examine it. The only other sport I know which has this quality is drinking. In both enterprises, an illusion is created, justified, and maintained over a period of time. While it lasts, you are a human being —in fact, one of the best!

DEEP-SEA FISHING

In its fleeting moments of glory game fishing provides surprise, adventure and beauty of an order unsurpassed by any other. According to those who know, the smashing attack of a blue marlin or the swift, rocketing run of a tuna or even the leaps of the relatively lightweight sailfish are thrills more potent than any you can get stalking lions in Africa, schussing the Headwall at Tuckerman Ravine, or sitting ringside at a championship fight. Ernest Hemingway, who presumably has experienced most of the fleshly and emotional excitements the twentieth century has to offer, has always ranked big-game fishing above all the rest. Some years ago, in *Esquire,* he wrote: "It [the excitement] comes from the fact they are strange and wild things of unbelievable speed and power and a beauty, in the water and leaping, that is indescribable, which you would never see if you did not fish for them, and to which you are suddenly harnessed so that you feel their speed, their force and their savage power. . . ."

A fascinating variation on the more familiar form of deep-sea fishing is bait casting at sea. To one who is a devotee of the artificial lure, used with light tackle in fresh water, this might prove an easy entree to the bigger stuff. The fresh-water bait-casting outfit, slightly modified, gives ideal sport in salt water. The light rig is just right for channel bass, striped bass, weakfish and blues. In the South you may reasonably expect to land tarpon up to five feet long.

A standard fresh-water bass fishing rod—say a six-ounce rod, five and a half feet long—will do, but it really ought to be six or eight inches longer. Four inches of that will be in the grip. You can cast farther two-handed, and you can rest the butt of the rod against your body in fighting a large fish. But the rod won't be much heavier. The reel is all right but you will put on it a hundred yards of fifteen-pound test silk or nylon line. Linen does not work well in salt water. Have a supply of one-foot gut leaders. Many salt-water fish have teeth or sharp gill covers, or both.

For lures you will need several metal spoons and a few plugs, slow sinkers and fast sinkers.

The rod for use down South is only slightly different—about a foot longer and a little sturdier than your fresh-water bass rod. On the reel you want a hundred yards of twenty-four-pound test silk or nylon. Different lures will be needed because this larger outfit won't cast a five-eighth-ounce play. Pick out a couple of lures made for king mackerel, a couple more of the kind designed for great northern pike and top these off with a shrimp plug. You may also take along a metal spoon. The plugs weigh around an ounce and a quarter.

From the ground, or from a pier or jetty, or from a boat, you can throw that plug a mile. You can watch for tarpon and cast at them when they strike or roll at the surface. Hooked on this tackle the big fish really goes to town, for you haven't a rig so heavy that you can slap him down flat and knock the fight out of him the first time he comes up out of the water.

It's a great game, this bait-casting in salt water. There is the pleasure of the cast itself, and a good cast has all the thrill of a well-hit golf ball. There is so much more thrill in the strike, because you always have a tight line and fish hit moving lures much harder than they do still baits. And there is the crowning pleasure of battling a fish on tackle that gives him a chance.

SURF FISHING

Until you have stood on a lonely October shore with the sedge grass reddening in the frosty air, and hurled your bait beyond the booming breakers, you still have one more fishing thrill to come.

Nighttime on the beach—then is the time to be abroad in search of striped bass in the summer time. The darkness and the evening chill have driven the last bather reluctantly from the water which now shimmers, darkly mysterious in the moonlight. The wide slope of sand is deserted, save for a party of picnickers around a flaring campfire. Their supper is over; they have heaped their charcoal fire high with driftwood which flames and crackles and throws their shadowy figures into silhouette, probably less grotesque than the originals. Later, they will sing, but now the only sound is the low boom of the surf, the surge and resurge of the wash across the phosphorescent sands. Far out on Ocean's tumbling bosom, the lights of a coasting steamer wink gravely at the stars and somewhere between you and the ship, your bait rises and settles gently to the pull of the breakers. It is like a telegraph line projected into a strange world, some denizen of which may send you a message, collect, at any second. It may be a skate or a sand shark. Or it may be a bass!

It may be that the next second, you will feel the unmistakable tug of a bass, followed by a strong, steady pull as he begins to run. You set the hook twice with all your might and hang on. A terrific surge runs through the line, bending the rod in a vibrant arc and then begins a battle royal, a battle not confined to a roped square of canvas but one which takes in wide spaces of beach and ocean as you stumble up and down the sand after your adversary, in and out of the surf for a desperate, panting half-hour until, if you are favored by the gods, a long comber will lift the tired fish and sweep him gently in to lie gleaming and quivering at your feet. If so, it is well worth the quest, the struggle and the toil of carrying him through the shifting sands to your car. And well worth it, next day, when cut into thick chunks, stuffed and baked, he reposes on the dinner table.

HAND-FISHING

As an added thrill, as a novelty, as a bit of variety and as a test of skill for the occasional day off, try bare-hand fishing. As pure thrill, this art, or sport, cannot be matched.

Catch a flounder, for simplest example, by hand. In summer or fall, when the flat fish comes closer and closer into shore for his food, he can be swooped up out of shallow tidal creeks without benefit of tackle.

To prepare the grounds for the hunt (which is what it amounts to) you have to travel upstream, stirring up the bed with your feet as you go to throw up a camouflage for the trip down. The waters must be clouded for the hunt to be successful, otherwise the flounder is apt to bury himself in the gravel at your approach, leaving only his two eyes staring out of the sand. And you won't know whether you have him or not.

Having stirred up the gravel for a distance upstream, you are ready for the chase. The return trip, by the way, requires considerable agility and is an excellent means of keeping down the waistline. You come downstream on all fours, your palms pressing down flat on the river bottom, your knees wherever they are most comfortable. Coming down in a swinging arc, like a traveling pendulum, your palms will find the fish. If the hand comes down over the head, you have him, for he will not be able to swim away. Merely close the fingers over the snout, lift out the prize and drop him into your bag. If, however, your hand falls on the tail, you will need both hands to complete the catch. Try lifting the flounder single-handed, and he'll scoot away downstream. Hold his tail, however, and bring the palm of the other hand up under him, and he's yours.

Hand-fishing for brook and speckled trout is slightly more complicated, demanding more patience and skill—you stretch out flat on a rock on the shore, making yourself as motionless as the stone itself; you slip your hand carefully into the water; you slowly, warily, coat your hand with seaweed or slime; and then you wait your chance to close your hand gently over an unsuspecting fish. This is a lazy man's kind of fishing, for it requires long stretches of lying motionless along the shoreline of a stream. There is nothing like it: the joy of watching the sunlight flecking the green waters with sprays of gold; the miracle of color when the darting trout flashes across the sunlight—and your close-up intimacy with it; the pleasure of eating such a catch, smoked over a willow smudge, its freshness and flavor sealed by searing the sides against the flames; and the sheer pleasure of battling the creature at even odds, and of outwitting him. It's real sport making a catch this way. Try it once and see. It requires all the skill, the wit, all the resources at the command of the "compleat angler." It has all the thrill of the primitive in it, a thrill no outdoor man will readily forego. For, after all, the thing that sends any man outdoors is the primitive urge.

HOW TO ENJOY FISHING

William J. Schaldach has the idea that joining an angling club is like reading a book; some people can take it, others just can't see the view for the mountains. Where do you fit in?

To get the most out of trout fishing one mustn't concentrate too intently on one's leader and flies. It is entirely possible to become overserious, to get so wrapped up in casting technique and angling problems that much of what is properly associated with a day on the stream passes by the gate unnoticed.

We pity the golfer who plays along serenely enough until the fateful day when he breaks eighty—and thinks he has caught the trick. Then for just weeks he can't get below the nineties. He sweats and groans, adopts new stances and swings, works himself into a lather. Golf is now a business and the joy has departed from life. Pathetic, isn't it? Well, while we're at it let us shed a tear for the angler who ties himself up in a knot over the matter of tackle and casting technique. It is surprising how easily one can get that way. Fishing is naturally conducive to it.

To illustrate, I present the sad case of John Butterworth. Butterworth represents a type. Since his graduation from college in the early twenties he has spent the bulk of his time boning at business. Recreation has been infrequent and brief, consisting principally of halfhearted participation in very

THE TOP FISHING REGIONS

 Atlantic Salmon / Brook Trout	Landlocked Salmon	Chinook Salmon / Coho Salmon	Rainbow Trout	Brown Trout	Large-mouth Bass / Small-mouth Bass
WHERE					
New Brunswick, Newfoundland, Nova Scotia, Maine, Quebec.	Maine, Quebec, New Hampshire, Vermont, Nova Scotia, Ontario.	Alaska, British Columbia, Washington, Oregon, California.	Idaho, British Columbia, Alaska, Oregon, Washington, Michigan, California, New Zealand.	Montana, Colorado, Wyoming, Michigan, New York, New Mexico, California.	Ontario, New Brunswick, Wisconsin, Minnesota, Arkansas, Georgia, South Carolina, Tennessee, Florida, Maine.
WHEN					
May through September but best in June and July. Often fast fishing in month of April for "black" salmon.	Spring and fall as a rule. Best just after ice-out and again in September. Some deep lakes are productive during summer months but check before planning.	As a rule, the months of July and August are best for chinooks, late September and October for coho, but it depends on where you go. Salmon can be had all year round, however, if you follow their migrations.	In general, April to October. Largest share of coastal rainbows (steelheads) caught in winter months (November and December). Summer-run steelheads from June through September.	In general, May, June and July are best months for prize winners. In the Far West good trout fishing begins with the eastern decline and lasts through fall.	In Southern waters from March through May; in North, July to October. Florida waters produce the big ones all year round but February, July and October are best.
HOW					
Fly-casting by law and preference. Angler can wade most rivers, but a good share of the fishing is done from guide boats or canoes. Wet or dry fly. Small trout patterns now popular.	Fly-casting, spinning gear. Some anglers troll small spoons and flies or use live smelt early in the season for lake fishing.	Fly-casting, spinning and trolling from skiff or rowboat. Chinooks don't respond to flies in *all* rivers but the coho is fly fisherman quarry. Polar bear, optic streamer flies may be cast among schooling cohos.	Fly-casting, spinning, bait-casting and trolling. To the fly fisherman the rainbow is principally a wet-fly fish. Very susceptible to spinners and spoons of all sorts.	Fly-casting, spinning, trolling and bait-casting in some of the larger rivers. The brownie is traditionally sought with the dry fly.	Fly-fishing, bait-casting, spinning and trolling. Bass is most sought game fish in America. The large-mouth is often found in mud-bottomed lakes, the small-mouth in gravel-bottomed waters.
TACKLE					
A 9-foot fly rod between 5¼ and 6¾ oz. in weight. Good, sturdy, single-action reel with 100 yards of 18-lb. test backing plus the fly line.	Long fly rod (9 or 9½ feet) preferable for casting from canoe. For wading, short rod should be light (4 to 5 oz.) as lakes are free of snags and fish can be handled with maximum sport in open water.	3-6 tackle (6-oz. tip and 6-thread line) 2/0 reel, spoons and plugs. For fly-fishing, a 9- or 9½-foot rod of 6 or 7 oz. in weight. At least 150 yards of backing.	A 5- to 7-oz. fly rod for most Western waters. Heavy spinning and bait-casting gear. Troll big lakes with 3-6 tackle. Torpedo head line recommended for Western rivers with nylon backing (100—150 yds).	Light to heavy weight fly rods, depending on size of water being fished and average size of trout. An 8½-foot, 4¾-oz. rod is standard. For spinning, a 7- or 7½-foot rod with 4- to 7½-lb. test line.	Nine-foot fly rod from 5 to 6¾ oz. Bait-casting rod from 4½ to 6 feet. Short rod popular in South, 5½- and 6-foot lengths for open, Northern waters where light lures are used. Standard spinning gear.
REMARKS					
Atlantic salmon fishing has been on the increase in Maine: The Dennys, Penobscot, Narraguagus, St. Croix and Pleasant Rivers are top spots. Record catch: 79 lbs. 2 oz., Tanaelu, Norway, 1928.	Best landlocked are in Maine's lakes and rivers. Record: Landlocked—22½ lbs., Sebago Lake, Maine, 1907; brook trout—14½ lbs., Nipigon River, Ontario, 1916.	Best Pacific salmon fishing on the continent is in Alaska and at Campbell River, B. C.	Maybe a 6-pounder or better in late fall (October-November) Michigan runs. Twenty-pounders run in Idaho's Lake Pend Oreille, May to November. Record: 37 lbs., Lake Pend Oreille, Idaho, 1947.	Although fishing for brown trout is good in U.S., the classic brown trout fishing is in the chalk streams of England, on a "beat" costing from $5,000 up. Record: 39½ lbs., Loch Awe, Scotland, 1866.	Florida's largest bass producer but an Arkansas "float trip" is a must for bass anglers. Record: Large-mouth — 22½ lbs., Montgomery Lake, Ga., 1932; Small-mouth—14 lbs., Oaklank, Fla., 1932.

Muskellunge	Channel Bass	Striped Bass / Bluefish	Tarpon / Bonefish	Bluefin Tuna / Broadbill Swordfish	Sailfish / Blue Marlin / White Marlin
Ontario, Wisconsin, New York, Minnesota.	New Jersey, Maryland, Virginia, North Carolina, South Carolina, Florida.	Massachusetts, North Carolina, New Jersey, New York, Rhode Island, Delaware, Maryland, Virginia, Pacific Coast.	Bahamas, Florida, Texas, Mexico.	Maine, Nova Scotia, Massachusetts, Bahamas, New York, California.	Cuba (north coast), Bahamas, Florida, Maryland, New York, New Jersey, Mexico, Pacific Coast (Pacific sailfish).
In general from June through October. Late fall fishing very spotty. Old-timers claim that the best fishing occurs immediately after the season opens.	March to December. September and October best north of the Carolinas. Month of August poor for big fish all over.	In general, June, July, and August; often good in September. Bluefish runs are spotty. First big run since 1936 occurred in 1947.	In general best fishing extends from April to early June. Florida tarpon fishing at best in May.	In general from June through September. The Bahamas, in June, Catalina in July and August, late July to mid-September at Nova Scotia.	February, March, and April are tops in Florida waters. July through September in the Bahamas. April top month for Pacific sailfish.
Bait-casting and trolling. The plug caster must learn to make the wooden minnow live if he hopes to dupe a musky, for muskies are fond of animated lures. The rule for trolling varies with the locale.	Surf casting and trolling. Red drum frequent inlets. Boats generally move alongside the schooling fish and the angler casts among them. Bait crabs, menhaden, squid, any trolled lure.	Trolling and surfcasting. Bait—squid, block tin squid, eel skins, feathered jigs, plugs.	Spinning, fly-casting, bait-casting and trolling. Heavy bait-casting gear now most popular for tarpon, fly-casting gear for bonefish. Use a skiff with outboard for bonefish. Fly casters like to wade tidal flats.	Trolling, still-fishing, or chumming, for tuna. Guides provide cut bait, herring, mackerel, squid. Best from rowboat; some use dories. Sight broadbill on surface, come up behind, circle bait in front of fish.	Trolling. Bait—mullet, squid, balao, bonefish, barracuda, feathered jig.
Heavy bait-casting tackle. Rod. 4½ to 5½ feet long. A 2/0 reel with at least 100-yard line capacity. Line 18- to 24-lb. test.	Standard surf tip, 6½ to 7 feet long. A 2/0 reel. Line—12 thread; 4- and 6-oz. sinkers; 7/0 hook.	Standard surf rod 6½ to 7 feet long. Very light rod can be used for blues. 2/0 reel and 9- or 12-thread line, 3-6 tackler for trolling. Need wire leaders for blues.	3-6 for trolling with 2/0 reel for bonefish, 2/0 or 4/0 for tarpon.	For tuna—a 23- to 36-oz. tip, a 12/0 or 14/0 reel, line 36 to 54 thread—rod should be equipped with roller guides. For broadbill, a 16- to 22-oz. tip, a 10/0 or 12/0 reel, 24- to 39-thread line, depending on tip size.	For sailfish use lightest tackle possible. The tackle limit is affected by the number of sharks in the water. 16-oz. tip, 24-thread for blue marlin; 12-oz. tip, 24-thread for white; 6-oz. tip, 9-thread for sails.
Men have fished for 15 years without getting a musky. Dubs often land five in a day. Best bet probably in north Wisconsin lakes and Lake-of-the-Woods area. Record: 64½ lbs., Lac du Flambeau, Wis., 1947.	Give the fish free rein—don't stand and fight it out. Never set the hook until his full weight is felt. They often pick up and drop bait. Record: 75½ lbs., Cape Hatteras, N. C., 1941.	Blues are considered by many as the hardest fighting fish in salt water. Record: Bluefish—no official record; striped bass—73 lbs., Vineyard Sound, Mass., 1913.	Fly-fishing for bonefish is quite new. Experts are using streamer-type flies in yellows and white. Record: Bonefish—13¾ lbs., Bimini, Bahamas, 1919; Tarpon — 247 lbs., Panuco River, Mexico, 1938.	Tuna hook themselves, so keep light drag on initial run. Never hold fish too hard—make him do the work. Record: Tuna—927 lbs., Ipswich Bay, Mass., 1940; swordfish—860 lbs., Tocopilla, Chile, 1940.	When marlin or sailfish first hit the bait, pay out slack. Fish will hit again. Record: Sailfish—106 lbs., Miami, Fla., 1929; blue marlin—737 lbs., Bimini, 1919; white marlin —161 lbs., Miami, 1938.

mild sets of tennis, a little swimming and an occasional sail on the Sound in a friend's yacht. With his domestic affairs satisfactory enough and a substantial rating in the financial world John found life very good. Storm clouds swept across his horizon, though, in a most unanticipated manner.

It started when he accepted an invitation to go trout fishing with a friend. Being city-bred and reared in an atmosphere of artificiality, Butterworth's outdoor experience had been largely gleaned from the sheltered surroundings of resorts. With him, Nature was a standardized sort of thing that one took in doses every so often.

On this first trouting trip, then, Butterworth found himself confronted by something totally different from anything he had ever known. His friend outfitted him with a good substantial fly-rod and tackle, taught him the rudiments of casting and turned him loose on a well-stocked pool, one of the choicest on the club property. There was some clumsy splashing of the line at first and once or twice flies got caught in clothing, but John, though not enthusiastic, was willing. With him diligence and perseverance were life rules. The trout were tame and didn't mind too much. Presently, one seized the fly, to John's utter amazement, and went dashing downstream in a frenzied rush. The novice tried to remember the rules he had been taught: keep the rod tip up; don't let him get slack line; lead him away from the fast water. And considering his lack of experience he didn't do at all badly. Things happened fast; by a miracle the leader held and the trout, a good pounder, was finally subdued and dragged to the net. John felt strangely excited as he scooped up the struggling, many-hued quarry. By evening, an entirely new world had opened for him. Conversion was sudden and complete.

After that, fishing trips became a regular thing. Butterworth purchased a reasonably good rod and equipment, practiced until he became a tolerably good caster and went at it with enthusiasm. His catches were usually very fair and there was no doubt but that he was having a loop. If he had only let it go at that he would probably be a happy man today; but he made the mistake of joining a club.

Now joining an angling club is very much like reading a book. Some people can take it, others can't. Butterworth couldn't. He was much too serious. He soon made the discovery that he had been naïve in believing that his days on the stream had been successful ones, merely because he had taken a few trout on flies and had enjoyed a good time as a result. Conversations with ultrascientific members showed where he was away off. That rod, for example; how had he ever managed to struggle along with it? And his flies! he had bought them in perfect innocence, taking the tackle clerk's word for it. It is true that they did take fish, but at the club everyone was discussing lateral hackling, single upright wings and bivisibles. The utmost importance was placed on the proper taper of the leader, calibrated every six inches from loop to tippet. Once a member raised an eyebrow ever so slightly when John quite innocently asked what a reverse taper line meant.

You begin to see the point? Poor Butterworth, being a fundamentalist basically, took all this entirely too literally. He began to buy rods with the zeal of a collector, only to discard them one by one because they did not meet his fancied requirements. The search for perfection led him into the field of flies. There he floundered around amid theory until his tackle room resembled a milliner's shop; feathers, tinsel, thread, chenille and mohair were scattered about in wild abandon. The final stage was the development of that faraway look in his eyes that his friends began to notice shortly after he had received a huge consignment of goods from a London tackle shop.

Lest the above seem too much like an exaggeration I wish to state that the case of Butterworth was very similar to my own, a few years back. Having passed through that hectic state I feel it almost a duty to warn those who may now be treading the borderline. The possession of a few items of fine tackle, such as a pair or so of handmade rods of varying weight and dimensions, lines to match, and a reasonable collection of flies, is to be desired. But once a man realizes that with such equipment he is ready for a day's sport under almost any circumstances he ought to let it go at that and be content.

More important, in the writer's opinion, is study of the stream and the habits of the quarry. A man should know where he may expect to find the various species of trout in a given water; that rainbows will use the fastest and heaviest rips, that brown trout are partial to a steady and even flow and that brook trout love shade and, usually, quiet pools. When to look for fish in the tail of the pool and at what times of the day to seek them in the shallow bright water are important considerations. A sketchy knowledge, at least, of aquatic insects is to be recommended, but it need not be at all scholastic. An angler should know a drake from a spinner, a May fly from a shad fly. If, however, he reaches the point where he carries a magnifying glass and collecting bottles you may be reasonably sure that he is teetering along the edge. He is about to enter the distracting field of entomology.

Here again lies a threat of danger, danger to one's amateur standing. It is so easy to become a professional fly-fisherman, and thereby to lose the whole point of the sport. If a man safely passes the tacklemania stage he may yet fall into the trap of trout stream theory. The symptoms are first manifested in an avid reading of everything that has been written on the subject; and that is plenty! His mind laden with the controversial writings of ten volumes dealing with the natural imitation theory, the question of whether or not trout are color-blind and the exact distance at which they can distinguish sound, the victim now finds himself in much the same position as the centipede that didn't know which leg came after which. Doubt and confusion creep in to ruin what should be a corking day, regardless of the outcome in creel results. When a man starts dashing about from pool to eddy with a thermometer, testing the water temperature to see if it checks with the advice of, say, His Grace, the Duke of Penningworth of Shropshire (who has done a twelve-hundred-page volume on the subject), the case is rapidly becoming grave. It would be a real blessing to find the poor chap's books and burn them, while there is yet time!

If what has been written sounds hard and overcritical let me say that my intentions are only of the kindest. Having experienced the various phases of nuttism discussed, and having passed through them with at least a measure of sanity remaining, I offer some suggestions which I hope may prove of value in obtaining the fullest enjoyment from a day spent along the river.

Every angler should be a collector of trout streams and the moods which overhang them. He should be an observer of beauty in a definite and conscious way. As he wades along and casts his flies he need not be so intent on the possibility of a rise that he misses the leap of white water, charging and singing over ledge rock.

One can well spare time out to listen to the song of a white-throated sparrow; and where the river opens out around a bend to reveal a broad valley, whose enclosing hills are bathed with enchanting light, there should the angler sit for a while and drink it in. These things give meaning to Izaak Walton's thought that angling is a contemplative sport.

It is impossible to spend a day along a trout stream without absorbing something of the atmosphere of Nature. But the point I make is that it is too often done in a subconscious and halfhearted manner. Zest for the sport itself may easily overwhelm a man. What fly to use? How to overcome drag in casting to that far bank? Is a 3x leader light enough? Problems, problems! After all, are these things *really* so important?

Of course we want to catch fish when we put on our waders and string up our rods. But at best a few will suffice. And under anything like normal conditions we need not be so terribly serious in order to take those few. It seems to me that a sensible division of the time spent during a day's fishing might read like this: attention to tackle and casting problems, 20 per cent; consideration of stream conditions and fish habits, 30 per cent. That is half of the time devoted to actual angling, leaving the other half to leisure for the pure enjoyment of the out-of-doors. Once this attitude is adopted it is possible to return from a trip empty-handed, yet perfectly content.

In other words, one need not always break eighty in order to have a good time.

An outstanding experience occurred several years ago, when in company with two companions I fished a lonely, half-forgotten mountain lake in the Catskills, over three thousand feet above sea level. To get there we drove up a rutted and rocky wood road with barely enough bedding to entitle it to the name. Most of the journey was accomplished by the use of low and second gears. At the end of a mile or so the alleged road petered out to an abandoned hay meadow, which through neglect had largely grown up to brush. There we tethered the car and took to the trail afoot. A steady climb of two more miles through a lonely and beautiful forested area brought us to a sparkling gem of a little lake.

Our fishing was done from an ancient boat, which had to be bailed constantly by one member of the trio. This left another to paddle while the third was free to fish. By taking turns we all had a chance. Like the road over which we had driven, the lake itself had gone to seed and trout were scarce and hard to rise. I don't recall accurately how many we did catch, perhaps in the neighborhood of a half-dozen. What I shall never forget, though, is the rare and unique charm of that little lake, nestled up there among the mountain ridges. From the deep woods great horned owls sent out their challenging calls; pileated woodpeckers, shy and retiring birds which have become rare in recent years, drummed a steady tattoo; and at evening a swimming mink crossed the calm water in the sunset, breaking its surface into bars of gold, burnished copper and purple.

Trout streams are like people. Each has a definite personality. Some are tricky and inclined to be mean. On such waters one must watch his step constantly to avoid trouble. I know one such spiteful little devil in Westchester County, New York. It drops a matter of seven hundred feet in a few miles, and for turbulence and tempestuousness it resembles nothing so much as an irascible old landlord. Yet, even as the latter may have his occasional soft moments, so this stream has given me some rare hours of fun—plus, I must admit, several cold baths.

The opposite conditions are found on the calmer and serener rivers of Michigan, of which the Pine and Little Manistee are good examples. They are open and frank. There one may fish through the long summer days, treading the even sand and gravel bottom as unconcernedly as one walks the city streets. A dry fly floats beautifully on much of this water, and there are some whopping browns and rainbows to be risen and hooked. Except where the rivers flow through swamps the fishing is easy and restful.

For brilliance of temperament, plus grandeur of surroundings, the fly-fisher is referred to the rivers of the West. Such streams as the Gunnison in Colorado, the Madison in Montana and the Rogue and Deschutes on the Pacific Slope offer the angler not scenic beauty alone, but unique problems as well. For there is no denying that the snow-fed waters of the mountain rivers influence the fighting qualities of the trout. But the sport is strenuous.

My taste runs more to a pastoral setting in a country of smaller mountains and hills. I like the patterned slopes that rise gently from the bottomlands, crisscrossed by rambling and weed-grown stone fences. I like mountain laurel and wild roses, fields of daises, paint brush and joe-pye weed. I even like poison ivy, because it thinks of the most decorative ways of draping itself around things. And cows. There should be cows somewhere near a trout stream. Of course one doesn't want them to be eternally wading in front of one's cast, but barring that, cows are undoubtedly an asset. The clanking ring of cowbells adds an indefinable quality to a day astream, and the varied tone of a herd seen against the soft green of pasture land is something to add to your list of impressions, which you are steadily collecting as you go about your fishing.

In the cool of evening, as you hopefully await the insect hatch, it is comforting to look far above to a hillside farm and see the thin blue curl of wood smoke arising from the red brick chimney of a neatly kept farmhouse. You feel that the simple people who dwell there aren't too greatly concerned about what the stock market is doing.

And for the final touch there should be a covered bridge. Where the water swirls against the moss-clothed, rocky abutment you are sure to find a fern-draped pool. If you place your fly carefully you are pretty apt to coax up a good trout.

Mention of the covered bridge reveals the place at once, for the few surviving examples of fine ones are to be found in New England and New York State, particularly in the Catskills. And the rivers that flow through this rugged but intimate land are the answer to the questing angler's doubts. Let the collector of trout streams wander as he will; if he has first tasted the delights of Catskill waters all is lost. He may think for a time that on such rivers as the Margaree (the upper reaches, where good trout are to be had) and the Cheticamp on Cape Breton Island, Nova Scotia, he has found the ideal; the waters of the lower province, with the possible exception of the upper St. Mary's River, will not hold him long. They are for the most part wilderness streams, grand in their way, but scarcely intimate or inviting. This also applies to most of the New Brunswick waters and many of the streams of Maine. Sport of a superb order is undoubtedly to be had there; trout average large in size, but wet-fly fishing from a canoe is the rule. The angler who likes to wade and prefers the dry-fly method will find something lacking.

To wet one's waders in such streams as the Beaverkill, the Willowemoc, the Neversink and the Mongaup in the Catskills is like returning home from China.

In my personal collection of trout streams the Beaverkill has come to represent the standard by which all waters are judged. If I were asked to give the reasons, they would probably sound silly. In the first place, all of us who know this grand stream will admit that trout are not nearly as plentiful as they were a dozen or more years ago. Again, the Beaverkill is no bed of roses to wade, particularly when there is a good head of water running. Erosion, too, due to the overcutting of forest land has all but ruined many of the finest pools. Finally, there is the question of competition, which grows yearly at an alarming rate. Whereas in the past a handful of anglers visited the river in May and June they now literally swarm from the Forks Pool to Beaverkill Post Office on the small river and down to below Cook's Falls on the big water.

But there is much left, those intangible things which are a part of the old river and which, happily, escape the current of a changing era. There are the pools, for one thing, all named and each with its own individuality, its records of triumph and defeat: The Forks, Barnhart's, Hendrickson's, Horse Run, Cairns, School House, Lockwood's, Mountain and so on down the river to Baxter's and beyond. Horse Run has a heavy rip, where rainbows may sometimes be caught, and Mountain Pool is fine to fish during the May-fly hatch, because of its currents. I suspect, though, that the biggest attraction of Mountain Pool for many of us is the way in which its far bank rises up straight from the water, in a series of mossy ledges, covered with ferns and accented by clumps of rhododendron. Looking across Barnhart's Pool one sees the finest light effects about seven in the evening, as the sun glows behind a mountain.

On lowery days, mist wraiths hover about and obscure the ridges so the landscape looks like the old engravings of the Highlands of Scotland that used to hang in Grandma's parlor. But when the sun shines brightly the atmosphere has an unbelievably brilliant quality. The water, too, in this region is so crystal-clear that it is possible to toss a dime into a ten-foot pool and note accurately whether it lands heads or tails.

During the past five years I can recall no really big catches, no exceptionally large trout having been taken either by my friends or myself. Competition has increased and difficulties have multiplied. Yet we return to wade and cast our flies year after year. Perhaps we are just sentimentalists, but on one point I am certain we would all agree: If the Beaverkill does not yield us the sport it formerly did it still affords a full 50 per cent of these abstract things which should be a part of the fly-fisher's day—beauty, charm and mood.

And if we do not take our sport too seriously, these things are sufficient. They represent the other side of trout fishing.

GUNNING

For the true connoisseur of the sport, hunting is a complex, highly disciplined sport that lures him into beautiful country at the time of year when Nature wears her brightest plumage. Not all that he bags is tangible. Nonhunters are likely to gauge the dividends in terms of the number of birds fetched home. These heretics don't know how to appraise the sun, clouds and color—the joy of seeing a pair of dogs freeze to a statuesque point, immobile against a brown backdrop of waving sedge. . . .

Mellow winter sunlight bathes the sleeping uplands of the South, transforming drab fields into living color. A gentle wind is just brisk enough to dispel the illusion of spring. Along the strip of sedge which borders a briery fence, a racing orange-ticked dog skids into a sudden stop. One step, another; then he freezes into a high-headed point. Ten yards behind, his brace-mate draws up with a backing point, honoring the find. In the tangle of grass and bramble ahead the alerted covey of quail lies, ready to burst on thundering wings and fan out across the field. This is the grand moment!

Each gun, each ground, each kind of game has its advocates, impassioned all. Here are a few, only a few, of the reasons why your peace too may lie behind a gun.

WING SHOOTING

The first man to kill a game bird on the wing experienced one of the greatest thrills in the annals of sport. It must have seemed a miracle. Beyond the gift of decent co-ordination and good eyesight the expert has nothing that anyone equally endowed can't acquire with practice. By shooting one learns to shoot. But to whatever practical terms and definitions we reduce the art of wing shooting there is still enough of the incredible in the performance to fascinate men who have shot all their lives. The dog finds at the edge of a patch of alders, and that by itself is something of an experience. As you come up with him there is a sudden, nerve-shaking roar of wings as the grouse gets up and darts away with the speed of a rocket. The matter is now in your hands. Your eyes must report the bird's speed and direction of flight, and the brain, if it is working as it should, takes these facts and makes instantaneous calculations as to where the gun should be pointed when the shot is fired. If the shot is successful you will realize that you've done considerably more than bag a pound and a half of the most delicious food on earth and partially satisfied your primordial passion for the chase. For once, at least, you have tasted the triumph of lightning-fast, perfect co-ordination as exemplified by your own nerves and muscles. It is an experience so very satisfying that you'll want to repeat it again and again.

Maybe that's why there are about fifteen million wing shooters in America. Some of these fifteen million are newcomers to the sport and are confused by the names tagged to our game birds. Seems no one wants to agree with the ornithologists.

In the sedge fields of the South, the natives swear that the quail, or bobwhite, is a "pa'tridge." Up in the hills of Maryland, Pennsylvania and northward, the farmers call the grouse a "partridge." As a matter of fact, the only "partridge" we have in this country is a foreigner that was first introduced to the prairies of Saskatchewan, Alberta and Manitoba a quarter-century or so ago—the European gray partridge. Because the first imported birds were brought over from Hungary, our wing shooters promptly misnamed the fat little bombshell with wings "Hungarian partridge." Yet this is the same "partridge" that roams the English heath.

If you must be technical about the game birds you hunt, the best thing to do is to consider the three classifications to which they have been relegated by the ornithologists: the gallinaceous birds, the shore birds, and the pigeons and doves.

The gallinaceous birds are king of the lot as far as upland shooting goes. This group includes the quail, grouse, turkey, pheasant and the Hungarian partridge. The last two are importations and are currently very much in the vogue, so much so a few million shooters swear they're the most sporty of all game birds.

These gallinaceous creatures are close kin to the barnyard fowl inasmuch as they're essentially ground dwellers given to much vigorous scratching of the soil. They are widely distributed, one or more varieties being found in most states. Most important fact is that every last one of this group is a delicacy for the palate.

The next group is the shore birds, and they are not rightly game fowl for they frequent the lowlands where marshes and inland waterways predominate. The shore birds include the woodcock, the plover, various sandpipers, jacksnipe and railbirds.

The woodcock is known by a variety of names. In the vicinity of Merrymeeting Bay in Maine, the natives refer to them as "timber doodles." In other areas they are known as wood snipe, night partridge, longbills, whistle-wings and other monickers.

It's no easy task to induce a woodcock to occupy a place on your dinner table. For one thing, he's a cleverly camouflaged fellow that sits tight and makes a setter or pointer work like a Trojan to find him. For another, he's just about the most unpredictable flier among all game birds. He may take off slow and easy, fast as a jet plane, straight as an arrow, then again he may zigzag upward with the most confusing display of flight pattern and wing action imaginable.

Finally, there are the pigeons and the doves. The mourning dove is the unexcelled master of flight acrobatics, and is the same bird you hear cooing so mournfully early in the morning and late in the evening. Years ago he had a cousin, the passenger pigeon. The cousin, however, was a dumb bird which fell easy victim to the market shooters and today the passenger pigeon no longer exists. This fate will doubtless never befall the mourning dove, for he is the swiftest-winged game bird and the trickiest. Manufacturers of shotgun shells bless the dove, for he's responsible for more bad shots than any other bird.

One reason dove shooting is so popular is because you don't need any fancy hunting rigs or highly trained dogs to hunt them. You simply station yourself at the edge of fields where the winged bullets come to feed. As the slate-colored fellow angles in for a landing you blast away—and usually miss. When you do drop one you have the reward of a small but highly delectable morsel.

Of all the game birds, the quail and the pheasant are probably the most sought after by the millions of hunters who hang a shotgun in the crook of their arm and go tramping across the fields.

The quail, the same bird that pipes a melodious "Bob White" during the languid summer months, is said to be the fastest game bird that flies—for the first sixty feet. Down in the deep Southland it's the hallmark of sport to journey afield on horseback with a good brace of setters and/or pointers working the sedge fields ahead of you. That's the plantation way of gunning for quail, but the majority of hunters leg it, getting plenty of exercise and thrills to boot as the highly trained dogs cast the coverts and freeze into statuesque "points."

Quail were once plentiful as far north as Maine, but their range has tightened to an area below the Mason-Dixon Line. They travel in coveys, from ten to as many as thirty birds. When flushed they are apt to startle you out of your wits by the drumming roar of beating pinions. They're so quick on the take-off, so sudden in the way they flush, that only the expert upland shooter can hope to drop a bird on every rise.

The ruffed grouse, which natives of the hills will swear is a "pa'tridge," but which definitely is not, is the bird most apt to make a fool out of any shooter. He's a handsome fellow that likes the mountain orchards and the laurel-grown draws and ravines of the mountain-ridge country. To hunt him you must have a setter or pointer. It's always fun to see a veteran quail shooter bring a perfectly trained quail dog into grouse country. The dog trained on quail likes to range freely, running fast, wide and handsome. Such a dog is a total flop when it comes to handling grouse. The hunting of grouse requires a bird dog that is trained for that job. These dogs hunt at close range, have chokebore noses and are able to pin a grouse under that nose.

A grouse is just about as scary a bird as there is. The best grouse shots I've seen walk through the timberland as though they have eggs in their shoes; careful, so very careful. When a grouse dog points, you better get there quick and be ready to shoot fast! The grouse booms into flight and presto! he's got a tree between you and himself.

And what about the "Chink"? He's the gaudy-hued fellow imported a few decades ago that has since taken over in more than a few states. In the summer the ringneck pheasant struts with all the aplomb of a peacock, but at the first crack of the first shot on opening day, he becomes a wily, thumbing-his-nose-at-you game bird.

A pheasant looks almighty big in flight, so much so that you think it's a spade you need to whack him down and not a shotgun. You get over the idea after you waste the first box of shells.

The exploits of a pheasant awing are enough to make you want to throw down your shotgun and scream angry blasphemy at the brilliant feathered cock-of-the-wild. There is a secret to bagging a mess of pheasant, though. It's a matter of "lead"; you have to learn how much space to leave between the gunsight and the outstretched head of the flying pheasant. Just shooting blindly because you're cutting loose with a shell full of small shot is no way to get yourself a meal, for if any bird can fly untouched through a hail of scatter shot, it's the ringneck.

He's as exasperating on the ground as in flight. For one thing, he'll run a ground race while other game birds will "stick" tight for the dog. He'll run and twist and slither through briers, brush and stubble like no other game bird in existence.

The smart bird dog makes a big swing, comes into the wind and nails the pheasant head on. Then and only then does the pheasant stay put.

Thanksgiving and Christmas are turkey-hunting time. In North Carolina turkey dogs are in vogue. They may be purebreds or the most ragged-looking cur dogs. They trail silently or openly. You shoot at a bronze-breast and hope for luck. Another way of hunting them is from "stations." You have ascertained beforehand where they feed, and in the early morning or late afternoon you crouch, wait and hope for a fat gobbler to put in an appearance. There's nothing like the feel of a twenty-pound wild turkey draped over your shoulder.

One of the worst things for anyone to attempt is to tell a fellow shooter what the best gun is for the game he shoots. What may be the ideal gun for you may be poison to him. You simply learn by dint of much wasted scattering of shot. Whether it's a double-barrel, a single-barrel, a pump gun or an automatic is up to you. It may be a chokebore piece or it may be open. The gauge may be .410, .20, .16 or .12.

Most game birds are dropped by the shooter within twenty yards of the take-off. If you're an amateur at the sport it's your own folly to try to drop them with a .410 or .20 gauge simply because those guns are light to carry. Equally true is the fact that if you miss with a .12 and keep right on missing after all kinds of practice, you'd better arrange to buy your pheasant for the plate from some commercial game breeder.

Where you shoot and when you shoot is dependent on the fatness of your wallet and the time you have. Some men travel hundreds and even thousands of miles in search of game birds when the shooting is practically in their own back yards. But the pastures still look green on the other side of the home fence.

And just for the sake of armchair dreaming you can start now to plan a trip that would begin in Maine in October with woodcock shooting; then to the Dakotas for pheasant shooting; to the prairies for Hungarian partridge; westward to the Pacific Coast for sage hen, and through the dry valleys bordering the Rockies for band-tailed pigeon, valley and mountain quail. On the homeward route there's scaled quail in the Southwest, jacksnipe in Louisiana and plentiful bobwhite and dove in Mississippi, Alabama, Florida and Georgia. Dream hard and you'll bag a turkey in the Carolinas and roaring-winged grouse in the Virginia, Maryland or Pennsylvania mountain country.

That trip's the dream of all wing shooters, but millions are discovering that the best sport is found on the last day of the trip, within harking distance from their doorstep. All of us are living on the doorstep of the wild. You don't have to make a trek of hundreds of miles to find good game-bird shooting. Whether you have hayseed in your hair or whether you live in an apartment building surrounded by the spires of skyscrapers, you can reach hunting territory in practically no time at all. Go, man!

BIRD DOGS

Not too many years ago a President of the United States, chatting with a group of friends, said: "There's only one thing more appealing than a beautiful woman. That is a bird dog on point."

Thousands feel about the same way. From the coupon clipper who spends thousands yearly having his dogs trained to the one-dog man who merely appreciates good things, the inner circle has grown into a large segment of sportsmen and pseudosportsmen who appreciate the beauty of a bird dog in action.

The fascination of watching this symmetry of motion, the brain, the body and the nose of the well-trained bird dog in action, has pleasant repercussions on wildlife conservation. For many it is more interesting and important than killing the game the dogs find. Some bird-dog men fire blank cartridges when the bird flushes; many find their pleasure in field trials. And those who do kill the birds their dogs find so accurately know they are aiding conservation by not leaving crippled birds—every bird shot is a bird found. Men who hunt without dogs cannot hope to make this claim.

Although bird dogs work on instinct, their training and molding is not easy. A man who wants a polished, well-broken dog must have first the love, patience and understanding. Know-how can be garnered from books. If one hasn't time for this training, he can send the dog to a good trainer for several months at a not exorbitant cost.

Watching bird dogs at work has become an important sport. Through the medium of field trials, where trained dogs are run in classes according to age, training and ability of their handler, many who have never heard of bird dogs before are becoming interested in the sport. Over four hundred formal field trials are held annually. These are the stiff trials where the majority of owners, handlers and judges follow the dogs to the bird field on horseback.

Bird dogs—the sleek, rangy pointer, the long-haired gentleman, the setter —can't justifiably be described as mere dogs. They are an expression, a sport in themselves.

WHY THE SAFARI?

What does a big game hunter get out of it all? Robert Ruark, reflecting on the not very tangible rewards to the professional "white hunter," put it this way:

There is a simple love of Nature, and of Nature's creatures, as against a hatred for the contrived living of cities, for the claustrophobic connivances of civilization, that drives a man to the vastnesses of Africa to fulfill some need of basic simplicity in himself. My friend Selby, hopelessly lost in the jungles of so small a town as Nairobi, is Moses leading his flock when all he can see is horizons and a lion or two. The complete love and trust of his blacks is testament to this.

He is happy in the dawn and in the tiny gleaming fires of the camp, and secure in his knowledge of domination of his element. He worships a buffalo or a lion or an elephant because he knows it can kill him painfully if he is not very careful. He builds his own bridges—makes his own roads. He still has the thrill of providing his own food, and the food of his friends. He recognizes the inevitability of death as an adjunct to life.

There are no more jealous people in the world than hunters. They have an intense pride in their work. A good white hunter will work himself into a breakdown to scare up a record bag for a man he despises. Hunters criticize each other constantly, and each man has his secret ground, a territory he endeavors, as long as possible, to keep from the ken of rival hunters. That personal pride prevents him from shooting the easy animal—what he wants is "heads."

"You are not shooting an elephant," Selby told me once, over a hot martini at the day's end. "You are shooting the symbol of his tusks. You are not shooting to kill. You are shooting to make immortal the thing you shoot. To kill just anything is a sin. To kill something that will be dead soon, but is so fine as to give you pleasure for years, is wonderful. Everything dies. You only hasten the process. But you remember we hunted rhino for three weeks, and never shot a single one we saw? That's what I mean. When you shoot a lion you are actually shooting its mane, something that will make you proud. You are shooting for yourself, not shooting just to kill."

This was an undue burst of eloquence from a usually taciturn young man, but I think I have his point, and the point of his brothers.

These few surviving men are largely Jasons, in search of the Golden Fleece, and they do not care who brings it down, so long as they are present at the chase. Selby, and his companions in arms, will actually work harder for a man they loathe than for a man they like and admire, because the ultimate end is noble in the mind.

Perhaps I invest the professional hunter with too much conscious sensitivity, which might be borne out by a banquet held by the hunters' association. One old gaffer, long since retired, was called on to talk. He fidgeted briefly, dug a finger into his boiled collar, and looked miserable. After great deliberation, he cleared his throat.

"Boy," he said firmly. "Bring the gin." And then he sat down.

SKEET

Skeet—an old Scandinavian word meaning "shoot"—requires skill and practice, but not so much a novice can't have fun at it, and it offers most delight to those who like to stand around and argue about the virtues of various bores, weights and makes of guns. It is a game likely to teach the "expert" field shot that he is not such a hot shot after all, and its practice is sure to reward any gunner with a higher co-ordination of mind and muscle.

The skeet field consists of two trap houses, placed forty yards apart, with trap openings for the targets facing each other. The first house has its target opening ten feet from the ground, to simulate the bird flying from high cover. The second house has an opening three feet from the ground, for the low-sprung bird. The clay disc, or bird, is flung from each house in an arc that carries it over the roof of the opposite house, to fall to the earth some twenty yards beyond. The traps are adjusted to throw the targets so that they reach a height of fifteen feet midway between the two trap houses.

Suppose these houses to be placed at the hours twelve and six of a clock. Each intervening hour is a shooting post, making seven posts, inclusive of the starting and finishing posts. The eighth post is right at the center of the clock face; that is, directly under the flight arc of the targets.

The trap puller sits behind three o'clock with a lever that leads to controls in both trap houses. Trap boys load the clay discs into the throwing machines. The shooter takes his place at twelve o'clock. When he is ready he gets his gun up to a "ready" or alert position, much as he would have it in the field if he were expecting a bird to jump from the bush at any instant. He says "Pull" or "Mark" to the trap puller, who, within the next three seconds, releases the clay bird. The three-second leeway is to make sure the gunner doesn't shoulder his weapon ahead of time; he must wait until he sees the released target.

Then he raises his gun and shoots at the bird coming out of the trap right next to him at sixty miles an hour. Pointing and shooting must take place in a fraction of a second; the best skeeters smash their birds before they pass the mid-mark, which is directly over the eighth post.

The second shot is from the same post, at a bird released from the opposite tower and coming toward the gunner. Thus he proceeds around the half-circle, taking two shots at each post, and then he takes two shots at the eighth post, right under the birds. That's the freak spot, which is said never to be duplicated in nature. It is necessary to shoot the bird before it gets overhead.

Having gone the rounds of the eight posts, with two shots at each post, the shooter returns to his first position for a pair of doubles. In doubles, the birds are released simultaneously from the two towers. The gunner fires first at the outgoing bird, then at the incoming bird. This, of course, requires fine co-ordination. The beginner is likely to muff his first shot in his anxiety not to let the second target get away; only with experience does he learn to be cool about the outgoing bird, concentrating on that kill before he swings for the second shot.

Double shots are made from the twelve o'clock, one o'clock, five o'clock and six o'clock posts.

In all, the gunner has expended twenty-four shots: sixteen in singles, and eight in doubles. He now takes a last fling, from any position he chooses, providing he names it before shooting. The optional shot is usually taken from the seventh post, though many sportsmen will select the post that is hardest for them, until they have mastered it.

Thus, twenty-five shots comprise a round. Anyone who breaks all the birds on a round is credited with a "straight," dubbed a twenty-five, and given a special button to wear. Average scores are around fifteen. If you run around twenty, you're an expert skeeter.

Beginners can enjoy skeet because a man who has never seen a gun before may step up and break six or eight targets in his first round. Those six or eight targets he breaks just as thoroughly and efficiently as a man who breaks all twenty-five of them. Imagine anybody making a good golf shot, or executing a first class forehand drive in tennis the first time he tries it!

Skeet shooters are not always practicing for real bird-shooting. Many of them like the sport for itself, and never go out into the field. You can shoot the clay all year round, while bird-shooting hereabouts is limited to forty days in the year. Skeeting is attractive because it is informal, and conversational. Shooting is usually done in squads of five, all members of the squad taking turns at each post before moving on to the next; kidding is not at all forbidden, though it is an unwritten rule to go easy on beginners. It is more leisurely and less costly than ordinary target shooting; in the old form of straight shooting one may kill from 150 to 200 clay birds in an afternoon; the skeeter will break from 50 to 75 targets.

The best way to learn the skeet shoot is not to go right out and shoot. As in most other sports, some preliminary study and practice will do a great deal more good than a pell-mell rush at the field of activity. Put a shotgun into the hand of a novice and he will probably take up a very awkward position, then follow the bird as it comes out of the tower until it is too late to shoot. When he does shoot, he will be considerably surprised at the kick of the gun. "She" will be even more surprised, and may decide to give up skeeting then and there.

A little preliminary explanation, some handling of the gun before a mirror, is of great help. The average person thinks of the shotgun as producing a spray as wide as a barn door; the reality, of course, is much closer to a handkerchief. Once the novice has got this in mind, he will have some notion as to the pointing of the gun. Then he must learn to lead, rather than follow, the bird. To swing up and shoot instantaneously; and when it comes to shooting doubles—

Just go out and try it.

HAND-TRAP SHOOTING

Skeet is a sweet sport, but for getting in trim for actual bird shooting nothing compares with hand-trap shooting.

Hand-trap shooting is a simple and economical sport—all you need is a gun, shells, a carton of clay birds, a hand trap and a companion.

The shotgunner can choose any type of shot, use any gun and about any shell. A rising grouse, a wink-quick black duck, a towering woodcock, a pheasant in full flight expressing out of sight; straightaway shots, dropping, quartering to right or left, the tricky grass cutters; you can simulate any type of game shot with a hand trap.

With a small expenditure and a bit of your time, you can polish up the old gun arm until it shines like the best of them. Get out the shotgun, buy a few shells and wham away!

SHOOTING THE PISTOL

What really, in the name of heaven, is that strange fascination which the pistol exerts over intelligent human beings (and they must be intelligent or the thing will be hopeless right from the start) so that they feel powerless to resist it? Is it the very difficulty of mastery? Is it the innate honesty which we encounter and love? We of the clan are unable to explain our complete immersion in the art—we just succumb!

When we are on the range, or in competition, we open our pistol case with tender care and view the black, sleek instrument of death with loving awe. We lift it out and heft it wordlessly. The beauty of its slender lines obliterates its terrible potency. We do not think of the murderous path of its bullet through flesh and bone, of the arrogant authority of the command which the spinning lead chunk sends to brain cells, to stop all the million delicate biological functions of mammal life, homo sapiens and other; of the sudden waste of individual education, culture, the promises of the future, of the appalling extent of sorrow, grief of mother, father, mate, children, of the awful irreparable finality.

We load the pistol matter-of-factly, take our stance, lift our gun hand, aim with micrometric accuracy and attend to the required expertness of trigger handling. Perfectly relaxed, with studious nonchalance, withal concentrated purposefulness, we release the shots.

Mastery of the pistol is just as exact a science as mathematics and just as much of an art as composing a symphony. Everyone of all the many biological centers must be submerged. All mental and physical purposes of the body converge to a pin point, to a concentration so profound that it seems removed from the sphere of earthly endeavor.

While part of our brain may perceive the operations of mechanics within the gun with diagrammatic logic, transmitting the necessary commands to the trigger finger with ever-changing modality, and while another part may supervise the micrometric alignment of the sights, a metapsychic spark is necessary to impulse with omnipotent force.

Until we learn to acquire the proper state of mind and master the bodily endeavors of holding, alignment and squeezing the trigger, we will only be dubs. These things can be reached with intelligent and stubborn practice, but the impulse must come from another sphere. It is in us all—but it is dormant. It must be kindled and it seems as if only absolute abandonment of one's self in our art were able to create the atmosphere so indispensable for its mysterious and benevolent existence.

12. ESQUIRE'S SPORTS SAMPLER

What? You haven't found it yet—the perfect sport, the ideal activity, the *very* enthusiasm your leisure cries for? Turn this page—and turn and turn and turn—for still more ideas. And when your eye lights on something you wish you were doing instead of just reading about, get up out of your chair and go *do* it. You can't learn younger!

DIVE!

Skin-diving in the ocean can furnish you with more exhilarating fun per grunt of expended effort than any other sport this side of paradise.

FASTER THAN THE WIND: ICEBOATING

Iceboat racing is packed with excitement, for spectator and competitor alike, and occasional spills are to be expected. The first time out in one of these winged creations might not convince you of the thrills the sport holds, in which case try a few more runs and learn the truth about the game.

Goggled against an ugly wind that keeps slapping your face and biting at ten fingers already numb, you huddle in a narrow cockpit, legs braced against a small cross-board for support. The taut canvas high above and the sharp runners below keep singing a weird song of danger ahead, but still you rocket along inevitably onward. Waiting, waiting.

Chin pops up from deep in a great muffler, but is pulled right down again for "Here she comes!" With an angry roar, a cutting blow from out the northeast crashes into your rigging and carries you up, UP, UP, then your boat heels over, one runner high off the ice. The tiller quivers and wriggles like something alive in your hand, but somehow you manage to hold on and the craft races along over the glassy surface—but on only one blade now.

After a tussle lasting a minute or two (it often seems like an hour) you slap her back down again and go skimming over a mirror at fifty miles an hour or better, the blurred surface flying by only inches beneath you.

That's really iceboat racing, an ancient sport replete with thrills, spills and chills. A sport for red-blooded sailors who like their weather stinging cold and their drinks piping hot.

ON THE ROCKS: FIGURE SKATING

The chief merit of figure skating, as with every other sport worth its salt, is that it is a sport that every able-bodied person can enjoy and can perform capably with far less than the six-hours-a-day practice that champs give it.

This isn't to say that Joe Doakes can do everything Dick Button does— even do it badly—but that he can give a fairly reasonable facsimile of many of the figures that stars like Button execute even in their big-time programs. There are only so many things that you can do on a pair of skates, just as there are only so many things that can be done in other sports. Gonzales can hit a tennis ball, and you can hit a tennis ball. You can't do it as well as he does, but you can do it, standing on two feet and using a racket just like Gonzales. That's the point.

And while you're trying to do it better, whether it's tennis or figure skating, you're enjoying yourself. Skating calls for patience and perseverance, if you want to be good at it. But if you're content just to skim along the ice, taking the crisp air into your lungs and working up a thirst, skating is just plain fun.

DIG THIS!

Let no man think garden making is sissy business. It is a mixture of art, sport, science and brute strength. It offers an opportunity for self-expression on the part of any male who might hesitate to portray his creative urges through adagio dancing or poetry and it is a swell substitute for routine setting-up exercises.

A garden that is something more than a collection of horticultural specimens, is the expression of an idea through the medium of plant materials. If you have that desire for self-expression smoldering within your hairy chest, and feel hesitant about going gardener because it has been woman-dominated in the past—just plunge in.

It is a sport, an art and a science, this garden game, a challenge to any man to exercise his aesthetic appreciation, his common sense and his muscles.

A fundamental difference between the woman-made garden and that which appeals strongly to a man lies in the fact that women seem to delight in fussing with detail. The primary strength of appeal in a garden that a man will like lies in its elements of design; in such things as lines, proportions, disposition of masses, the organization of basic framework embodied in garden paths, the placing of colors of such power as will give added accent to design forms.

Men appreciate telling forms and lines, an air of spaciousness, the expression of strength in design.

Gardening is a man's game, if he will play it.

EN GARDE!

As an athletic diversion fencing has much to offer. It requires no elaborate court or playing field. Instruction is to be had at reasonable rates and the cost of all necessary paraphernalia is negligible. It provides splendid exercise without placing too great strain on the individual who is out of training. Handicaps of age and technique can be offset by skill and experience. Above all, fencing develops muscular co-ordination, speed of judgment and a sense of timing, to a degree not surpassed by any other sport.

"Fencing is complex and all-fulfilling," says Georgio Santelli, famed coach of Olympic fencers. "It appeases vanity. One good touch does wonders for the ego. It exposes character, bringing out our basest and most altruistic impulses. La! la!" He brandishes an imaginary sword. "A few lunges and parries and the inner man is revealed, noble, cowardly, brave, petty, whatever he is. He cannot hide it. The sport flatters virility in the male. There is nothing like a sword in hand to make him feel like a warrior of old. Fencing is an excellent purge for all sorts of tension. It strengthens the weak and humbles the strong. And, once you have achieved proficiency (a matter of two to five years for most people), it becomes intellectual as well as physical. It is a violent chess game, shot with strategies and intrigue, with the brain busier than the blade. Fencers have more fun than anybody."

And hear Paul Gallico: "Fencing really is a game for the middle-aged and mature. Unlike tennis or handball or most other man-to-man athletics which demand more-or-less constant and sustained expenditures of energy, fencing calls for fleeting bursts that do not strain the heart."

The type of fencing taught in this country has gained general acceptance in international competition and is mainly French in origin. It provides a choice among three weapons each of which requires its peculiar technique.

The foil, most familiar of the lot, has a slender, rectangular, tapering blade set in a weighted handle. The blade of the epée, or dueling sword, likewise tapering, is trifoil in section and longer and less flexible than that of the foil. The saber has a flattened, rectangular blade of diminishing thickness, like a blunt knife. The grips of foil and epée are curved to fit the hand and their guards usually hemispherical. The saber has a straight grip and a hilt which envelops the hand as does that of a cutlas.

Certain general conditions govern the use of all three weapons. The contest takes place on a strip of rubber or cork, three feet wide and thirty feet long. It is presided over by a referee or director with the assistance of either two or four judges. The latter determine when and how a contestant has been struck, announcing their observations by cries of "Touch" or "Foul." The director arbitrates disputed points, awarding a touch in favor of the contestant who in his opinion scored first, or, at his discretion, disallowing the point entirely. He gives the signal to start the play and interrupts it in response to the judges' exclamations, or whenever it seems to him desirable to do so.

With both foils and saber, the bout usually lasts until one contestant scores seven times, whereas an epée bout is completed by the landing of a single touch, or when, if no point has been made, some previously determined time limit has been reached.

The epée bout adheres closely to the procedure of actual dueling. A touch, if made with the tip of the weapon, may be scored on any part of the anatomy. This fact, coupled with the consideration that victory and defeat are only one point apart, induces a degree of caution in epée fencing which detracts in large measure from its appeal to the spectator.

The foil's target is restricted to the torso. Touches on the limbs or neck constitute fouls and are not counted. When a foul has been made, however, a halt is called and play resumed at the center of the strip. The area to be defended being greatly reduced and the margin of safety increased to seven touches, far greater latitude of movement is possible with foil than with dueling sword. Foil technique is the most difficult to master, but is essential to progress with the other weapons.

Saber fencing is the most spectacular of all. The entire body above the waist is vulnerable to attack which may be delivered with either the point or the edge of the blade. Wide, overhand slashes are parried and returned in quick succession. The ring of steel against steel, or the stinging thwack of blows landed on tight canvas jackets lend a warlike glamour to the saber bout. A sense of reality is imparted by the knowledge that every unparried blow contains a more potent threat than the mere sting of defeat.

JUDO: GENTLE (?) ART

Judo, of course, is not fighting. It is a game. It's exercise, it's physical training, it's discipline, it's a code of ethics, it's a philosophy, it's modified jujitsu, but it's not fighting.

No. Not fighting, but a swell thing to know if you see a fight coming.

What is Judo?

In feudal Japan a system of defense and attack exercises without the use of weapons developed and was known as jujitsu. Jujitsu means *the gentle art,* and gets its name from the principle, embodied in many of the tricks, of appearing to yield, in order to get your opponent to apply his strength in the direction you wish to use it.

Say you hold your clenched fist out rigid from your side. I wish to make you lift that fist suddenly. Do I try to push it up? No, instead I push it down until I feel you resisting, trying to maintain your fist rigid in place. As soon as you are pushing against me hard enough, I stop pushing, and your fist flies up of its own accord—helped, if necessary, by such force as I may wish to apply. That is the principle of *the gentle art*—jujitsu.

Dr. Jigoro Kano, in formulating his science of Judo, embodied an extraordinary wealth of attributes in his new adaptations of the old, feudal jujitsu. Consider the following: Judo, unlike gymnastics, has meaning and purpose, and so, interest. It has secondary benefits added to physical culture: when you've learned Judo, you've got more than just a good physique. You have the incentive of attaining skill—a feature wanting in gymnastics. You have a *symmetrical* exercise, like swimming, which develops every muscle of the body evenly and naturally, without muscle-binding. You have an exercise or game which requires no equipment—an old coat and a soft lawn will suffice. You have a sport which is electric in its tension: the slightest relaxation from watchfulness may find you on the mat; thus you develop a natural alertness that becomes second nature. Your mind is challenged constantly in play to devise ways to entrap your watchful opponent. You become, in the words of Dr. Kano, "earnest, sincere, thoughtful, cautious and deliberate in all your dealings." Your imagination is stimulated.

If this sounds like the enthusiasm of the zealot, drop down some night and watch the contests at the Dojo. You will be struck with the laughing you hear. The sly thrust foiled; the tables turned on the confident aggressor; the horseplay, the remarks from the sidelines, the spontaneous applause for an unusually well-turned point—this laughter has a quality of sheer joy you'll like.

You learn psychology, too. After all, life is a contest. You see the hothead wearing himself out, being played like a trout by the skillful, but more patient veteran. You see the futility of opposing sheer strength to science. You learn, in short, that there is a single, sensible way to attack any problem, and that is to sit down and work it out on the basis of maximum mental and physical efficiency.

Aesthetically, too, Judo has much of the satisfaction of the dance. The efficient application of strength produces always the most graceful postures, and gives to the performer the rhythmic timing that is the dance's appeal.

Judo clubs are active now in almost all large cities and very popular on the West Coast. Some headquarter in YMCA's, others in local gyms; usually they have Japanese coaches. A good judoist can sweep you up and crash you flat so ferociously the walls tremble. If you're a judoist yourself, you arise as cheerfully as the magician's assistant who has just been sawed in two; if you're not, heaven help you.

WHY CLIMB A MOUNTAIN?

James Hilton gave this answer, not so long ago:

To this question every climber has his own reply. Mallory said he climbed mountains "because they were there"—and not in the spirit of ambition or conquest. "Have we conquered an enemy? None but ourselves," he added.

There must be some primitive human urge that finds spiritual comfort in "up" rather than "down"; it cannot be mere chance that heaven and hell are so placed. Probably there are Freudian or Fraserian roots in this. Maybe among our ancestors of a million years ago it was the rule to hide in underground caves when wild animals threatened, but the rare fellow would climb the hills up to steep rocks or the snowline where animals could not follow. Anyhow though men would explore the bottom of the sea if they could, it is doubtful if they would get that curious *élan* that comes from the opposite movement.

Even to those who, like myself, have reached no higher than half the height of Everest and on peaks offering no special difficulty, there may have come the kind of occasional mountain experience easier to remember than to analyze—some momentary clairvoyance that sets the mind swinging free like a compass needle—perhaps a product of physical exhaustion giving an effect of disembodiment. But they are special moments, no more to be counted on than divine visitations to the Saint. For the main, if I were asked why I make the modest ascents accessible to me, I would answer that they offer a maximum of striving with a minimum of competition. Mingling ardors and arduousness, mountain climbing is perhaps the most enchanting way of not keeping up with the Joneses.

THE CHAMPAGNE OF THRILLS

At the bobsled run the very air is charged with excitement and danger. There are voices which drone out from the giant megaphones at each of the hazardous curves. The noise of tractor engines and shouting voices fills the air with sharp, staccato notes.

"Clear the track . . . they're ready to start . . . Satan at the tape . . . they're off! . . . taking Eyrie Corner high . . . they're in, diving high up close to the rim . . . they're out!"

Far up the track you see the bob flying down, the four members of the crew bobbing in rhythmic unison—-a feat reminiscent of crew racing in a shell. You stand at one of the turns and watch the sleds take the iced curves with geysers of snow which spew up behind as the runners cut through the ice. Some of the bobs have conical hoods and resemble nothing more closely than the fantastic rockets fashioned for the journey to Mars. All of them are as minutely fashioned as streamlined racing cars. Some of the teams wear heathenish red masks and hand guards which are gruesome and warlike in appearance. A sign with monolithic letters greets your eye. ALL PERSONS USING THIS BOB RUN DO SO AT THEIR OWN RISK.

Few persons, enjoying this thrilling winter sport sandwiched in between a licensed driver and brakeman, with nothing to do but hold on to the straps and "bob" in the straightaways, have paused to consider what constitutes the sporting proposition of bobsled racing on the days when the runs are closed to joy riders. The thrill of mere speed on a snow-and-ice packed course which is diversified by long and short straightaways, winding turns, and sharp curves of hairpin, "S" or horseshoe form, is enough to satisfy the most critical of sports followers in the high mountain valleys.

But when you try to clip off seconds from a normal, breath-taking flight of a minute and a half down the side of a great mountain, the thrilling ride ends and the sporting proposition begins. In the case of bob racing the increase of speed becomes an athletic feat.

Bobsled racing owes its sporty thrill to the fact that machinery is eliminated, to the fact that there are self-imposed hazards which must be met in the path, to the fact that the danger of a spill increases with every additional mile per hour that the crew adds to its pace. It is a crew game, where smooth work in bobbing and skill in negotiating the high-banked curves cut off the fractions of seconds which are necessary to win. "Four" racing is more spectacular and more sporting, because of its higher rate of speed, because of its rhythmic team performance.

This racing bob weighs around five hundred pounds. The sleds are equipped with powerful saw-toothed brakes, operated by the rearmost member of the team. The front man steers and captains the team. All riders are required to wear safety armour, or at least a heavy leather padded helmet.

At the starting point, to pick up seconds, two or sometimes three of the crew run alongside the racing bob, sending it across the tape which operates the timing device with their added weight and push, leaping into their racing positions. The cry goes up: "They're off!"

Bobbing, an athletic feat readily acquired by the novice, will cut off many seconds on the straightaways, where the track is of glare ice covered with a thin frosting of snow so that the sled runners will bite in and hold the track. The brakeman strokes the crew, calling out above the rush of wind, "One, two, bob!" At one, the three members of the crew lean back, and continue to lean back during the count of two. At the command, "bob," they bring their bodies forward, pressing hard against the foot rests, so that the entire force is applied against them. Just when the pressure is greatest they lift slightly out of their seats. On a dash down a long straight this performance looks like crew racing in a shell.

The driver's judgment in gauging the parabolic easement curves will mean a gain or loss of seconds in the sharp curves of hairpin, "S" or horseshoe form. At times the pilot may call for brakes before the more treacherous curves, and still save seconds through skillful running of the gauntlet of ice.

Fighting the curves is bob racing's cardinal sin. The crew should let the corners take them around, and not take themselves around the corners. The members of the crew lean away from the bank in the sharp turns, to counteract the centrifugal force, being careful not to disturb the balance which the driver has earned on the easement curves, entering or coming off. There is a heretic technique, originating on the circular curves in the Alps, which calls for a position far out from the bob and leaning back—which, though beautiful in performance, more often results in disturbing the steersman's course.

In this sport, as in no other, practice makes perfect, for the tricks of each corner may be virtually mastered. Weight is undoubtedly an important factor, though by no means a determinant of speed. A steady nerve is essential in driving the comets of the ice up the thirty-foot walls of ice at the high rates of racing speeds. The most experienced teams on the best-built runs will reach maximum speeds of more than a mile a minute, and at such speeds as these occasional spills are inevitable. But their likelihood may be minimized by correct engineering design of the run, and by the proper training of licensed bobsled pilots.

FOR MADMEN ONLY

There is a special type of mentality which discovers in sheer terror a kind of ecstasy. For such a man—*The Cresta.*

The Cresta is a run for skeleton sleds—a refined species of tobogganing. Now, a skeleton sled differs from a bobsled in one very significant respect: it has no mechanical device of any sort for braking or for steering. The rules of the Cresta Club permit you to use any kind of sled you please—any kind of sled, that is, provided it has nothing on it which will enable you to stop it or to steer it. Cresta riding differs further from bob running, itself no sport for sissies, in that you go down alone. And you go down head first, instead of sitting up. You go down, when you get really going, at something better than eighty miles an hour. And what you go down is a narrow trough, harshly banked, sharply curved, surfaced with ice, three-quarters of a mile in length. In this three-quarter-mile distance, it takes a drop of 514 feet.

This Cresta Run is unique. It exists only in Saint-Moritz. And perhaps no other locality in the world affords the requisite combination of altitude, incline and temperature which serve to distinguish *The Cresta* from the ordinary toboggan run. St. Moritz has high altitude (above six thousand feet), perilously steep slopes, and a temperature which does not vary from December to March. The Run is built in a steep valley between two hills, shielded from the sun until noontime. This is important because it must be ice-coated. At dawn it is watered, and the intense cold insures immediate freezing; it is open for use only in the mornings.

Saint-Moritz, the winter sports center of the world, draws each season a greater number of sportsmen of that special temperament which finds its fun in almost dying. Some tease Destiny on skis; some sneer at Death on bobsleds. These are games for girls and boys. Certainly the most ingenious of these sensation-seekers are the reckless few who form the exclusive little organization known as the Cresta Club. They are of many nations. They are men who are in love with speed and danger. They are men who have grown tired of racing boats or cars or horses, men who have become names in other sports and sought something still more hazardous. Aviators appear to find a particular fascination in *The Cresta*. Amateur racing-car drivers are among the most enthusiastic riders. Taken all together, the Cresta Club's membership constitutes a kind of combined International Who's Who, Social Register and Lost Battalion.

And they are all men. *The Cresta* is possibly the world's one remaining exclusively masculine sport.

Cresta riding demands strength, skill and, of course, above all, nerve. It is by no means simply a matter of lying on a sled and coasting down a groove to the bottom. A sled started from the top would never reach bottom by itself. Somewhere, on the way, it would inevitably pitch over one of the banked corners and go crashing to a splintered destruction. It wants "riding." It wants cool, precise control. And this is achieved, since it has no steering wheel, by the agile shifting of the rider's weight. It is not only more dangerous to ride than a bobsled; it is also more difficult. The sled customarily used by Cresta riders consists of two steel runners, the forward portions of which are rounded, the rear portions of which are grooved and knife-edged, so that they will bite into the ice surface. Mounted between these is a small rubber-cushioned sliding seat on which the rider lies as though he were taking a belly whopper on an ordinary flexible flyer. At the start and on a straightaway he keeps this sliding seat forward, throwing his weight on the rounded front portion of the runners. He gains his speed solely by the force of gravity. On turns, he shifts the seat rearward, so that the grooved rear of the runners will grip the ice; and he slews his body round to lean in the direction he wants to turn, shoving the nose of the skeleton hard downward with the other arm. The maneuver sounds fairly simple. But there are ten corners to be accounted for within the frenzied minute or so between top and bottom.

He has, however, one other means of controlling his toboggan. Screwed to the bottom of each of his shoes, projecting beyond the toe, is a sharply pointed steel rake, fan-shaped. His legs trail behind him, so that he can, when need arises, drag these rakes along the ice surface, using them to check speed or to aid in shifting direction.

A racing rider, however, never uses his rakes for braking, because they slow him up; he uses one or another of them dexterously, as a kind of rudder, to help him round a curve. The less he rakes, the faster he goes, of course. The novice, however, is exhorted to use the rakes to his heart's content.

Accidents on *The Cresta* occur, in almost every case, from recklessness. There is always the temptation, when one is trying to break a speed record, to cut corners—or, in other words, to save time by hitting the banks as late as possible, instead of anticipating them.

On *The Cresta*, however, it really doesn't pay. The consequences are too disagreeable. Accidents are of two kinds. There is, first of all, the danger of a spill inside the Run itself.

But the really harrowing danger in riding *The Cresta* lies in going over one of the banks and crashing outside the Run. This comes to about the same thing as bailing out of an airplane without a parachute. The Club makes a nice propitiatory gesture toward the gods by putting a good deal of straw outside the turns; this is a help no doubt—if you happen to land in the straw. If you don't . . . Well, the first really bad series of curves on the way down is called Church Leap. Shoot over this and you land neatly among the tombstones of the little Saint-Moritz cemetery. And, in all probability, that is where you stay. The gray stone crosses are visible from the Run, quiet cautioners.

That fatal or serious accidents are as infrequent as they actually have been in a sport essentially so dangerous as *The Cresta* is due to the elaborate precautions on which the Club insists. To guard against falls, every rider is required to wear a special costume.

This consists, first of all, of a heavy leather crash helmet, not unlike the headguard worn by college football players. A chin guard is also prescribed. It is not hard to understand the importance of this chin guard, if you bear in mind that the rider's face, when he is whisking down that runway at eighty miles an hour, is just about four inches above the ice.

Heavy elbow and heavy knee pads are worn to protect him from the sides of the run, which he often scrapes along or hits with tremendous force. His hands are gloved in thin, supple leather, the back of the hand protected by a kind of round aluminum basket which looks like the hilt of a dueling sword.

The Run itself has gradually been improved during the fifty years of its existence, its curves and banks scientifically perfected. It takes about a month to build and condition *The Cresta* for racing. Generally it is opened toward the end of December—but only in part. The lower third, from Stream Corner to the bottom, is put into use first. A little later, the second third is opened from a point known as Junction. The entire Run from the Top is usually not ready for riding until late in January.

Riders who wish to compete in further races must first qualify from Stream

finish line. You take this all out simply because you have no strength left to do anything else. Then suddenly you find yourself hurtling uphill around a long, steep incline to the left, your speed slows, you become aware of things about you once more; you slow down, you stop. An attendant appears with a long hook and captures the thunderbolt you have been riding to keep it from sliding backward. He knows you are too tired to dig in your spikes yourself.

You gasp for air, letting out breath with a whoosh that carries with it a solemn vow never, never, never to do this again. Then you suddenly realize that you have been *holding your breath all the way down,* that in the entire passage down hell's frozen corridors you have not once *dared to breathe.*

The broadcast voice of the observer and announcer in the tower high up on the hill, three-quarters of a mile away, gives your time of descent: "Eighty-eight and six-tenths seconds!"

What? you say to yourself, getting up from the fatal contraption, your legs trembling with fatigue and your mortal soul still shaken. *One minute and twenty-eight seconds? What in the La Hell took me so long? Why that's almost twice the time it took Doug Conner, the champ, to come down. Say, maybe if next time I kept from banging into the walls on the straightaways, and came off the curves sooner. . . . Next time? What am I saying?* Yup. The old Cresta's got you and you'll never be the same again. You suddenly find yourself worried that you won't be able to get back up to the top before they close off the run for the morning as the sun mounts and softens the track.

Yes, from then on you eat, live, sleep, dream the Cresta run, working out ways to beat its dangers and subtleties, at first cutting seconds from time of descent and then being grateful for tenths and hundredths.

At my age, this is ridiculous, but older men than I do it and seem to survive, and so I am content to join the group of old fools whose lives are made happier and more zestful.

RUN!

Running is still the supreme conditioning exercise of mankind.

If any man wants to improve his physical condition, add to his health, increase his endurance and chances of living a longer, more satisfactory life, he should add running to his exercise regimen.

This sounds forbidding to Americans, to recommend running. Besides, it sounds dangerous. Isn't running hard on the heart? And isn't it a young man's game exclusively? The facts: running is not hard on the heart; anyone organically sound from fifteen to fifty can run to his heart's content, not with danger, not with discomfort, but with pleasure. Running is not a young man's game. To the contrary. The best distance runners are men who are twenty years past their athletic prime for other athletics.

The running we are talking about isn't competitive running at all. It is health running; running you do because it is fun to run and is healthful at the same time. You need never train except for running; need never follow a daily schedule. Running is the most natural form of activity there is.

When you start, take it easy, ever so easy, in the beginning. At first, don't even run. Jog. A jog is the next gentlest gait to a walk. Barely lift your feet as you cover the ground. Glide over it. Act lazy. Whenever you feel out of breath in the least, slow down to a walk, and walk until you have recovered. Then jog again. Continue in this way—jog until you feel "winded," walk until you feel rested, jog again, walk again.

If you haven't ever run before, you had better jog for a month or six weeks before you ever so much as think of stepping out at a run.

After you have jogged for a while, you will notice the results of running in everything you do. You will feel better. Your appetite will improve. Better digestion will be yours. If you have been subject to colds and coughs, that tendency will disappear. And your physical development all over will increase—even to the arms.

There are three main styles of distance running—landing toe first, landing flat-footed, and landing heel first. For a marathon distance, the flatfoot style is the most economical of energy. The Finns use the heel-first style, and there are no greater distance runners than the Finns. But for just padding along as you will for fun, the toe-first style is probably best. It's fun, though, to try all three; each is a refreshing change from the other.

Bend the elbows as you run, clench the fists lightly and let the arms swing gently. No stiffness or strain anywhere. Stiffness, strain are fatal. Everything should be ease, naturalness.

No matter how busy you are, no matter where you live, no matter what your occupation, you can run—if you want to.

And if you try it just once—you will want to!

JUMP!

Ski jumping calls for more nerve than any sport we can think of—flying, polo, bobsledding and motorcar racing not excepted. It is a lone wolf game. You climb to the roof of the world and catapult yourself down a precipitous runway into an aching, dazzling void of sun-reflected whiteness all by yourself. You have no team mates with whom to share your qualms. Misery loves company, as any novice bobsledder knows.

The jumper, courageous though he may be, always hopes that his judgment at the take-off will not be too soon or too late. His landing at all times is hazardous, for there are many things to be contended with during his flight in mid-air and upon landing.

There may be bad weather to cause uncertainty, there may be the difficulty of picking up increased speed on the inrun, which could result in disaster; and there may be some troublesome conditions on the transition or landing slope. Many times, too, expert skiers have been hurtling through the cold air at a seventy-mile-an-hour clip and suddenly felt the binding of one of their ski clamps break. Then what?

They are at the mercy of the powers that be! Only brilliant skill in executing a landing on one ski and making a safe spill can save them.

Still, they do it, and do it again. There must be something about that flight through space. . . .

SWIM!

When you get the hang of it, you find a quite endurable pleasure in swimming a quarter of a mile with the overarm stroke and the flutter kick. It fixes those ailing lungs. It swells those shrunken muscles and it sends the blood pounding to all parts of the body. It even, if gone at hard enough, makes you sweat. Some toe dunkers never really get the slightest taste of that strange, indefinable thrill that comes with timing, co-ordination and relaxation in the water. If you learned to swim before today's free-style stroke was developed, or before the dolphin replaced the old breast stroke, expose yourself to a little instruction. Once you get the bug of learning the new strokes, and feel the exhilaration that comes from effective propulsion in the water, nothing will keep you from your daily eight or ten laps in the pool.

Smoothness is the essence of swimming. Speed comes with relaxation and properly applied power. It is not the power derived from straining every sinew like a wrestler breaking a grip, but of relaxing all but the working muscles. If the champions enjoy swimming these new fast strokes, in competition and against the driving hand of the stop watch, the swimming dilettante, will, if he makes the effort, get all kinds of exercise and pleasure out of mastering the butterfly stroke, the dolphin locomotive process or the graceful orthodox breast stroke.

GO DOWN TO THE SEA

Where there's enough water you'll see him. Bag of sails in one hand, tennis shoes, old dungarees and a battered cap—a man going down to the sea for a week end. He's an amateur, but he knows his boat—plastic hull or plywood —because he's been scraping, varnishing and swearing at it since last winter's snows began to melt.

After sandpaper, copper paint, maybe some new canvas, or even a complete reconditioning job in the shipyards, the *Star* or the cutter or the schooner is ready to go and so is the skipper.

Subject to more conventional descriptions than home and mother, the boat is always *she* to him. And the combination of skipper, *she* and the sea —known as yachting—is forever luff and line and Beauty with a capital "B." The words and methods are a part of hallowed tradition—and, somehow, all of the phrases seem to fit. Surely a ship *is* like a woman, with beautiful lines and an exciting mind of her own. Full of whims and close to nature, she's tame—almost—when the right man is at the helm. Ask the skipper of any sailing craft if he thinks there is anything more beautiful than a day when the breeze is up and sails are full across a clear sky. Because all of this is true, sailing is one of the fastest-growing sports in America.

OUTBOARD MOTORBOATING

The outboard is a mechanical gadget, simple and efficient, that a man can carry as easily as a suitcase, attach it to the stern of a boat and *really get away!*

Countless millions of our people have never seen sailboats nor yachts, and very few of the populace could tell, without research, the difference between a ketch and a yawl. But outboards! Any sort of inland puddle, pond, lake or stream will do. A flask of gasoline with some motor oil mixed in, a shell of a boat—skiff, dory, canoe, rowboat—anything that will float, and you're prepared to be an outboard bug.

If you are a quiet soul, you'll get your fun out of a simple one- or two-cylinder motor, light and easily carried, attached to the stern of a square-sterned canoe or dinghy, and used for brief explorations, picnicking, fishing or duck shooting.

But if once you get the racing urge, you'll need a more complicated motor and a shingle-like hull. You will fare best if you are a composite made up of the finest qualities of a mechanic, bull fighter, football player and aviator, with perhaps a smattering of the swimmer thrown in. Your *nom de guerre* will doubtless be "grease monkey."

ARCHERY

It's true that unless you hunt big game with the bow, archery does not contain such an element of physical danger and personal contact as does football, for instance. Neither does tennis, or the shot-put or golf or pistol shooting. And in the qualities demanded by any of these sports—accuracy, endurance, exquisite muscular and nervous control—archery is way ahead of most of them. In addition you have the one weapon that makes hunting a genuine sport, and the one for which (in most states) there is no closed season for any kind of game.

As a matter of fact a good archer will beat a good pistol shot at his own game every time and a good golfer most of the time.

In an archery-golf match, archer and golfer start from the tee together, the archer firing his second shaft from where the first lands, and counting the number of shots it takes him to land an arrow in the cup as the golfer counts his strokes. The archer will get about the same distance off the tee—a good flight arrow travels around 250 yards—and much more accuracy; but on the putting green things even up, thanks to the fact that the ultimate target is set down in the ground and offers an aiming point which, seen from the archer's position, is a flat oval, the hardest of all objects to hit with an arrow. Going around the course with bow and arrow keeps many a golfer happy during the winter season: snow is no deterrent to arrows.

Bows are rated by a system of poundage which has nothing whatever to do with weight. The poundage is determined by putting a spring scale on the string and using it to pull the bow as far as it would be drawn in launching an arrow. The reading on the scale then represents the amount of pull necessary to shoot the bow, and if it is sixty pounds, means you have a sixty-pound lift to make with one hand and a sixty-pound push with the other every time you fire an arrow from that bow. Doing this a hundred or more times in an afternoon (necessary for a "York round" of target archery) would develop muscles on a grasshopper.

In practice the sixty-pounder is much too heavy for the average man.

A thirty- or thirty-five pounder will do quite as good work up to 125 yards, which is as far as anyone can shoot well without a good deal of experience, the heavier weight producing only muscle strain, quivering and consequent inaccuracy.

Most hunters with the bow prefer to use a forty- or forty-five-pounder in the field. It has enough power to drive the heavier killing arrow at about the same angles of flight as the thirty-five does a target shaft.

Even in the bows of lighter "weight" it takes a handsomely muscled individual to pull the feathered broadhead to its razor-sharp barb, hold it there for the instant required to take aim, and send it on its flight.

If you are going in for archery you had better buy your bow, as making them is a difficult and recondite art. With arrows it's different. They are expensive, you're always losing them, breaking them, or tearing the feathers off. The sooner you learn how to make and repair your own, the better. The raw materials are dowel rods and cartridge cases which you can get in the hardware store for very little and turkey feathers, which you can get in the butcher shop for nothing. And once you do learn to fletch your own arrows you will find archery the most inexpensive, enthralling and healthful of sports. Yare! And let free the clothyard shaft.

An archery target on three legs may have its sulky off days, but it never was known to charge. It gives the archer a chance to think, to estimate distance, to be precise. Game is altogether different. The hunter lifts, draws and releases his bow as the bobcat springs, by instinct. Be the game large or little, the archer has no time to think, and no time to lay down a tapeline.

Big game, with the bow and arrow, is a most impressive theme. You can hold the world by the ear for an hour with the tale of a giant slain.

Yet the dull, dusty truth forces us to admit it is mainly a matter of stalking.

The real hunting with bows, the job that takes speed and skill, is pinking small creatures, not big ones. You can't miss a bull moose at thirty-five yards, unless your hand shakes with buck ague.

But you can't hit a squirrel half the time. When you hit him, however, he is yours for keeps. The buzzards and ants do not share him.

True sportsmen have pride in their handicap hits. They seek no easy slaughter.

If you are the best hunting shot in America with a gun, you will split one in four when you try mallard ducks on the wing. Few archers drop one in a dozen.

So your bag will be light, but the game you do get will not rise in your plate to reproach you. You gave him big odds, and then won.

ROQUE

Roque is to croquet what chess is to checkers, only more so. The London *Spectator* once called it "The most scientific of outdoor games. It is more exciting and more intellectual than golf, and involves the very maximum of pressure on the nerves and temper allowable by the regulations of civilized society."

The court is usually of hard clay, carefully levelled, and sprinkled lightly with sand, sixty feet long by thirty wide, with six-foot diagonals at the corners to give it an octangular shape. It is enclosed in a border four to six inches high, first made of wood, later of cement and rubber, and now usually of steel "I" beams. The arches are constructed of rigid half-inch steel, embedded in blocks of cement buried under the surface of the court.

The arches are three and one-half inches wide, except the two in the center called the cage, which are three and three-eighths inches, and the balls, of composition material, are three and one-quarter inches in diameter! Instead of the inch or more of clearance that croqueters found difficult to manage, the roque boys have never more than a quarter-inch, and in the national championship tournament, all the arches are of the smaller size, which means only one-eighth inch of clearance.

The mallet is a highly efficient instrument. Its shaft is ten to sixteen inches in length, varying according to the stance and reach of the player, but short enough in any case to let him sight his stroke accurately (and also to make him stoop or kneel, for the benefit of his waistline) and the head, which doesn't fly off, is seven to ten inches in length and two to two and three-eighths inches in diameter, bound with steel ferrules. One end of the mallet is hard and the other is capped with soft rubber, somewhat like a flattened tip on a billiard cue, and useful in much the same way.

For generally speaking, a roque player can make just about the same shots with a roque ball that a billiardist can make with the ivories. He can carom or bank pretty much as he pleases. Double or triple caroms are frequent, and a shot that caroms five times is not uncommon. With the soft end of the mallet he can put english on the ball and bank it at all sorts of angles. He can produce the equivalent of a massé shot by striking the ball at a downward angle, and players have been seen to "jump shot" a ball over an arch ten inches high and fourteen feet away and hit another ball behind the arch that stymied them.

In old-fashioned croquet, if you can make yourself remember it, as many as four people could play, each playing one ball, and the object was simply to get your ball through all the arches and to the home stake before the other fellow could get there. You could impede him by croqueting him out of bounds, or you could, on occasion, send him out of position and advance yourself by "splitting" your ball off his and winning an extra shot for yourself, but by and large you just tapped and socked, and argued about which arch you had to go through next.

In a roque game there are rarely more than two players but each plays two balls, and he must get them both home to win. It is because of this that the tactics of roque are so complicated as to make those of croquet look like rummy compared to contract bridge.

There is no croqueting and no split shot, as such, though of course it is desirable to send your opponent's ball out of position whenever you can without losing ground yourself. Instead, the playing ball is used to drive the other into position, and the problem of keeping the opposing balls back and your own advancing together is one that demands a lot of headwork as well as physical skill and nervous control. But there aren't any arguments as to which arch you're headed for. Each player has a clip of his own color which he affixes to the arch at which he is aiming, and the clip stays there until he has gone through the arch. The clips have a front and a back side, to show whether the player is going out or coming in.

Roque isn't very strenuous, of course, but is golf, really? And it has this on golf: in roque you and your opponent can legally do something to stop each other, whereas in golf the only person you battle against is yourself. And if you think that blasting out of a sand trap or sinking an eighteen-foot putt takes skill, just try driving a roque ball through an arch with a quarter-inch clearance, sixty feet away!

WHAT IS THE ROUGHEST SPORT?

The roughest sport of them all—a sport requiring more strength, courage and better physical condition of its players than any other competitive event —is water polo.

The game requires but few physical properties. All that is necessary is a pool or tank "not greater than seventy-five feet nor less than sixty"; a white rubber ball not less than seven nor more than eight inches in diameter which "should be inflated seven-eighths full . . . so that a good grip may be had on it with one hand"; and two four-foot goal boards to be hung just above the water at each end of the tank.

The two teams of six men each stand at their respective ends of the tank: two Forwards, two Backs, a Center and a Goalkeeper. When the ball is thrown by the referee into the center of the pool the players dive in and strike out for the ball. The object of the game is simple. Each team, by smart and scientific passing, or by sheer brute strength, endeavors to touch or throw the "ball of contention" against the opponent's goal board. A touch goal equals three points, a thrown goal two and a free throw after a foul one point. The game is divided into two halves of eight minutes each, with a five-minute rest period between halves. In case of a tie as many extra periods of three minutes each are played as is necessary to break the tie. And, though the game is a combination of mayhem, wrestling, football and water-rioting, only four substitutions a game are permitted.

The rules governing the play of the game are stark in their simplicity. Gouging, biting and, occasionally, slugging are regarded as rather extreme measures. Everything else goes.

Tries for thrown foul goals are awarded on a purely technical basis, such as tackling a player who is not within four feet of the ball, use of abusive language, or engaging in gladiatorial combat while holding on to the side of the pool. The gentle spirit of the game is perhaps best illustrated by the rule which, while awarding a foul for holding under water more than ten seconds any player within four feet of the ball, makes the following exception, "A player who has possession of the ball may be held under *as long as* he retains possession of the ball." An innocent-appearing rule, except that any player who would release a ball to avoid drowning would thereafter be shunned by his team mates as a craven and a man unworthy of the society of his fellow beings.

The underwater tactics of two grappling players are anything but gentle. In fighting and wrestling certain holds are barred. But not under the water. You can punch, heel, kick, use *jujitsu,* thumbs, fingers and arm holds, or use the toe and strangle holds which are barred in wrestling. Anything and everything goes.

No actual drownings are on record but many players have been out for a few hours.

If you like thrills in sports water polo will provide you with all you can ask for. The leading club teams are located in New York, Boston, Philadelphia, Chicago, Los Angeles and San Francisco. The leading college teams are Yale, Columbia, Michigan, Northwestern and Leland Stanford. Watch any of these teams in action and you'll quickly understand why water polo is known as the roughest and most strenuous of sports.

And if you are thinking of taking up the game yourself, remember that the cardinal principle of water polo is—if a man gets a hold on you that you can't break, go down to the bottom of the tank with him and wait to see who drowns first.

"DANCE, TO RELAX" SAYS TOM HARMON

Dancing helps an athlete as much as any single activity I know. It gives him a sense of rhythm, which every athlete must have, regardless of the sport he is playing. It teaches him footwork, which also is one of the most important factors in every sport. The idea of dancing being sissy is a lot of bosh. If you want to see a surprised look on someone's face, take a peek at the face of the girl who starts dancing with an athlete for the first time. When the athlete does not step all over her feet she looks as though she has had a revelation. I can name quite a few athletes who not only know their way around an athletic field but can do as well as the best of them on a dance floor. Dancing is only one of the many ways for an athlete to relax after a game, but it is one of the best and most enjoyable. There are several other sports such as bowling, ping-pong, etc. that are all good for relaxation and still help the athlete keep his edge. The main point of my argument is to learn how to relax, as a major feature of your training program, both during the game and also after it is over.

SAND SAILING!

On the wind-swept, water-leveled, hard-packed sands of Florida's Daytona Beach, where once the roar of Sir Malcolm Campbell's Bluebird made history and Major H. O. S. Seagrave pushed the accelerator of his speedwagon to the floor, the horizon is now filled with the colors of the plastic sails of the land yachts invented by the Ely brothers—ex-coast guardsmen and sailing enthusiasts. This twentieth-century contribution to the world of sport and romance is a sail on wheels. The boat is handled much in the same way as the water sailboat. The wind is its main propulsion; but the tiller is attached to the rear wheel of the tricycle. Almost anyone familiar with basic sailing technique can learn to handle the sand sailboat in about the time it takes to say, "I'll rent one of those land sailboats for an hour." The novice can find himself whipping along the beach at speeds ranging from fifteen to twenty miles per hour. This may seem like a good seventy-five miles an hour to the novice, since he's sitting only a foot above the ground. He hasn't really tried anything, though, until the wind gets at his plastic sails and he moves along at a neat seventy-five miles per hour (which really feels like only a little over six hundred miles per hour)—a speed that has actually been clocked on the beach. So far even Superman hasn't managed to go that fast in the old-fashioned sport of sailing on water.

ANOTHER VOTE FOR SURF FISHING

You plant your booted feet firmly in the white sand and watch the surf breaking out ahead, suddenly lashing in and boiling white around you; then the long cast, the strike, and the exciting play. If your luck is in, you'll probably come walking back out of the surf foam with the fine spray of salt in your nostrils and a striped bass, a channel bass, a red drum, a pompano or a weakfish in your hand.

Surf fishing is grab-bag fishing. You never know what is coming out of the sea. It could be any of a dozen fighting, excellent-tasting fish, or it could be something deadly and dangerous, like a sting ray.

But for the fisherman who finds still-fishing, trolling, and boat fishing too tame and too slow, surf fishing is the answer. Action is the constant keynote. Naturally enough, the old fisherman's standard piece of equipment, luck, is needed, but just as necessary are method and manner.

Probably the gamest fish you'll hook while beating the surf will be the bluefish. He's not big, but he's a scrapper. Other fighters who go nicely between knife and fork are the channel bass, red drum, the striped bass, weakfish, snook, pompano, permit, king mackerel or kingfish, pollack, bonefish and wahoo. There are others that may strike your line, and it is even a possibility that a shark, hunting in close, may give you a tussle you'll remember all your life.

Once you sink your feet in the sand and watch the lash of the surf, feel the strike of a bluefish, and battle him to shore, you'll recognize the call.

You've been hooked as securely as the bluefish. You, my friend, are a surf fisherman. One of the elite.

HUNTER'S CHOICE

Go for woodcock, like this enthusiast:

We had a sharp frost last night. The hilly pasture that rises abruptly from the back of the house has taken on a pearly cast. Goldenrod skeletons and clumps of sweet fern, faded New England asters, hardhack and bracken are woven decoratively throughout the acres of frosty meadow grasses to form a gigantic Persian rug.

The air has a nip that penetrates to your toes as you breathe in deeply. It is strangely exciting. The old setter feels it, too. He has shaken off the lethargy of summer and is prancing around like a pup. He looks at you pleadingly with eager brown eyes, paws you impatiently and wonders what you are waiting for. Then suddenly it dawns on you; it is mid-October and the woodcock are down!

Woodcock fever is a good deal like malaria. There is no permanent cure; only palliative measures, which must be repeated with each outbreak. And these spells are sure to occur at regular intervals throughout the autumn. But the treatment is pleasant indeed, and I have never known a victim to object to frequent and large doses.

The appeal of woodcock hunting is intangible, like a mist-shrouded mountaintop. I have often wondered what there is about this long-billed, dumpy, bug-eyed inhabitant of the thickets that can exert such a powerful pull on those of us who love a dog and a smooth-bore gun. It can't be his looks. He has neither the charm of the oriole nor the sleek loveliness of the wild mallard. And, in the matter of intelligence the woodcock certainly does not rate with the grouse; nor is he as smart as that chicken-like creature, the ringneck pheasant. But looks and brains are not everything. There is another quality that always pulls down the gallery, and this the woodcock has— mystery. Now you see it, now you don't. That is what gets us and keeps us coming.

There are men who enjoy precision work with the rifle but have no taste for competition or the formalized routines of target shooting; who have in them also a deep feeling for the outdoors, but care little for the slapdash of most field shooting. If you are one of these, try woodchuck hunting, for you can shoot with all the hair-splitting accuracy you can develop and find it not too good, and you can hunt during Nature's softer moods—from spring to early fall.

We're not offering the woodchuck as a substitute for deer, sheep or grizzly bear. In hunting him there will be no supreme thrill comparable to the securing of a fine trophy after weeks of hardship and back-breaking toil. There will be no trophy to mount and display to your admiring friends. In fact, your friends may think you're a little screwy to spend your time hunting such worthless game. But you'll be led into quiet places which will be good for you, and you'll find a peculiar satisfaction in living up to the motto of the chuck hunter: *"The shot's the thing!"*

Hunt out of season, too:

If you're a bird hunter the chances are October is the red-letter month of the year for you, maybe with November running a close second.

October is the time when the woodcock flight comes down through New England, and the foliage begins to thin out in the grouse woods of Wisconsin. It's the season when local ducks pull out of the marshes and the first mallards and bluebills of the fall flight come tumbling in from the northern breeding grounds, heralded by a day or a night of wild and windy weather. It's also the month that sees the ringneck pheasant at his best, alike in the valleys around Philadelphia and on the green rain slopes of the Cascades, and all the way across the continent between. There's even some topnotch quail shooting in the northern half of the bobwhite range at that same time of year.

The air is full of feathers in October, both in the marshes and the uplands, and in most sections the shooting hangs on into November and stays pretty fair until Thanksgiving or a little later. Then there's a lull. Of course, if you're one of the favored, you'll likely plan to run down to Georgia or Mississippi for quail in February. But the big majority of bird hunters who live north of the Mason-Dixon figure to put their guns away and lock the cases sometime before Christmas. The law says no dice on pheasants and grouse by that time. The fun is over on northern quail and the rest of the upland list. The last woodcock and jacksnipe went through weeks earlier and only a few of the hardier ducks are left, rafting far out on big water, sticking it in the face of cold storms and the first snow, hard to decoy and hard to kill. The curtain is down. Bird shooting is done for the year. Until October paints her red and tawny murals in the uplands again there's little for the wingshot to do save sit by the fire and dream.

To most bird hunters it never occurs that all-winter wing shooting is at hand for the asking. Wing shooting calls for a feathered target, big and canny and fast enough to be worth bothering with, and one that the law will let you take. But the bulk of the birds have gone now and on those that do remain the season is closed.

All save one. There's one that stays north all winter, that flies fast enough to test your trigger eye even if you break twenty at skeet, that's got as many brains as a wild goose or a pheasant—and that's plenty—one whose neck the law has no wish to save. He's the crow.

If you live in crow country winter wing shooting is no harder to get than October wing shooting. It's good, lively, you-give-the-odds hunting, too. Shoot black pirates from a snow blind, at a time when no other feathered game is legal, and you'll have the answer to a bird hunter's closed season prayers!

THE END

. . . is only the beginning, we trust (we can almost *promise*), of a happier, healthier, more vigorous life for you. Yes, you who can still brag about your cast-iron stomach (follow this book's program and you'll rustproof it), no less than you who fear that men of your age are supposed to look that way (you're not!). The only tough part of what we've asked you to do—no fooling—is simply to *get started*. There'll never be a better time than right

NOW!

INDEX

Set in Linotype Caledonia
Format by Nancy Etheredge
Lithographed by The Murray Printing Co., Forge Village, Mass.
Bound by The Haddon Craftsmen, Inc., Scranton, Pa.
Published by HARPER & BROTHERS, New York